The New Practical Guide to Canadian Political Economy

The New Practical Guide to Canadian Political Economy

EDITED BY
Daniel Drache &
Wallace Clement

James Lorimer & Company, Publishers
TORONTO 1985

ISBN 0-88862-785-8 paper
ISBN 0-88862-786-6 cloth

Design: Dreadnaught

Canadian Cataloguing Publication Data

Drache, Daniel, 1941–
   The new practical guide to Canadian political economy

Includes index.
Updated edition of: A practical guide to Canadian political economy / Wallace Clement & Daniel Drache.

1. Canada - Economic conditions - Bibliography.
I. Clement, Wallace. A practical guide to Canadian political economy.   II. Title.

Z7165.C2C58 1985 016.330971 C85-098328-2

James Lorimer & Company, Publishers
Egerton Ryerson Memorial Building
35 Britain Street
Toronto, Ontario M5A 1R7

Printed and bound in Canada

6 5 4 3 2 1   85 86 87 88 89

Contents

VII: STATE AND POLITICS

Acknowledgements

The inspiration for bringing out this new edition of the *Guide* came from Peter Saunders, who insisted that a revision would be timely. For this he deserves our collective thanks, as does Mel Watkins, another early enthusiast, who was very helpful at different stages of the project. Jim Lorimer and Ted Mumford, our editor, also get a hearty thank you for their encouragement. This bibliography could not have been assembled, however, without the generous cooperation of all the contributors. They minimized the difficulties of coordinating such a project, and we are most appreciative. To our colleagues who actually sent their section of the bibliography in on time, encore merci.

Assembling a bibliography is an exacting science requiring endless hours of intensive work. Liz Dobson, our bibliographer, with the help of Isabelle Gibb, checked and verified each and every entry, paying scrupulous attention to each comma, date, place of publication, and author's name or names. All of us are in her debt, for it was she who transformed the hundreds of entries supplied by the contributors into the state of the art of bibliographic excellence.

Publication of this guide was assisted by a grant from the Publications Division of the Ontario Arts Council and another from Studies in Political Economy of Canada. In the spirit of the collective nature of this undertaking, all royalties will go to SPEC, which is committed to supporting new work in the field of Canadian political economy.

Daniel Drache and Wallace Clement

Introduction:
The Coming of Age of Canadian Political Economy

Since the publication of the first edition of the *Guide*, the field of political economy has undergone rapid change and development. For more than a decade, creative and important contributions to Canadian social science have come from historians, economists, sociologists and political scientists working in the tradition of Canadian political economy. A quick glance at the range of new entries confirms that, as an area of study, Canadian political economy has come into its own.

Not only have Canadian political economists produced exciting new work on women, labour process, foreign investment, culture and regionalism, in the last ten years, but they are also becoming recognized internationally as distinguished scholars on non-Canadian subjects: John Saul and Bonnie Campbell on African studies,[1] Richard Lee on anthropology,[2] Leo Panitch on corporatism,[3] the late Stephen Hymer on the theory of the multinational corporation,[4] Robert Cox,[5] Harry Glasbeek[6] and Doug Hay on industrial relations and legal history,[7] Jean-Marc Piotte and Gilles Dostaler on Marxist theory,[8] Wally Seccombe on gender, reproduction and housework, and Mary O'Brien on feminist theory.[9] These recent contributions follow the pioneering work of C.B. Macpherson on liberal democratic theory and that of the late Herbert Norman, acknowledged for his seminal Marxist study on the origins of modern Japan.

Political Economy: More Than a Discipline

What does *political economy* encompass? This question has never been an easy one to answer. As practised in Canada, political economy is not simply a discipline, nor is it merely a preserve for a single political or ideological tradition. It is simultaneously a "tradition," a field of study and a paradigm. As a tradition, political economy stems from two intellectual streams of thought: most notably the liberal writings of Harold Innis, Donald Creighton, W.A. Mackintosh and Vernon Fowke and the theoretical and historical work of Marxists C.B. Macpherson, H. Clare Pentland and Stanley Ryerson.[10] As a field of study, political economy draws on contributions from social scientists in all disciplines by recombining the disparate "disciplines" of economics, history, cultural studies, political science, sociology and anthropology in its own distinct theoretical tradition of materialism. As a paradigm, the political economy perspective provides a way to understand the dynamic relationship between people within a specific society by identifying how that society has unfolded historically and, in particular, how its economic system is organically linked to the social/cultural/ideological/political order. Political economists study the laws and relations of the capitalist system, either critically from the Marxist perspective or from the more traditional liberal view.[11]

That political economy has become accepted academically is without question. Now, however, it faces some critical challenges and must answer to some probing questions, the most important being: Is political economy still viable as a discourse of critical theory?

Beyond Dependency Theory

Canadian political economy is at a crossroads because the issue of American domination, once the central problematic, is no longer the overriding theoretical preoccupation of political economists. In the 1970s, a deep interest in dependency theory by Wallace Clement, Tom Naylor, Kari Levitt, and Abe Rotstein forced English Canadian political economists to acquire a national perspective on Canadian economic development, elites, American imperialism and the state. In a nutshell, what dependency theory explained was how the ensemble of forces of advanced capitalism blocked the economic and cultural development of societies at the "margin" of the international economic system. Those who found the stress on dependence and domination inadequate, used dependency as a spur to develop alternative perspectives to explain the larger setting of the economic and social relations of Canadian capitalism. With the enormous changes that have taken place in the economy in the last decade alone, dependency theory is no longer adequate for understanding our relations either with the U.S. or with other countries. Clearly, neither dependency theory nor any other single theory can explain the variety of forces defining the relations between the world economy and the national economies. However, the rejection of dependency theory by Canada's state theorists and most of the new labour historians as the unifying perspective in the discipline has left a void that remains to be filled. This has had at least one benefit: where once a core issue dominated debate and discussion, a genuine pluralism of viewpoints and issues now exists that has given a certain vitality to this "golden age" of Canadian political economy.

The extent of this pluralism is evident in the number and range of the ongoing debates in the field. They cover such topics as the new labour history, commercial dominance, wages for housework, industrial strategy versus free trade, elite linkages, nationalism, regionalism, foreign ownership, Canadian multinationals and technology. What is interesting to note is that political economists are intent on exploring various of these fields and refuse to be limited by the approaches and/or extent of their former writings. This has meant an enormous amount of dynamic and evolving thought and a change in viewpoints often resulting in collaboration between former antagonists or individuals with sharply opposing points of view. For instance, David Wolfe, a lukewarm Innisian, and Mel Watkins, an unrepentant Innisian, teach a joint course in political economy at the University of

Toronto; and at York University, Leo Panitch and Daniel Drache, with their sharply divergent views on Canada and Marxism, teach together, as do Reg Whitaker, one of Canada's leading neo-Marxist political theorists, and Don Smiley, the dean of Canadian liberal political economy. Clearly, much must have changed to make this possible, and it is hoped that current attempts to transcend past ideological divisions augur well for the future.

Questioning the Innis Paradigm

Despite the decline of dependency theory, it still has some relevance to the debate on Innis's contribution and his paradigm of political economy. By examining the debate initiated by an article in the special issue, autumn 1981, of *Studies in Political Economy*, "Re-Thinking Canadian Political Economy" by Leo Panitch, and the rejoinder in autumn 1983 in the *Canadian Journal of Political and Social Theory*, "Beyond Dependency Theory" by Daniel Drache, one can see just how far political economy has come. In brief, the major thrusts and counterthrusts were as follows:

- *Theory*: The two positions represented fundamentally opposing assessments of the eclectic nature of Canadian political economy. Classically oriented Canadian Marxists, such as Panitch, charged that combining Schumpter, Innis, Marx, Grant, Porter, etc., made it very difficult to systematically explain the development of classes and Canadian capitalism. In particular, Panitch claimed that this haphazard mix of Marxism and liberalism prevented Canadian political economy from distancing itself sufficiently from the staples tradition and therefore rendered it incapable of treating Canadian society as a totality. Drache, on the other hand, believed that the strength and innovative character of the new political economy lay in its theoretical and conceptual willingness to break with more traditional Marxist theory and that the heterodox tradition of Canadian political economy had the flexibility to grasp the national specificity of Canadian development. Canada has many of the structural features of a dependent economy and yet is not a Third World country.
- *Focus*: Panitch, as a Marxist, was principally concerned with class relations and class conflict, that is, the way a class-divided society is constituted and reproduced. On the other hand, Drache as an Innisian-inspired Marxist began with capitalist development and capital accumulation and focused on explaining the evolution and transformation of a settler resource colony into an industrial society — one that has an open economy and depends on trade for its prosperity.
- *Methodology*: Because Marxists stress the similarity of social relations of all advanced capitalist societies, Panitch examined Canada through the lens of a universal model of capitalist society. This model has as its primary relations the class relations between labour and capital, which are in turn mediated by the labour market, wage labour and the private ownership of production. By contrast, the Innisians do not stress convergence but rather the specific relations in a given capitalist society and the reasons for that specificity. In Canada, dependency is a central feature of capitalism and capitalist devel-

opment, not only because of Canada's domination by first Britain and then the U.S., but also because, in the words of Eric Kierans, dependency is a condition "when the resources and revenues from markets and production accrue largely to others."[12] It is this condition of dependency that Innisians believe must be added to Marxism's traditional focus on class and labour.

The difference between these Marxist and Innisian perspectives becomes clearer when one examines the work of Tom Naylor on business elites and industrialization. Panitch makes a powerful argument that Naylor's seminal work on Canadian business is flawed for both theoretical and empirical reasons. He objects to Naylor's claim that there is no sharp opposition between commercial and industrial capital. Panitch also believes that theoretically Naylor's position is erroneous because it does not give sufficient weight to indigenous factors, such as wage rates, nor does it explain why by the 1920s Canadian industry was able to compete with American industry. Drache, on the other hand, claims that commercialism is the pivotal force in Canadian economic life and that Naylor's theory of commercialism remains the most useful and original perspective developed by Canadian political economy to explain the behaviour and strategy of Canada's elites, not only in the nineteenth century but also in the twentieth. The fortunes of the Canadian capitalist class have been based on commercial, trade and resource-related activities at home, as well as on its intermediary activity in the world economy.[13]

From the positions articulated in this exchange, it is clear that Marxism, à la Panitch, singles out indigenous rather than external forces as the impetus for change. Conversely, it is also apparent that the Innisians à la Drache place externalities at the centre of their paradigm. At issue is not whether one or the other is "correct" in some narrow sense of the word, but whether class struggles not only condition, but are conditioned by Canada's place in the international division of labour.

This controversy brings to the fore other issues that require further research. These include: the role of labour in Canadian development (in particular, the central importance of wages and work conditions to Canadian industrialization and the importance of industrial relations as an instrument of state policy); the reasons for a state policy that has always had both an industrial and commercial counterpart; and the effect of that policy on the formation and fragmentation of both the working class and independent commodity producers.

Reconceptualizing the Issue of Canadian Development

The fundamental question is how to explain the complex process of development in Canada. As Tom Traves has rightly admitted, this process poses very real problems for Canadian political economy because "the links between the staple and the industrial economy were both more complex and less direct than usually acknowledged." After a decade of debate, there is a real need for a fresh conceptual approach. While the concept of dependency continues to be a powerful one and, as Mel Watkins has justly noted, while the staple approach constitutes a distinctive Canadian perspective to a general theory of growth, a narrow economic focus on staple-led growth cannot add to our knowledge of the ways in which the structures of advanced capitalism block the economic development of settler societies or the reasons why Canadian development occurs despite being constantly exploited by centre capitalist economies. The most troubling question is: Why hasn't the original work on Canadian dependency and development evolved into a much more sophisticated perspective capable of recognizing the plurality of factors — ethnic, institutional, social and cultural — that shape each stage of development? For example, the systemic analyses of the structural origins of the world crisis by Emmanuel Wallerstein and Ferdinand Braudel, show that dependency theory is not just an economistic doctrine for analyzing the ways in which the structures of advanced capitalism block the economic development of marginalized societies; it also shows how power is deployed between classes, nations and, perhaps most important, between economic blocs of countries globally. Yet Canadians have been blind to the full potential of dependency theory as a systemic approach to explain social and economic development.

A recent article by Michel Beaud[14] that reconceptualizes what is meant by "development" is an important and relevant breakthrough. His work is particularly germane to Canadian political economy because it provides powerful analytical alternatives to what is normally meant by such terms as "development," "dependency" and "underdevelopment." By distinguishing between what he calls the condition of dependent development and the condition of dominant development, he identifies the process and dynamic of growth which, theoretically, can occur anywhere in the world economy and is not time-bound by a static centre/periphery model of political economy.

Dependent Development/Dominant Development

According to Beaud, dependent development has the following characteristics: the resources, the process of industrialization, and the modernization of the economy are subject to the global trends that correspond to the decisions and the strategies of the states or groups within the dominant industrial countries. Development that is dominated by these externalities results in sudden specialization in one or two sectors of the economy. More generally, it also results in an extraverted economy in which the industrial and advanced sectors are not responding to national needs but rather to demands orginating from the dominant economies: mineral or agrarian production for export, the implantation of industries corresponding to the shift in industrial production from the advanced bloc or to the strategy of the multinational firms. Crucial for Beaud's theory is that this kind of deformed development destructures and disaggregates the existing local or regional economies without leading to a new national coherence.

In sharp contrast, dominant development is characterized by a mastering of advanced technologies, production methods and principal markets at each stage of growth. It also translates into a capacity to exercise a predominant influence on domestic markets and on the conditions of exploitation of its resources, and the ability to influence the industrial policies of other states and other international organizations in order to control and benefit from the principal technological, financial and commercial transfers. This implies a production system and as comprehensive a national technological capacity as possible. More particularly it means having a level of social coherence between the state and the producing classes and a state apparatus that is respected politically, militarily and monetarily at the world level. Beaud adds that actually this is only the case for the U.S., the USSR and Japan, the three countries that can be considered "outsiders" in the world system.[15]

If we are to apply Beaud's insights to the situation in Canada, we need to take a radically different tack than the ones offered by either dependency theory or class analysis. As we have seen, the single-minded focus of either the Innisians or Marxists leads inevitably to a static and selective view of the way a society evolves, since both foci underestimate how a given system of economic regulation takes hold, matures and declines. What is missing is an adequate understanding of the relationship among the institutional processes, the existing level of social and economic cohesion and Canada's role in the North American economy. Among the questions that need to be addressed are these: How was the Canadian system of macroregulation, one dependent on export-led growth, irrevocably transformed during the nineteenth and twentieth centuries? And how were the structural weaknesses of a staples economy reproduced in each successive phase of development? These are two pieces of the puzzle of Canadian development that have yet to be theorized and understood.

Keynes Comes to Canada: Continuity in Change

In a more contemporary vein, it is necessary to pose these same kinds of questions about postwar development in Canada. For example, how well did the new Keynesian system adapt to Canadian needs given the constraints inherited from an older system of competitive capitalism? Why would Keynesian management strategies, normally the means to promote the growth of indigenous industry in the advanced capitalist economies, in the case of Canada open the door to American investment and the establishment of branch plants on an unprecedented scale? How would the Canadian state adapt Keynesian stabilization policies to operate in an open economy subject to the constant pressures of resource booms and slumps? How would the virtuous Keynesian cycle of productivity-growth-investment-consumption be altered and nationalized in Canada?

Of the two staples theorists, Innis and Mackintosh, it is Mackintosh who tells us more about these major policy issues and who provides the stimulus for reconceptualizing such fundamental issues as economic growth and change. It is a striking fact that Mackintosh, the creator of the "staple theory," was one of the key persons to bring Keynesianism to Canada. As a leading architect of postwar state policy, he believed that Keynesian policy instruments made possible a new fit between resources and industry. The extensive work of David Wolfe on state policy[16] shows how the strategy of export-led growth became an essential part of the Keynesian "success story" of rapid growth, rising incomes, high levels of consumer demand and increased penetration of the Canadian economy by American capital.

Adapting Keynesian stabilization policies to Canadian conditions proved to be much more difficult than Mackintosh anticipated. In a country with so much of its economy dependent on the American business cycle, it was questionable whether the Keynesian macro-instruments of stabilization would be effective in stabilizing the swings of the business cycle and stimulating the economy. Economists such as Scott Gordon concluded that from a Keynesian standpoint, federal fiscal policy was appropriate in only four of the nineteen years surveyed. Other economists argued that for a third of the time, budgetary policy between 1945 and 1963 was actually pro-cyclical rather than counter-cyclical. The most intractable problem was Ottawa's inability to wrestle to the ground Canada's persistently high levels of unemployment. It never came close to building an economy based on full employment. The high levels of unemployment in the mass production industries stemmed from the continual growth in import-penetration of the Canadian market. By 1980, 36 per cent of all manufactured goods in Canada were imported. For the U.S. the same figure was 10 per cent and for all other industrial countries, imports constituted only 16 per cent of goods consumed. Nor did trade respond to Keynesian medicine. While world trade in manufactured goods increased at an 11 per cent rate between 1958 and 1973, Canada's share only marginally improved. Compared to resource exports, the industrial side of the economy remained the weak link in Canada's economic performance.

The Keynesian Growth Model in a Resource Economy

What was unexpected about the Keynesian cycle of growth was that rising incomes and the spread of mass consumption didn't end Canada's historic reliance on resource exports, as Mackintosh and others had anticipated. Nor was the modernization of Canadian industry particularly effective in correcting past weaknesses. The persistent gains in real ouput (averaging almost five per cent between 1947 and 1967) and in real productivity (growing significantly at 3.5 per cent in the first decade after World War II before levelling off in the Sixties) did not translate into a golden era for Canadian mass consumer or capital goods industries. Even though Canadian manufacturing expanded and employed a record number of Canadians, it was outperformed by the export industries. What made this situation even more puzzling was that until 1968 Canada remained a low-wage economy in light of American industrial wage rates, with Canadian industrial workers being paid as much as 25 per cent less than their American counterparts.

At the institutional level, collective-bargaining arrangements were only minimally up to Keynesian standards. The post war reforms to collective bargaining and industrial relations didn't reflect the increased power of the working class; nor did they give labour a larger share of the national income. In fact, there was no shift in economic power to labour, and the overall share of national income going to wages and salaries in Canada between 1930 and 1970 remained remarkably constant.[17] Nationally, labour simply didn't have the bargaining muscle to demand a share in productivity gains. Between 1946 and 1977, productivity shot ahead of the rise in real earnings and output. But, as Uri Zohar concludes in his seminal study on productivity and technological change, there was "a definite structural change,'' given that labour's share of the value-added decreased from 61 per cent in 1946 to 49 per cent in 1977.[18] This meant that, proportionately, capital increased its share from 39 per cent in 1946 to 51 per cent in 1977.

Given these outcomes, does it make sense to speak of a Keynesian revolution? To what extent did state policy mark a fundamental break with an earlier system of wage relations based on a model of growth and development of competitive capitalism? Why were Canadian markets more fragmented than many of our competitors'? More fundamentally, why did the economy and state policy not succumb to Keynesian macro-therapy?

The fact is that Keynesian stabilization policies served to legitimize an open door policy to American capital and, therefore, reproduced most, if not all, of the economic problems that were intrinsic to a classically oriented import-export market economy of an earlier era: trade imbalances, a stop-and-start economy, minimal rights for workers to organize themselves collectively, a low wage economy for the more than two-thirds of the work force in the unskilled and non-unionized sectors, the continual outflow of profits and, most crucially, a lack of indigenous technology. Because the Canadian variant of Keynesian-inspired theories had built-in stabilizers that put a floor on how low the economy could go when the business cycle bottomed out, Canada's state policies appeared to fit the general conception that the state would replace the market as the principal mechanism of adjustment. "The optimism that the new role for the state would ensure confidence and healthy levels of investment in a continued free enterprise world"[19] meant that as long as the formula for short-term success did produce results that were acceptable both to business and the bureaucracy, there was no need to formulate other solutions to Canada's structural problems, or even to discuss the need for long-term change. As long as the Canadian economy rode on the back of the American business cycle, there were "real and achievable opportunities for growth through trade."[20]

Seen in these terms, it is now obvious that under the postwar system of regulation, Canada became both more developed and more dependent, though not in equal proportions. The economy had both a Keynesian and a Mackintosh growth pole. When the economy repeatedly faltered, the state looked to a leaner and meaner version of staple-led growth to get the economy back on track: wage controls and wage restraint programs to strengthen the international competitiveness of Canadian industry, an excessively generous system of capital transfers to the private sector to reinforce trade policy, numerous state-assisted megaprojects to exploit Canada's rich supply of raw resources and, most recently, a reduction of state expenditures to restore business confidence in the economy.

An economy subject to the vicious cycle of export-led growth is ill-equipped to respond to far-reaching changes in the international economy. For the state, which links development to the export of its resources in the most mechanical fashion, guarding Canada's international trade advantage is the principal preoccupation. In a world in which there is little likelihood of a return to prolonged rapid growth, Canada's economic prospects are anything but buoyant. The question is how will the state attempt in the climate of the 1980s to intervene to expand export markets, attract new investment capital and assist business. The search for flexibility takes a variety of forms but the most important on the state's agenda is to move towards free trade with the U.S. and, at the same time, to reduce labour costs in the workplace on the assumption that this tough medicine will force all sectors of the economy to perform up to capacity. In a society in which trade and cheap labour costs are seen by government as "the vital link between the economy and the international competitive environment," the state mechanism of adjustment can only be blunt, crude, coercive and indifferent to the real dangers and costs of this kind of economic restructuring.

Where does this leave macropolitical economy? What lies ahead?

New Theoretical Questions for the 1980s

The broad concerns, such as foreign ownership, branch-plant economy and corporate concentration, which political economists such as Kari Levitt in her path-breaking study *Silent Surrender: The Multi-national Corporation in Canada* identified, haven't lost any of their importance. Canada remains on an economic and political collision course with the U.S as each country seeks to protect its standard of living and searches desperately to restructure its economy by increasing exports to the other. In the race to be competitive, Canada is doubly handicapped: it cannot rely on the goodwill of American foreign capital to either sustain a recovery or to improve Canada's trade balance. While Canada is an advanced society, able to function on an industrial footing, it is becoming less and less firmly anchored in the industrial world and has only a minimal amount of economic and political freedom with which to manoeuvre. The end of Keynesian management policies now means that political economy must shift its focus from the "slide into dependency" to the more complex set of policy issues imposed by economic restructuring. These are the issues that will have a far-reaching impact on the social fabric of Canadian society. Given Ottawa's commitment to free trade, there will be greater Americanization of the economy and culture, not less. As the multinationals reorganize their operations in Canada, most frequently by closing down operations and prolonged layoffs, the growing inequalities of the labour market for men and women will come sharply into focus, particularly for those people working in the primary labour market and those in the secondary sector working in part-time and low-skilled jobs. The continuing attack by the state and capital on labour's entitlements also sets the stage for bitter confrontation, both nationally and regionally.

These new trends raise the most fundamental kinds of questions about the principal social actors in Canada and their role in the economy and in society. Studies of the elites need to be updated and broadened. What are the interests of the economic elite in the 1980s? How has the wave of takeovers, mergers and shutdowns changed the strategy of the leading edge of corporate Canada? How has "paper entrepreneurialism" altered the elite linkages between Canadian and American capital?

This return to market-based policies also forces a reconsideration of state theory. The state's ever greater concern with the question of distribution has put the boots to Keynesianism. What kind of state is being created? Will it be less interventionist or more? As it is able to control more of the political process, what kind of political initiatives is it likely to take? Most critically, what kind of cross-class consensus is possible as the state becomes less autonomous and more subservient to the immediate needs of business? In the grim days ahead, what future does labour have in the new social order? Is the labour movement capable of being more than a trade union movement? How is it going to relate to what Gorz calls the "non-class" of workers, those who will likely be part-time, low paid, and without job security of any sort? Turning to the economy, the exhaustion of Keynesian management policies raises questions about economic rationality and economic planning techniques as ends in themselves. As the bishops' statement "Ethical Reflections on the Economic Crisis",[21] pointedly asks: "What values should economics realize or serve?" Should the market be the unique institution for promoting production and distribution of wealth? Does the economy serve basic human needs or does it merely increase the domination of the weak by the strong? Are people to be perceived solely in terms of their economic function or in terms of the value and dignity of their labour?

In Search of a Research Agenda

To answer these and other fundamental concerns requires new research and new theoretical perspectives. In the first edition of the *Guide*, Clement proposed an ambitious agenda of research, much of which has in fact been accomplished. In the 1980s, such an agenda would be very different and difficult to draw up because of the growth and diversity that have occurred within the field of Canadian political economy. Indeed, it would be naive to think that one research agenda could suffice. Each area of study needs to create its own.

At a more fundamental level, it is an open question whether political economy will speak with the same confident voice that it did in the 1970s, combining scholarship with relevance. Since the economic crisis, political economists face a range of new challenges both from within and from without the discipline.

Marxism

The first of these challenges comes from within Marxism, the theoretical foundation of political economy, that is itself in a period of flux and reappraisal. Many leading Marxists, such as Claus Offe, Samuel Bowles and Herbert Gintis, have abandoned, in the words of Michael Piore and Charles Sabel, "the singular emphasis on one of Marxism's basic assumptions, namely an overriding belief in the logic of capital," which says in effect that "market competition and technological change determine the trajectory of economics and political developments."[22] The central thrust of this autocritique is to take a hard look at the major tenets of Marxism in order to begin to grapple with its "received" theoretical limitations. For this reason, it does not come as a shock to have someone of the stature of the German theorist Claus Offe openly question the core assumptions of classical Marxism in terms of both the central role of labour and the Marxist model of class conflict. In his recently published book of essays, *Contra-*

dictions of the Welfare State, edited by John Keane, Offe singles out four major tenets that he regards as sociologically and politically misleading. These are:

- In advanced capitalist societies, wage labour is no longer an equalizing and homogenizing process, "on the basis of which a politically conscious proletarian 'class for itself' would be formed.... The increased heterogeneity of the working class constitutes a serious problem for the collective action of the working class."
- The work identity and social identity of workers is diverging to such an extent that "the ideal-typical figure of the classical Marxian analysis, namely, the productive wage-labourer has cost much of its original relevance and appeal." It has to be recognized that political conciousness is derived less from the fact of individuals being workers and more from their role as consumer, man/woman, citizen/client, inhabitant of a territory or ecosystem.
- "There is no one central condition that causally determines all other conditions in a base-superstructure or primary/secondary manner. The work role is only partially determinative of social existence."
- "Workers' struggles have no necessary priority over popular and democratic struggles.... Social conflicts arising from the role of citizenship — citizens as both politically active beings and recipients and consumers of state services — can be of great significance and should not be dismissed as superficial or 'superstructural'."[23]

As Offe's challenge shows, it makes little sense to speak about a Marxist tradition or to intone that "Marxist theory tells us that...." Such assertions reduce Marxism's ability to analyze the contemporary wage-labour relationship in any given setting or to identify the emerging opposition to capital in a specific country. It is precisely these two factors that are central to the contemporary agenda and that traditional Marxism is often ill-equipped to handle.

Feminist Theory

A second challenge comes from feminist theory. Political economy continues to suffer from being a male-dominated "professional ghetto." While some progress has been made, it is true that feminist theory is often treated as marginal to the macroconcerns of political economy. All too frequently, only the slightest attempt is made to integrate the innovative new work by feminist theorists into the teaching of political economy. The issues of women, women's work and gender are given only token attention in most political economy courses, often relegated to the end of the course! Despite this, the women's movement and feminist theory are redrawing the cultural and political map, taking over terrain once occupied by the male political intelligentsia and the revolutionary political movements. Their work is essential to the future development of political economy because, in questioning the traditional gender division of labour, they assert the centrality of non-economic activity as an essential condition of the modern era. This is a major breakthrough and one that is providing an impetus for a powerful new language of public discourse.

The Rise of the Right and the Disappearance of the "National Question"

A third challenge comes from the rise of the political right in Canada following Brian Mulroney's election victory. At the political level, the federal government seems intent on dismembering some of Canada's most basic social welfare programs by radically altering the concept of universality. These and other measures mark an end to the cross-class consensus that has shaped Canadian social democracy since the postwar years. Of equal importance is the fact that these initiatives come at a time when Quebec no longer occupies the centre stage of Canadian politics. The combined effect of the defeat of the referendum, the signing of the Constitution without Quebec's agreement and, most recently, René Lévesque's own repudiation of sovereignty as the principal goal of the PQ, has left a political vaccuum at the centre of Canadian political life. In the past, a focused, Quebec-based radicalism was often the inspiration for parallel movements in English Canada. The current decline of militant working-class politics in Quebec has had serious repercussions beyond its borders. Now that Quebec has lost its determination to fight for a new political status, one of the major constraints on Ottawa has been removed and English Canada can no longer lean back and count on Quebec nationalism to act as a counterweight to Ottawa's authoritarian attempts to centralize power at the expense of the provinces. In the 1980s the dynamics of Canadian federalism have radically swung in favour of the central government. The precipitous decline in Quebec nationalism creates a politically dangerous situation for English Canada and for English Canadian political economy.

English Canadian political economists have never found it easy to come to terms with Canada's national question. For the better part of two decades, there was never any significant debate among political economists on the type of partnership that English Canada might establish with Quebec.[24] While some left-wing political economists were sympathetic towards Quebec nationalism, there was no broad consensus on acceptance of Quebec as an equal. Indeed, there was much support for Ottawa's attempt to contain Quebec's aspirations for a new political status. Even though it makes less and less sense to see the field of political economy, in Garth Stevenson's words, "polarized between 'centralists' and 'provincialists'," political economists have paid a high price for not dealing with Quebec nationalism and Canada's national question in terms that went beyond treating Quebec as an ethnic community in the Canadian mosaic. The absence of any new theoretical and analytical work on Canadian federalism has only served to reinforce the two solitudes of Canadian political economy.

Political Economy and Public Discourse

Given these challenges from Marxism, feminist theory, Quebec and the rise of the political right, what kind of contribution can political economists realistically expect to make? Outside the university, political economists will only have a critical role to play in evaluating the social and economic consequences of state and private sector policy if they are prepared to intervene in public debate and raise difficult issues that are not being addressed. As Innis astutely remarked, the concentration of power in the hands of the few has meant that Canadian "political life has become a blazing furnace burning off material which might have been used for the development of a broad cultural base."[25] In a country with such an abysmally low level of political debate, it is essential that the language and content of public discourse change to reflect the reality of Canada both socially and culturally. To neglect the importance of discourse only contributes to the marginalization of political economy in the country at large.

Loosely defined, discourse means little more than the articulation of a general sensibility. More formally, as Frank Stark noted in a recent paper, "it is the language of communication and discussion that goes on in everyday political struggles and interaction."[26] If discourse is not encouraged in a capitalist democracy, the essential vitality of society is lost and social change is slowed to a snail's pace.

Canadian discourse remains narrowly elitist and technocratic, dominated by business interests and largely unmarked by the marginal or the unpredictable world of gender, class and ethnicity. John Porter was intrigued by English Canada's lack of a free-standing, popular and innovative language of politics. He once remarked that what distinguished Canadian liberalism is that it had no defensive values and it sought to protect only universal ones. The absence of a clearly defined political project in English Canada (unlike Quebec) has reinforced Canadian liberalism's hegemonic control over public discourse in two ways: first, by devoting its enormous resources to attacking ideologies such as populism or nationalism, that do have something positive to offer politically and culturally; second, and ironically, by its seemingly infinite capacity to absorb the symbols and language of these very same ideologies (such as nationalism and, more recently, feminism) for short-term state ends. It has, as well, consistently refused all dialogue with Marxism, ignoring its humanizing influence as well as its more powerful theoretical concepts and concerns. Canadian socialism, however, is not above reproach, since it failed to force liberalism "to explain itself" and thus evoke the same sort of broad centrist response from the state and elites that has occurred in Europe. As Gad Horowitz so perceptively writes, this has meant "a situation where the centre and the left dance around one another, frustrating one another and living off the frustration; each is locked into the dance by the existence of the other."[27] Small wonder, given our political culture, that the work of political economists is hardly known outside the university and that Marxist political economy continues to be excluded from the mainstream of political life.

The "closed" character of public discourse has had far-reaching consequences in Canada, a country with multiple political arenas in which issues are perceived differently. Only with the greatest effort is it possible to generate any stable, broad-based majority consensus on a specific issue. While there is a strong intellectual tradition, from Harold Innis to George Grant, among others, of mounting a sustained critique of the state and North American liberalism, the rejectionist wing of liberal thought, to borrow Arthur Kroker's phrase, has never offered a viable alternative to late capitalism. The failure to articulate a nationally applicable alternative has frequently encouraged a narrow regional perspective and intellectual autarky. In Gorz's words, "Communal autarky always has an impoverishing effect: the more self-sufficient and numerically limited a community is, the smaller the range of activities and choices it can offer its members. If it has no opening to an area of exogenous activity, the community becomes a prison."[28]

Tilling Society's Memory

The analogy of a prison is apt. A people without a capacity for self-realization inhabit a "closed" universe in the Sartrian sense. In this condition, how does the social scientist, in Margaret Atwood's words, "see what is there"? The fundamental challenge is not only to describe what is there, but also to see it in a more powerful way. In the language of Anne Hébert, "Society's memory has to be tilled like a plot of land. You have to fire it from time to time. Burn the weeds down to the roots."[29]

Novelists and writers help us understand that society is imperfectly cohesive and that there are substantial areas of indeterminancy and freedom. But for a society to act upon what it knows intuitively, it needs tools, categories and a larger framework that interprets its particular structured system. Such a system "is not the product of free and voluntary co-operation. Individuals do not produce it starting from themselves. They adapt themselves to the jobs, the functions, skills, environments and hierarchical relations pre-established by society to assume its cohesive functionning."[30]

The 1980s are placing new demands on the discipline of political economy. The state and elite want to appropriate the strategic resource of teaching and research for their own political ends. Political economists who hope to contribute to a new language of discourse must be prepared to ask the most basic questions about political economy and about their own part in generating social meaning if they intend to help develop this society's capacity for self-reflection and, ultimately, social change. As social scientists, do they have the values and norms which generate mass loyalty to the political system, or are they prepared to reject "the whole logic of expertise and dependence which dominates our contemporary culture?"[31] Are political economists to define themselves in highly individualistic terms and be seen to be non-partisan, value-free social scientists divorced from social and political conflicts? Are they to be interpreters for the state, which, in Sartre's words, "is so thoroughly delighted in seeing itself mirrored...because it recognizes the notions it has about itself; it does not ask to be shown for what it is, but it asks rather for a reflection of what it thinks it is."[32] Or are political economists to be principally interested in undermining, in Offe's words, "the false empirical assumptions and beliefs upon which the dominant normative images of the social order implicitly rely?"[33]

With more contestation and conflict on the way, political economists have a special contribution to make to public debate. There is no shortage of issues. They range from deindustrialization to free trade; from the attack on existing social entitlements to business's search for new flexibility in the workplace; from women's demands for equal pay for work of equal value to the creation of a non-class of part-time workers largely unprotected by existing legislation; from the legalization of politics to the decline of social movements; from peace activists demanding disarmament to the rise of militarism at home and abroad; from wage restraint programs to the new urban and working poor; from demands for a just society to the multinationals' relentless search for profits and deregulation. Pushed by the international crisis, the state and capital are intent on massively restructuring the economy and dismantling the postwar consensus. As Innis once wrote, quoting Herodotus, the worst fate for the social scientist is "to have much insight and power over nothing." For political economists there are alternatives to this terribly fatalistic view of the role and influence of the social sciences and the social scientist. In the days ahead, the challenge is be as inventive and as vigilant as possible by learning to combine scholarship with relevance.

How to Use This Guide

This guide is intended primarily to introduce students to various aspects of the field of political economy. It is not written for specialists and is inherently a cooperative undertaking, drawing on the insights of its contributors. Each contributor was asked to list about one hundred of the most significant yet accessible works in his/her area of specialization. The brief introductions highlight current debates and the leading edge of research in each sub-field of political economy. These introductions are intended to stimulate interest and indicate the major work in progress.

The *Guide* has been designed to be relevant to the way political economy courses are generally taught. Political economy must be both diffuse and yet coherent, for the strength of the tradition lies in its ability to integrate the research from various disciplines. When an item was included in more than two contributors' lists, we attempted to designate it to the most appropriate field. Given the nature of political economy, there are many unavoidable instances of cross-referencing, which is why an author index is included at the end. Students wanting to generate their own reading list on a specific topic should consult several fields. For example, to explain the issue of wage and price controls, students should consult the sections on state policy and politics, economic crisis, and industrial and commercial policy.

Notes

[1] John S. Saul, *The State and Revolution in Eastern Africa* (New York: Monthly Review Press, 1979); Bonnie Campbell, *Liberation nationale et construction du socialisme en Afrique, Angola, Guinée-Bissau, et Mozambique* (Montreal: Nouvelle Optique, 1977).

[2] Richard Lee, *The !Kung San: Men, Women, and Work in a Foraging Society* (Cambridge: Cambridge University Press, 1979).

[3] Leo Panitch, *Social Democracy and Industrial Militancy: The Labour Party, The Trade Unions and Incomes Policy 1945-1974* (Cambridge: Cambridge University Press, 1976).

[4] Stepan Hymer, *The Multinational Corporation: A Radical Approach*, Robert B. Cohen et al. (ed.) (Cambridge: Cambrdige University Press, 1979).

[5] Robert Cox, *Power and Production* (New York: Columbia University Press, forthcoming).

[6] H.W. Arthurs, D.D. Carter and H.J. Glasbeek, *Labour Law and Industiral Relations in Canada* (Toronto: Butterworth, 1981).

[7] Douglas Hay, "Property, Authority and the Criminal Law," In Doug Hay et al., *Albion's Fatal Tree: Crime and Society in Eighteenth Century England* (London: George Allen and Unwin, 1975).

[8] Jean-Marc Piotte, *Marxisme et socialistes, essais* (Montreal: VLB, éditeur, 1979); Gilles Dostaler, *Valeur et prix: l'histoire d'un debat* (Paris: Presses Universitaires de Grenoble et François Maspero, 1978).

[9] W. Seccombe, "The Housewife and Her Labour under Capitalism," *New Left Review* 83, 1973, pp. 3-24. Mary O'Brien, *The Politics of Reproduction* (London: Routledge and Kegan Paul, 1981).

[10] See Daniel Drache, "Rediscovering Canadian Political Economy," in Wallace Clement and Daniel Drache, *A Practical Guide to Canadian Political Economy* (Toronto: James Lorimer, 1978).

[11] For a useful discussion of the political economy tradition, consult C. Chattopadhyay, "Political Economy: What's in a Name?" *Monthly Review*, April 1974.

[12] *Globalism and the Nation-State*, Massey Lectures (Toronto: CBC Enterprises, 1983), p. 104.

[13] For a contemporary view of the question of commercial capitalism in an American setting, consult Robert B. Reich, *The Next American Frontier* (New York: Times Books, 1983).

[14] Michel Beaud, "Pour le codeveloppement," *Le Monde Diplomatique*, janvier 1985.

[15] The preceding paragraphs follow Beaud's discussion of the principal features of dominant and dependent development. Ibid., p. 9.

[16] See David Wolfe's recent article, "The Rise and Decline of the Keynesian Era in Canada," in Michael Cross and G. Kealey, eds., *Modern Canada*, vol. 5 (Toronto: McClelland and Stewart, 1983).

[17] *Report of the Task Force on Labour Relations* (Ottawa, 1968), p. 25.

[18] Uri Zohar, *Canadian Manufacturing: A Study in Productivity and Technological Change* (Toronto: Canadian Institute for Economic Policy in association with James Lorimer, 1982), p. 34.

[19] Robert Campbell, "Post Keynesian Politics and the Post-Schumpterian World," *Canadian Journal of Political and Social Theory* 8:1-2 (1983).

[20] *Canadian Trade Policy for the 1980s: A Discussion Paper* (Ottawa: Minister of Supply and Services, 1983), p. 6.

[21] Gregory Baum and Duncan Cameron, *Ethics and Economics* (Toronto: James Lorimer, 1984).

[22] Michael J. Piore and Charles F. Sabel, *The Second Industrial Divide* (New York: Basic Books, 1984), p. 9.

[23] Claus Offe, *Contradictions of the Welfare State* (London: Hutchinson, 1984). In particular, see pages 282-87 for Offe's discussion of the contemporary state of Marxist theory. The quotations are drawn from pages 282 and 283 respectively.

[24] Daniel Latouche has written an important study of Canada-Quebec relations, *Le Canada et le Québec: Un Essai Retrospectif et Prospectif*, which will be published shortly by the Macdonald Commission.

[25] The quotation is taken from Reg Whitaker's paper on the political theory of Innis, presented to the H.A. Innis Symposium, Simon Fraser University, March 30-31, 1978.

[26] Frank Stark, "Symbols, Institutions and the Canadian State." Paper presented to the Canadian Political Science Association, Guelph, Ont., June 1984.

[27] Gad Horowitz, "Conservatism, Liberalism and Socialism," in Hugh G. Thorburn, ed., *Party Politics in Canada*, 5th ed., (Scarborough: Prentice-Hall, 1984), p. 69.

[28] André Gorz, *Farewell to the Working Class* (London: Pluto Press, 1980), p. 102.

[29] Anne Hébert, *Kamouraska* (Toronto: PaperJacks, 1974), p. 71.

[30] Gorz, *Farewell*, p. 76.

[31] Patrick J. Monahan, "Mistaking Moral Growth: The Constitutional Mythology of Michael Perry," *Queen's Law Journal*, 9, no. 2 (Spring 1984): 324.

[32] Jean-Paul Sartre, *What Is Literature?* (London: Methuen, 1967), p. 69.

[33] Offe, *Contradictions*, p. 260.

1
Resources and Staples

WALLACE CLEMENT

Much pioneering work in Canadian political economy has focused on resources and staples because of their central role in Canada's development. The classic writings of Harold Innis, A.R.M. Lower, Vernon Fowke and W.A. Mackintosh, and the more recent writings of H.G.J. Aitken, Mel Watkins and Daniel Drache, have proven the staples tradition to be a dynamic locus for theorizing and explaining Canadian political economy. As might be expected, there have been major debates about the ordering of explanatory factors, including the character of the staple, capital formation, the role of technology, the significance of international markets, the availability of labour and the centrality of class struggle.

The field of resource studies is grounded in the staples tradition founded by Harold Innis, whose studies of fur, fish, forest products, minerals, agriculture and energy are the cornerstones of the Canadian political economy tradition. It must also be said that there are literally hundreds of studies on these staples written by people of various theoretical persuasions.

The material basis for the proliferation of such studies resides in the fact that resources are the foundation of the Canadian economy. Canada's early development was a direct result of the search for the staple — fish, fur, square timber, wheat and placer mining, to name the most important. Indeed, it is the commercial staple that had a marked impact on the national infrastructure of roads, canals, ports and railways in the nineteenth century. In the twentieth century, this reliance on and the pursuit of staples shaped the country's development, particularly following the Paley Report's *Resources for Freedom* of the 1950s, filed by a U.S. presidential committee after the Korean War, which, by identifying twenty-two resources crucial to U.S. development and targeting Canada as the primary source for twelve, intensified the exploitation of this country's industrial resources. In particular, the forest, mining and energy industries became the focus for export-led development.

The essential problem of a staples-based economy is the country's ability to capitalize on the benefits of forward, backward and final demand linkages that follow from the resource's exploitation. More recent investigators have tended to focus on the implications of the booms and busts of staples development for labour as well as for capital, placing each within its international context.

There has been much new research on the social and economic consequences of staple-led growth. There has been a renewed interest in the fur trade, particularly in terms of the role of women, the role of native peoples and the evolving relations between trappers, intermediaries and production. Fisheries also continue to be a centre of research for class transformations, gender, race and region. As with all staples, the international market for products and the role of state policies have been the subject of many government commissions reporting on the possible restructuring of the fisheries. Agriculture as a staple also remains an area for theoretical debate on class transformations and class politics. Most critical is the role wheat plays in internal uneven development and international marketing. Both classic and contemporary research on the mining industry has focused not only on resource communities and international markets, but also on class relations, technological change and issues such as health and safety. Research on the forest industries in British Columbia, Ontario, Quebec and the Maritimes has focused on similar issues, including state development policies and fluctuations in labour force demand. The focus of the energy industry has been on the impact of state policy, at both the federal and provincial levels, and on resource development, as well as on regional disparities and class formation.

As long as Canada relies upon resource exports as the basis of its economy, this area will continue to generate debates about the nature of Canada's political economy. The following list offers a sampling of both classical and contemporary writings in the area of resources and staples.

Aitken, H.G.J.
American Capital and Canadian Resources. Cambridge, Mass.: Harvard University Press, 1961.

Alexander, David
The Decay of Trade: An Economic History of the Newfoundland Saltfish Trade, 1935-1965. St. John's: Institute of Social and Economic Research, Memorial University of Newfoundland, 1977.

Apostle, Richard; Kasdan, Leonard; and Hanson, Arthur
"Political Efficacy and Political Activity Among Fishermen in Southwest Nova Scotia." *Journal of Canadian Studies* 19 (Spring 1984): 157-65.

Barrett, L. Gene
"Underdevelopment and Social Movements in the Nova Scotia Fishing Industry to 1938." *Underdevelopment and Social Movements in Atlantic Canada*, pp. 127-60. Edited by Robert J. Brym and R. James Sacouman. Toronto: New Hogtown Press, 1979.

Barrett, L. Gene, and Davis, Anthony
"Floundering in Troubled Waters: The Political Economy of the Atlantic Fishery and the Task Force on Atlantic Fisheries." *Journal of Canadian Studies* 19 (Spring 1984): 125-37.

Berger, Thomas
Northern Frontier, Northern Homeland: The Report of the Mackenzie Valley Pipeline Inquiry. Ottawa: Supply and Services Canada, 1977.

Bertrand, Robert J.
Canada's Oil Monopoly: The Story of the $12 Billion Rip-off of Canada's Consumers: Highlights from the State of Competition in the Canadian Petroleum Industry, the Government Report that Alleges Monopoly Practices by Canada's Big Oil Companies. Toronto: James Lorimer, 1981.

Bourgeault, Ron
"The Indian, the Métis and the Fur Trade: Class, Sexism and Racism in the Transition from 'Communism' to Capitalism." *Studies in Political Economy*, no. 12 (Fall 1983), pp. 45-80.

Bradbury, J.H.
"State Corporations and Resource Based Development in Quebec, Canada: 1960-1980." *Economic Geography* 58 (January 1982): 45-61.

"Class Structures and Class Conflicts in 'Instant' Resource Towns in British Columbia — 1965 to 1972." *BC Studies*, no. 37 (Spring 1978), pp. 3-18.

Bradwin, Edmund W.
The Bunkhouse Man: A Study of Work and Pay in the Camps of Canada, 1903-1914. Toronto: University of Toronto Press, 1972. (First published 1928.)

Britton, John N.H., and Gilmour, James M.
The Weakest Link: A Technological Perspective on Canadian Industrial Underdevelopment. Background Study no. 43. Ottawa: Science Council of Canada, 1978.

Brown, Jennifer S.H.
Strangers in Blood: Fur Trade Company Families in Indian Country. Vancouver: University of British Columbia Press, 1980.

Buckley, Kenneth
"The Role of the Staple Industries in Canada's Economic Development." *Journal of Economic History* 18 (December 1958): 439-50.

Burley, Kevin H., ed.
The Development of Canada's Staples, 1867-1939: A Documentary Collection. The Carleton Library, no. 56. Toronto: McClelland and Stewart, 1971.

Cameron, S. Donald
The Education of Everett Richardson: The Nova Scotia Fishermen's Strike, 1970-71. Toronto: McClelland and Stewart, 1977.

Canada. Commission on Pacific Fisheries Policy
Turning the Tide: A New Policy for Canada's Pacific Fisheries: The Commission on Pacific Fisheries Policy Final Report. (The Pearse Report.) Vancouver: The Commission, 1982.

Canada. Royal Commission on Canada's Economic Prospects
The Outlook for the Canadian Forest Industries. Hull: Queen's Printer, 1957.

Canada. Task Force on Atlantic Fisheries
Navigating Troubled Waters: A New Policy for the Atlantic Fisheries. Ottawa: Supply and Services Canada, 1983.

Clark, Melissa Helen
"The Canadian State and Staples: An Ear to Washington." Ph.D. dissertation, McMaster University, 1980.

Clarkson, Thora Kerr
Miners and Prospectors of Canada: A Bibliography. Toronto: T.K. Clarkson, 1982.

Clement, Wallace
"Canada's Coastal Fisheries: Formation of Unions, Cooperatives and Associations." *Journal of Canadian Studies* 19 (Spring 1984): 5-33.

Clement, Wallace (con'd)
"Transformations in Mining: A Critique of H.A. Innis." *Class, Power and Property: Essays on Canadian Society*, pp. 172-93. Toronto: Methuen, 1983.

"Transformations in Mining: A Critique of H.A. Innis." *Class, Power and Property: Essays on Canadian Society*, pp. 172-93. Toronto: Methuen, 1983.

Hardrock Mining: Industrial Relations and Technological Changes at INCO. Toronto: McClelland and Stewart, 1981.

Davis, Anthony, and Kasdan, Leonard
"Bankrupt Government Policies and Belligerent Fishermen Responses: Dependency and Conflict in Southwest Nova Scotia." *Journal of Canadian Studies* 19 (Spring 1984): 108-24.

Denison, Merrill
The People's Power: The History of Ontario Hydro. Toronto: McClelland and Stewart, 1960.

Deverell, John
Falconbridge: Portrait of a Canadian Mining Multinational. Toronto: James Lorimer, 1975.

Drache, Daniel
"Harold Innis and Canadian Capitalist Development." *Canadian Journal of Political and Social Theory* 6 (Winter-Spring 1982): 35-60.

"Staple-ization: A Theory of Canadian Capitalist Development." *Imperialism, Nationalism and Canada*, pp. 15-33. Edited by John Saul and Craig Heron. Toronto: New Hogtown Press, 1977.

Fowke, Vernon Clifford
Canadian Agricultural Policy: The Historical Pattern. Toronto: University of Toronto Press, 1946.

Galbraith, J.S.
The Hudson's Bay Company as an Imperial Factor, 1821-1869. Toronto: University of Toronto Press, 1957.

Glenday, Daniel
"Thirty Years of Labour Relations in the Mining Industry in Rouyn-Noranda, Quebec, 1934-1964." *De l'Abitibi-Témiskaming 5*, pp. 77-119. Cahiers du Département d'histoire et de géographie, no. 5. Rouyn, Qué.: Collège du nord-ouest, 1979.

Goulding, Jay
The Last Outport: Newfoundland in Crisis. Ottawa: D.F. Runge, 1982.

Hann, Russell
Farmers Confront Industrialism: Some Historical Perspectives on Ontario Agrarian Movements. 3rd. rev. ed. Toronto: New Hogtown Press, 1975.

Hartland, Penelope
"Factors in Economic Growth in Canada." *Journal of Economic History* 15:1 (1955): 13-22.

Hayward, Brian
"The Co-op Strategy." *Journal of Canadian Studies* 19 (Spring 1984): 48-64.

Heath, Caroline, and Lane, Patrick, eds.
"Canadian Working Class Poetry." *Canadian Dimension* 15 (February 1981): 22-41.

Higgins, Larratt
"The Alienation of Canadian Resources: The Case of the Columbia River Treaty." *Close the 49th Parallel, Etc.: The Americanization of Canada*, pp. 223-40. Edited by Ian Lumsden. Toronto: University of Toronto Press, 1970.

Hill, Arnold Victor
Tides of Change: A Story of Fishermen's Co-operatives in British Columbia. Prince Rupert, B.C.: Prince Rupert Fishermen's Co-operative Association, 1967.

Innis, Harold A.
Essays in Canadian Economic History. Edited by Mary Q. Innis. Toronto: University of Toronto Press, 1956.

The Fur Trade in Canada: An Introduction to Canadian Economic History. Rev. ed. Toronto: University of Toronto Press, 1956. (First edition 1930.)

The Cod Fisheries: The History of an International Economy. Rev. ed. Toronto: University of Toronto, 1954. (First edition 1940.)

Settlement and the Mining Frontier. Canadian Frontiers of Settlement, vol. 9, part 2. Edited by W.A. Mackintosh and W.L.G. Joerg. Toronto: Macmillan, 1936.

Irvine, William
The Farmers in Politics. Toronto: McClelland and Stewart, 1976. (First published 1920.)

Jenness, Diamond
The Indians of Canada. 7th ed. Toronto: University of Toronto Press, 1977.

Kierans, Eric
Report on Natural Resource Policy in Manitoba. Prepared for the Government of Manitoba. Winnipeg: Queen's Printer, 1973.

Kilbourn, William
Pipeline: TransCanada and the Great Debate: A History of Business and Politics. Toronto: Clarke, Irwin, 1970.

Knight, Rolf
Indians at Work: An Informal History of Native Indian Labour in British Columbia, 1858-1930. Vancouver: New Star Books, 1978.

Work Camps and Company Towns in Canada and the U.S.: An Annotated Bibliography. Vancouver: New Star Books, 1975.

Laxer, James
Oil and Gas: Ottawa, the Provinces and the Petroleum Industry. Toronto: James Lorimer, 1983.

Laxer, James, and Martin, Anne, eds.
The Big Tough Expensive Job: Imperial Oil and the Canadian Economy. Erin, Ont.: Press Porcepic, 1977.

Legendre, Camille
"Les Débuts de la rémuneration à la pièce dans l'industrie forestière." *Recherches sociographiques* 20 (septembre-octobre 1979): 301-35.

Leyton, Elliott
Dying Hard: The Ravages of Industrial Carnage. Toronto: McClelland and Stewart, 1975.

Lorimer, Rowland, and McMullin, Stanley E., eds.
Canada and the Sea. Canadian Issues, vol. 3, no. 1. Willowdale, Ont.: Association for Canadian Studies, 1980.

Lower, A.R.M.
Great Britain's Wood Yard: British America and the Timber Trade, 1763-1867. Montreal: McGill-Queen's University Press, 1973.

The North American Assault on the Canadian Forest: A History of the Lumber Trade Between Canada and the United States. Toronto: Ryerson, 1938.

Lucas, Rex
Minetown, Milltown, Railtown: Life in Canadian Communities of a Single Industry. Toronto: University of Toronto Press, 1971.

Macdonald, David A.
Power Begins at the Cod End: The Newfoundland Trawlermen's Strike, 1974-75. St. John's: Institute of Social and Economic Research, Memorial University of Newfoundland, 1980.

MacDowell, Laurel Sefton
'Remember Kirkland Lake': The History and Effects of the Kirkland Lake Gold Miners' Strike, 1941-42. Toronto: University of Toronto Press, 1983.

Mackintosh, W.A.
"Economic Factors in Canadian History." *Approaches to Canadian Economic History: A Selection of Essays,* pp. 1-15. Edited by W.T. Easterbrook and M.H. Watkins. Toronto: McClelland and Stewart, 1967.

MacMillan, James A.; Gislason, G.S.; and Lyon, S.
Human Resources in Canadian Mining: A Preliminary Analysis. Kingston, Ont.: Centre for Resource Studies, Queen's University, 1977.

Macpherson, C.B.
Democracy in Alberta: Social Credit and the Party System. 2nd ed. Toronto: University of Toronto Press, 1968. (First edition 1953.)

Main, O.D.
The Canadian Nickel Industry: A Study in Market Control and Public Policy. Toronto: University of Toronto Press, 1955.

Marchak, M. Patricia
Green Gold: The Forestry Industry in British Columbia. Vancouver: University of British Columbia Press, 1983.

Mathias, Philip
Takeover: The 22 Days of Risk and Decision that Created the World's Largest Newsprint Empire, Abitibi-Price. Toronto: Maclean-Hunter, 1976.

McCallum, John
Unequal Beginnings: Agriculture and Economic Development in Quebec and Ontario until 1870. Toronto: University of Toronto Press, 1980.

McFarland, Joan
"Changing Modes of Social Control in a New Brunswick Fish Packing Town." *Studies in Political Economy,* no. 4 (Autumn 1980), pp. 99-113.

McKay, Paul
Electric Empire: The Inside Story of Ontario Hydro. Toronto: Between the Lines, 1983.

McMullan, John L.
"State, Capital and Debt in the British Columbia Fishing Fleet, 1970-1982." *Journal of Canadian Studies* 19 (Spring 1984): 65-88.

McNally, David
"Staple Theory as Commodity Fetishism: Marx, Innis and Canadian Political Economy." *Studies in Political Economy*, no. 6 (Autumn 1981), pp. 35-63.

Mendels, M.M.
The Asbestos Industry of Canada. Montreal: McGill University, 1930.

Mitchell, Don
The Politics of Food. Toronto: James Lorimer, 1975.

Moore, E.S.
American Influence in Canadian Mining. Toronto: University of Toronto Press, 1941.

Muszynski, Alicja
"The Organization of Women and Ethnic Minorities in a Resource Industry: A Case Study of the Unionization of Shoreworkers in the B.C. Fishing Industry, 1937-1949." *Journal of Canadian Studies* 19 (Spring 1984): 89-107.

Nelles, H.V.
The Politics of Development: Forests, Mines and Hydro-Electric Power in Ontario, 1849-1941. Toronto: Macmillan, 1974.

North, George
A Ripple, A Wave: The Story of Union Organization in the B.C. Fishing Industry. From a draft manuscript by George North. Revised and edited by Harold Griffin. Vancouver: Fisherman Publishing Society, 1974.

Ontario. Royal Commission on the Health and Safety of Workers in Mines. *Report.* (The Ham Commission.) Toronto: Ministry of the Attorney General, 1976.

Otter, A. den
"Social Life of a Mining Community: The Coal Branch." *Alberta Historical Review* 17 (Autumn 1969): 1-11.

Parker, Ian
" 'Commodity Fetishism' and 'Vulgar Marxism': On 'Rethinking Canadian Political Economy'." *Studies in Political Economy*, no. 10 (Winter 1983), pp. 143-72.

Pearse, Peter H., ed.
The Mackenzie Pipeline: Arctic Gas and Canadian Energy Policy. Toronto: McClelland and Stewart, 1974.

People's Commission on Unemployment
'Now That We've Burned Our Boats...': The Report of the People's Commission on Unemployment, Newfoundland and Labrador. St. John's: Newfoundland and Labrador Federation of Labour, 1978.

Pratt, Larry
"Energy: The Roots of National Policy." *Studies in Political Economy*, no. 7 (Winter 1982), pp. 27-59.

The Tar Sands: Syncrude and the Politics of Oil. Edmonton: Hurtig, 1976.

Pratt, Larry, and Richards, John
Prairie Capitalism: Power and Influence in the New West. Toronto: McClelland and Stewart, 1979.

Radforth, Ian
"Woodsworkers and the Mechanization of the Pulpwood Logging Industry in Northern Ontario, 1950-1970." Canadian Historical Association. *Historical Papers: A Selection from the Papers Presented at the Annual Meeting Held at Ottawa* (1982), pp. 71-102.

Ray, Arthur J.
Indians in the Fur Trade: Their Role as Trappers, Hunters, and Middlemen in the Lands Southwest of Hudson Bay, 1660-1870. Toronto: University of Toronto Press, 1974.

Ray, Arthur J., and Freeman, Donald
'Give Us Good Measure': An Analysis of Hudson's Bay Company Post Accounts to 1763. Toronto: University of Toronto Press, 1978.

Rich, E.E.
The Hudson's Bay Co., 1670-1870. 3 vols. Toronto: McClelland and Stewart, 1960.

Richardson, Boyce
James Bay: The Plot to Drown the North Woods. Toronto: Clarke, Irwin, 1973.

Ryerson, Stanley
"Conflicting Approaches in the Social Sciences." *Marxist Quarterly* (Toronto) 1 (Spring 1962): 46-64.

Sinclair, B.; Ball, N.R.; and Petersen, J.O., eds.
Let Us Be Honest and Modest: Technology and Society in Canadian History. Toronto: Oxford University Press, 1974.

Sinclair, Peter R.
"Fishermen of Northwest Newfoundland: Domestic Commodity Production in Advanced Capitalism." *Journal of Canadian Studies* 19 (Spring 1984): 34-47.

Smith, Philip
Brinco: The Story of Churchill Falls. Toronto: McClelland and Stewart, 1975.

Swift, Jamie
Cut and Run: The Assault on Canada's Forests. Toronto: Between the Lines, 1983.

The Big Nickel: Inco at Home and Abroad. Kitchener, Ont.: Between the Lines, 1977.

Tataryn, Lloyd
Dying for a Living. Ottawa: Deneau and Greenberg, 1979.

Trudeau, Pierre Elliott, ed.
The Asbestos Strike. Toronto: James Lorimer, 1974. (First published in French 1956.)

United States. President's Materials Policy Commission (The Paley Commission)
Resources for Freedom: A Report to the President. 5 vols. Washington: U.S. Government Printing Office, 1952.

Van Kirk, Sylvia

'Many Tender Ties': Women in Fur-Trade Society in Western Canada, 1670-1870. Winnipeg: Watson & Dwyer, 1980.

Veeman, Terry, and Veeman, Michele

The Future of Grain. Toronto: James Lorimer in association with the Canadian Institute for Economic Policy, 1984.

Warnock, Jack

"Potash in Saskatchewan: Keeping It Safe for the 'Multi-Nationals'." *This Magazine* 7 (January 1974): 3-9.

Warriner, G. Keith, and Guppy, L. Neil

"From Urban Centre to Isolated Village: Regional Effects of Limited Entry in the British Columbia Fishery." *Journal of Canadian Studies* 19 (Spring 1984): 138-56.

Watkins, Mel

"The Innis Tradition in Canadian Political Economy." *Canadian Journal of Political and Social Theory* 6 (Winter-Spring 1982): 12-34.

"The Staple Theory Revisited." *Journal of Canadian Studies* 12 (Winter 1977): 83-95.

"A Staple Theory of Economic Growth." *Canadian Journal of Economics and Political Science* 29 (May 1963): 141-58. (Reprinted in *Approaches to Canadian Economic History: A Selection of Essays*, pp. 49-73. Edited by W.T. Easterbrook and Mel Watkins. Toronto: McClelland and Stewart, 1967.)

Williams, Rick

"Inshore Fishermen, Unionization, and the Struggle Against Underdevelopment Today." *Underdevelopment and Social Movements in Atlantic Canada*, pp. 161-75. Edited by Robert J. Brym and R. James Sacouman. Toronto: New Hogtown Press, 1979.

Willson, Bruce F.

"An Assessment of the National Energy Program 1980." *Journal of Business Administration* 13:1 & 2 (1982): 29-55.

Wilson, Barry

Beyond the Harvest: Canadian Grain at the Crossroads. Saskatoon: Western Producer Prairie Books, 1981.

Wood, Louis Aubrey

A History of Farmers' Movements in Canada. Toronto: University of Toronto Press, 1975. (First published 1924.)

2
Banking, Finance and Capital Accumulation

R.T. NAYLOR

Since the first edition of the *Guide* was issued in 1978, there has been a twofold revolution in the literature concerning the Canadian financial system. On the one hand, there has been an enormous burst of published work, only part of which can be reflected in this brief summary and list of titles. On the other hand, the financial environment has been transformed by the triumph of monetarism and/ or supply-side religion in the leading centres of ideological and political power and, ipso facto, by the defeat of sound practical sense in the formulation of economic policy. Simultaneously, of course, has come a rapid evolution of the structure of Canadian banking and financial institutions, paralleling the global march towards the financial services supermarket. As yet, the literature does not adequately reflect this development.

More specifically, at the time of the first edition of the *Guide*, much policy debate still centred on the nature and role of the transnational corporation as an instrument for affecting international financial transfers. Since then, Canadian banks have been participating heavily in the explosion of international banking activity. While the developments have started outside Canada, the relevance for Canadian political economy clearly cannot be underestimated.

The following titles have been subdivided into categories for convenience of reference, but it should be understood that there is much overlap between them.

While English-language titles have been selected, there is a wealth of literature in French on many of the topics treated.

A. CAPITAL ACCUMULATION IN A HISTORICAL CONTEXT

Aitken, Hugh G.J.
  American Capital and Canadian Resources. Cambridge, Mass.: Harvard University Press, 1961.

  "A Note on the Capital Resources of Upper Canada." *Canadian Journal of Economics and Political Science* 18 (November 1952): 525-33.

Buckley, Kenneth
  Capital Formation in Canada, 1896-1930. The Carleton Library, no. 77. Toronto: McClelland and Stewart, 1970. (First published 1955.)

McCallum, John
  Unequal Beginnings: Agriculture and Economic Development in Quebec and Ontario Until 1870. Toronto: University of Toronto Press, 1980.

Myers, Gustavus
  A History of Canadian Wealth. Vol. 1, 1st Canadian ed. Toronto: James, Lorimer, 1972. (First published 1914.)

Naylor, R.T.
  "Canada in the European Age." *Canadian Journal of Political and Social Theory* 7 (Fall 1983): 97-125.

  "The Canadian State, the Accumulation of Capital and the Great War." *Journal of Canadian Studies* 16 (Fall-Winter 1981): 26-55.

  "The Rise and Fall of the Third Commercial Empire of the St. Lawrence." *Capitalism and the National Question in Canada,* pp. 1-41. Edited by G. Teeple. Toronto: University of Toronto Press, 1972.

Pentland, H. Clare
  Labour and Capital in Canada, 1650-1860. Edited and with an introduction by Paul Phillips. Toronto: James Lorimer, 1981.

  "Physical Productivity in Canada, 1935-52." *Economic Journal* 64 (June 1954): 399-404.

  "Further Observations on Canadian Development." *Canadian Journal of Economics and Political Science* 19 (August 1953): 403-10.

  "The Role of Capital in Canadian Economic Development Before 1875." *Canadian Journal of Economics and Political Science* 16 (November 1950): 457-74.

B. HISTORY OF THE CANADIAN BANKING AND FINANCIAL SYSTEM

Denison, Merrill
  Canada's First Bank: A History of the Bank of Montreal. 2 vols. Montreal: McClelland and Stewart, 1966-1967.

Hammond, Bray
  "Banking in Canada Before Confederation, 1792-1867." *Approaches to Canadian Economic History: A Selection of Essays,* pp. 127-68. Edited by W.T. Easterbrook and M.H. Watkins. Toronto: McClelland and Stewart, 1967.

McIvor, Russell Craig
  Canadian Monetary, Banking and Fiscal Development. Toronto: Macmillan, 1958.

Naylor, R.T.
  The History of Canadian Business, 1867-1914. Vol. 1. Toronto: James Lorimer, 1975.

Neufeld, Edward Peter
  The Financial System of Canada: Its Growth and Development. Toronto: Macmillan, 1972.

Neufeld, Edward Peter, ed.
Money and Banking in Canada: Historical Documents and Commentary. The Carleton Library, no. 17. Toronto: McClelland and Stewart, 1964.

Ross, V.
A History of the Canadian Bank of Commerce. Vols. 1 and 2. Toronto: Oxford University Press, 1920-34.

Shortt, Adam, and Doughty, Arthur George, eds.
Canada and Its Provinces: A History of the Canadian People and their Institutions by One Hundred Associates. 23 vols. Toronto: printed by T. & A. Constable at the Edinburgh University Press for the Publishers' Association of Canada, 1913-1914. (Reprinted Toronto: Glasgow, Brook, 1914-1917.) (See various articles on the history of Canadian currency, finance and exchange, summarized from articles by A. Shortt in the *Journal of the Canadian Bankers' Association*, 1901-1908.)

Schull, Joseph, and Gibson, J. Douglas
The Scotiabank Story: A History of the Bank of Nova Scotia, 1832-1982. Toronto: Macmillan, 1982.

Trigge, A.
A History of the Canadian Bank of Commerce: Vol. 3, 1919-1930. Toronto: The Canadian Bank of Commerce, 1934.

C. BUSINESS CYCLES AND ECONOMIC POLICY

Barber, Clarence L., and McCallum, John C.P.
Unemployment and Inflation: The Canadian Experience. Toronto: James Lorimer in association with the Canadian Institute for Economic Policy, 1980.

Baum, Gregory, and Cameron, Duncan
Ethics and Economics: Canada's Catholic Bishops on the Economic Crisis. Toronto: James Lorimer, 1984.

Gonick, Cy
The Great Economic Debate. Toronto: James Lorimer, forthcoming.

Inflation or Depression: The Continuing Crisis of the Canadian Economy. Toronto: James Lorimer, 1975.

Gordon, H. Scott
The Economists Versus the Bank of Canada. Toronto: Ryerson, 1961.

Innis, Harold A.
Problems of Staple Production in Canada. Toronto: Ryerson, 1933.

Kierans, Eric
Globalism and the Nation-State. C.B.C. Massey Lecture Series. Toronto: C.B.C. Enterprises, 1984.

Lamontagne, Maurice
Business Cycles in Canada: The Postwar Experience and Policy Directions. Toronto: James Lorimer in association with the Canadian Institute for Economic Policy, 1984.

Laxer, James
Rethinking the Economy. Toronto: NC Press, 1984.

League for Social Reconstruction
  Social Planning for Canada. The Social History of Canada, no. 26. Toronto: University of Toronto Press, 1975. (First published 1935.)
Safarian, E.A.
  The Canadian Economy in the Great Depression. The Carleton Library, no. 54. Toronto: McClelland and Stewart, 1970. (First published 1959.)

D. CANADIAN ECONOMIC THOUGHT

Brecher, Irving
  Monetary and Fiscal Thought and Policy in Canada, 1919-1939. Toronto: University of Toronto Press, 1957.
Goodwin, Crawford D.W.
  Canadian Economic Thought: The Political Economy of a Developing Nation, 1814-1914. Durham, N.C.: Duke University Press, 1961.
Johnson, Harry G.
  The Canadian Quandary. Toronto: McClelland and Stewart, 1977.
Naylor, R.T.
  "Johnson on Cambridge and Keynes." *Canadian Journal of Political and Social Theory* 5 (Winter/Spring 1981): 216-29.
Neill, Robin
  A New Theory of Value: The Canadian Economics of H.A. Innis. Toronto: University of Toronto Press, 1972.
Watkins, Mel
  "The Economics of Nationalism and the Nationality of Economics: A Critique of Neoclassical Theorizing." *Canadian Journal of Economics* 11 (November Supplement 1978): 87 + .

E. FOREIGN INVESTMENT IN CANADA

Brecher, Irving
  "The Flow of United States Investment Funds into Canada Since World War II." *The American Economic Impact on Canada*, pp. 100-26. Edited by H.G.J. Aitken et al. Durham, N.C.: Duke University Press, 1959.
Canada. Task Force on the Structure of Canadian Industry
  Foreign Ownership and the Structure of Canadian Industry: Report. (The Watkins Report.) Ottawa: Information Canada, 1968.
Canada. Trade and Commerce
  Foreign Direct Investment in Canada. (The Gray Report.) Ottawa: Queen's Printer, 1972.
Caves, Richard E., and Reuber, Grant L.
  Canadian Economic Policy and the Impact of International Capital Flows. Toronto: University of Toronto Press, 1969.
Field, F.W.
  Capital Investments in Canada: Some Facts and Figures Respecting One of the Most Attractive Investment Fields in the World. 2nd ed. Montreal: Monetary Times of Canada, 1914. (First edition 1911.)

Hartland, Penelope
"Canada's Balance of Payments Since 1868." *Trends in the American Economy in the 19th Century*, pp. 717-55. Princeton: Princeton University Press, 1960.

Levitt, Kari
Silent Surrender: The Multinational Corporation in Canada. Toronto: Macmillan, 1970.

Marshall, Herbert; Southard, Frank; and Taylor, Kenneth W.
Canadian-American Industry: A Study in International Investment. The Carleton Library, no. 93. Toronto: McClelland and Stewart, 1976. (First published 1936.)

Naylor, R.T.
"Dominion of Capital: Canada and International Investment." *Domination*, pp. 33-56. Edited by A. Kontos. Toronto: University of Toronto Press, 1975.
The History of Canadian Business, 1867-1914. Vol. 2. Toronto: James Lorimer, 1975.

Paterson, D.G.
"European Financial Capital and British Columbia: An Essay on the Role of the Regional Entrepreneur." *BC Studies*, no. 21 (Spring 1974), pp. 33-47.

F. THE BANKING AND FINANCIAL SYSTEM

Baum, Daniel Jay
The Banks of Canada in the Commonwealth Caribbean: Economic Nationalism and Multinational Enterprises of a Medium Power. New York: Praeger, 1974.

Belford, Terrence
Trust: The Greymac Affair. Toronto: James Lorimer, 1983.

Canada. Parliament. House of Commons. Standing Committee on Finance, Trade and Economic Affairs
Bank Profits. Issue no. 109 of the Minutes of Proceedings of the Standing Committee, 1st session of the 32nd Parliament. Ottawa: Supply and Services Canada, 1982.

McQueen, Rod
The Money-Spinners: An Intimate Portrait of the Men Who Run Canada's Banks. Toronto: Macmillan, 1983.

Nagy, P.
The International Business of Canadian Banks. Montreal: Centre for International Business Studies, 1983.

Naylor, R.T.
Political and Structural Factors Behind the Bank Profits Enquiry. Ottawa: Canadian Centre for Policy Alternatives, 1982.

Riis, Nelson A., and Orlikow, David
Report on the Inquiry into Chartered Bank Profits. Ottawa: New Democratic Party, 1982.

Stewart, Walter
Towers of Gold, Feet of Clay: The Canadian Banks. Toronto: Collins, 1982.

G. MONETARISM AND ITS AFTERMATH

Cornwall, John, and Maclean, Wendy
Economic Recovery For Canada. Toronto: James Lorimer in association with the Canadian Institute for Economic Policy, 1984.

Donner, Arthur W., and Peters, Douglas D.
The Monetarist Counter-Revolution: A Critique of Canadian Monetary Policy, 1975-1979. Toronto: James Lorimer in association with the Canadian Institute for Economic Policy, 1979.

Hudson, Michael
Canada in the New Monetary Order: Borrow? Devalue? Restructure! Montreal: Institute for Research on Public Policy; distributed by Butterworth, 1978.

Naylor, R.T.
Monetarism and Canadian Policy Alternatives. Ottawa: Canadian Centre for Policy Alternatives, 1982.

Rotstein, Abraham
Rebuilding From Within. Toronto: James Lorimer in association with the Canadian Institute for Economic Policy, 1984.

Torrie, Jill
Banking On Poverty: The Global Impact of the IMF & World Bank. Toronto: Between the Lines, 1983.

H. BIG BUSINESS AND THE FINANCIAL ELITE

Clement, Wallace
Continental Corporate Power: Economic Elite Linkages Between Canada and the United States. Toronto: McClelland and Stewart, 1977.

Chodos, Robert
The C.P.R.: A Century of Corporate Welfare. Toronto: James Lorimer, 1973.

Foster, Peter
Other People's Money: The Banks, the Government and Dome. Toronto: Collins, 1983.

Fournier, Pierre
The Quebec Establishment: The Ruling Class and the State. Montreal: Black Rose Books, 1976.

Lorimer, James
The Developers. Toronto: James Lorimer, 1978.

Newman, Peter
The Canadian Establishment. 2 vols. Toronto: McClelland and Stewart, 1975, 1978.

Niosi, Jorge
Canadian Capitalism: A Study of Power in the Canadian Business Establishment. Toronto: James Lorimer, 1981.

Park, Libbie, and Park, Frank
Anatomy of Big Business. Toronto: James Lorimer, 1973. (First published 1962.)

Wismer, Catherine
Sweethearts: The Builders, the Mob, and the Men. Toronto: James Lorimer, 1980.

3

Class Formation

PAUL PHILLIPS AND ERIN PHILLIPS

Canadian political economy has traditionally followed two paths: the older, more established staple approach associated with its leading exponents, particularly Innis, Mackintosh, Fowke and Creighton; and the more radical class analysis usually identified with the writings of Ryerson and Pentland. In the last decade or so, a new generation of scholars has been exploring some of the interconnections between the two, particularly in the context of the debates over the national question and over the predominance of the role of commercial, financial or industrial capital in the origin and form of Canada. In their search for explanations, those who favour a staple approach tend to seize upon the dependency model from development economics; those who favour the class approach are more apt to use the traditional "two-class" Marxist model.

The fact is, neither approach is in itself superior or satisfactory. The staple model does not make the distinction between a staple *trade* (where mercantile capital controls the terms of exchange) and a staple *industry* (where industrial capital controls the means of production). Similarly, the class analysis has tended to ignore the fact that, at least until the Second World War, the majority of Canadians were neither capitalists nor wage workers but were independent commodity producers or artisans, subcontractors (what are now known as dependent contractors), petty merchants, professionals or bureaucrats. Indeed, among some *habitant* sectors of Quebec in the nineteenth century and among the aboriginal population, a state of near self-sufficiency existed in which contact with either commercial or industrial capital was of relatively minor importance.

The literature on class formation, therefore, is comprised of a wide variety of work, including, of course, the writing on wage labour and industrial capital, much of which will be referred to in other sections of this guide. Therefore, more attention will be given here to agrarian and other non-wage, non-industrial capital formations than would otherwise be warranted. The first subsection in this list deals with more general works, while the second is concerned with the working class. The third subsection deals with independent commodity production (including agrarian movements), and the final one with capitalist class formations.

With thanks to Jean and Gerry Friesen for their help.

A. GENERAL

Bourque, Gilles, and Laurin-Frenette, Nicole
    "Social Classes and Nationalist Ideologies in Quebec, 1760-1970." *Capi-*

talism and the National Question in Canada, pp. 185-210. Edited by G. Teeple. Toronto: University of Toronto Press, 1972.

Brodie, M. Janine, and Jensen, Jane
Crisis, Challenge and Change: Party and Class in Canada. Toronto: Methuen, 1980.

Brym, Robert J., and Sacouman, R. James, eds.
Underdevelopment and Social Movements in Atlantic Canada. Toronto: New Hogtown Press, 1979.

Caldarola, Carlo, ed.
Society and Politics in Alberta: Research Papers. Agincourt, Ont.: Methuen, 1979.

Cooper, John Irwin
"The Social Structure of Montreal in the 1850's." Canadian Historical Association. *Report of the Annual Meeting Held at Montreal, June 6-8, 1956, with Historical Papers* (1956), pp. 63-73.

Craven, Paul, and Traves, Tom
"The Class Politics of the National Policy, 1872-1933." *Journal of Canadian Studies* 14 (Fall 1979): 14-38.

Cuneo, Carl J.
"A Class Perspective on Regionalism." *Modernization and the Canadian State*, pp. 132-56. Edited by Daniel Glenday, Hubert Guindon and Allan Turowetz. Toronto: Macmillan, 1978.

Drache, Daniel
"The Crisis of Canadian Political Economy: Dependency Theory Versus the New Orthodoxy." *Canadian Journal of Political and Social Theory* (Special Issue: "Beyond Dependency") 7 (Fall 1983): 25-49.

"Harold Innis and Canadian Capitalist Development." *Canadian Journal of Political and Social Theory* 6 (Winter/Spring 1982): 35-60.

"Rediscovering Canadian Political Economy." *Journal of Canadian Studies* 11 (August 1976): 3-18.

Ehrensaft, Philip, and Armstrong, Warwick
"The Formation of Dominion Capitalism: Economic Truncation and Class Structure." *Inequality: Essays on the Political Economy of Social Welfare*, pp. 99-155. Edited by Allan Moscovitch and Glenn Drover. Toronto: University of Toronto Press, 1981.

Friesen, Gerald
Prairie West: The History of a Canadian Region, 1640-1980. Toronto: University of Toronto Press, 1984.

Getty, Ian A.L., and Lussier, Antoine G., eds.
As Long as the Sun Shines and Water Flows: Reader in Canadian Native Studies. Vancouver: University of British Columbia Press, 1983.

Guindon, Hubert
"Social Unrest, Social Class and Quebec's Bureaucratic Revolution." *Prophecy and Protest: Social Movements in Twentieth-Century Canada*, pp. 337-46. Edited by Samuel D. Clark, J. Paul Grayson, and Linda Grayson. Toronto: Gage, 1975. (First published in *Queen's Quarterly* 71 [Summer 1964]: 150-62.)

Johnson, Leo A.
"Precapitalist Economic Formations and the Capitalist Labor Market in Canada, 1911-71." *Social Stratification: Canada*, 2nd ed., pp. 89-104. Edited by James E. Curtis and William G. Scott. Scarborough, Ont.: Prentice-Hall, 1979.

History of the County of Ontario, 1615-1875. Whitby, Ont.: Corporation of the County of Ontario, 1973.

"The Development of Class in Canada in the Twentieth Century." *Capitalism and the National Question in Canada*, pp. 141-83. Edited by G. Teeple. Toronto: University of Toronto Press, 1972.

Johnston, William, and Ornstein, Michael D.
"Class, Work and Politics." *Canadian Review of Sociology and Anthropology* 19 (May 1982): 196-214.

Katz, Michael B.
The People of Hamilton, Canadian West: Family and Class in a Mid-Nineteenth-Century City. Cambridge, Mass.: Harvard University Press, 1975.

"Social Structure in Hamilton, Ontario." *Studies in Canadian Social History*, pp. 164-88. Edited by Michiel Horn and Ronald Sabourin. Toronto: McClelland and Stewart, 1974.

Mahon, Rianne
"Canadian Public Policy: The Unequal Structure of Representation." *The Canadian State: Political Economy and Political Power*, pp. 165-98. Edited by Leo Panitch. Toronto: University of Toronto Press, 1977.

McKay, Ian
"Capital and Labour in the Halifax Baking and Confectionery Industry During the Last Half of the Nineteenth Century." *Essays in Canadian Business History*. Edited by Tom Traves. Toronto: McClelland and Stewart, 1984.

"Class Struggle and Mercantile Capitalism: Craftsmen and Labourers on the Halifax Waterfront, 1850-1902." *Working Men Who Got Wet: Proceedings of the Fourth Conference of the Atlantic Canada Shipping Project, July 24-July 26, 1980*, pp. 287-320. Edited by Rosemary Ommer and Gerald Panting. St. John's: Maritime History Group, Memorial University of Newfoundland, 1980.

Mealing, S.R.
"The Concept of Social Class and the Interpretation of Canadian History." *Canadian Historical Review* 46 (September 1965): 201-18.

Ouellet, Fernand
Economic and Social History of Quebec, 1760-1850: Structures and Conjunctures. The Carleton Library, no. 120. Ottawa: Carleton University, 1980.

Panitch, Leo
"Dependency and Class in Canadian Political Economy." *Studies in Political Economy*, no. 6 (Autumn 1981), pp. 7-33.

Pentland, H. Clare
Labour and Capital in Canada, 1650-1860. Edited by Paul Phillips. Toronto: James Lorimer, 1981.

"The Development of a Capitalist Labour Market in Canada." *Canadian Journal of Economics and Political Science* 25 (November 1959): 450-61.

Phillips, Paul
"Unequal Exchange, Surplus Production and the Commercial-Industrial Question." *Explorations in Canadian Political Economy: Essays in Honour of Irene Spry*. Edited by Duncan Cameron. Ottawa: University of Ottawa Press, 1984.

Pratt, Larry, and Richards, John
Prairie Capitalism: Power and Influence in the New West. Toronto: McClelland and Stewart, 1979.

Prentice, Alison
The School Promoters: Education and Social Class in Mid-Nineteenth Century Upper Canada. Toronto: McClelland and Stewart, 1977.

Rea, J.E.
"The Politics of Class: Winnipeg City Council, 1919-45." *The West and the Nation: Essays in Honour of W.L. Morton*, pp. 232-49. Edited by Carl Berger and Ramsay Cook. Toronto: McClelland and Stewart, 1976.

Ryerson, Stanley
"Quebec: Concepts of Class and Nation." *Capitalism and the National Question in Canada*, pp. 211-27. Edited by G. Teeple. Toronto: University of Toronto Press, 1972.

Unequal Union: Confederation and the Roots of Conflict in the Canadas, 1815-1873. Toronto: Progress Books, 1968.

Schecter, Stephen
"Capitalism, Class and Educational Reform in Canada." *The Canadian State: Political Economy and Political Power*, pp. 373-416. Edited by Leo Panitch. Toronto: University of Toronto Press, 1977.

Teeple, Gary
"Land, Labour and Capital in Pre-Confederation Canada." *Capitalism and the National Question in Canada*, pp. 43-66. Edited by G. Teeple. Toronto: University of Toronto Press, 1972.

Williams, G.
"The National Policy Tariffs: Industrial Underdevelopment Through Import Substitution." *Canadian Journal of Political Science* 12 (June 1979): 333-68.

B. WORKING CLASS

Avery, Donald
"Dangerous Foreigners": *European Immigrant Workers and Labour Radicalism in Canada, 1896-1932*. Toronto: McClelland and Stewart, 1979.

Bercuson, David J.
"Labour Radicalism and the Western Industrial Frontier: 1897-1919." *Canadian Historical Review* 58 (June 1977): 154-75.

Bleasdale, Ruth
"Class Conflict on the Canals of Upper Canada in the 1840s." *Readings in Canadian Social History*. Vol. 2: *Pre-Industrial Canada, 1760-1849*. Edited by Michael S. Cross and Gregory S. Kealey. Toronto: McClelland and Stewart, 1982. (First published in *Labour/Le Travailleur*, no. 7 [Spring 1981], pp. 9-39.)

Clement, Wallace
"Transformations in Mining: A Critique of H.A. Innis." *Class, Power and Property: Essays on Canadian Society*, pp. 172-93. Edited by Wallace Clement. Toronto: Methuen, 1983.

Copp, Terry
The Anatomy of Poverty: The Condition of the Working Class in Montreal, 1897-1929. Toronto: McClelland and Stewart, 1974.

Drache, Daniel
"The Formation and Fragmentation of the Canadian Working Class: 1820-1920." *Studies in Political Economy*, no. 15 (Fall 1984), pp. 43-89.

Duncan, Kenneth
"Irish Famine Immigration and the Social Structure of Canada West." *Studies in Canadian Social History*, pp. 140-63. Edited by Michiel Horn and Ronald Sabourin. Toronto: McClelland and Stewart, 1974. (Reprinted from *Canadian Review of Sociology and Anthropology* 2 [February 1965]: 19-40.)

Frank, David, and Reilly, Nolan
"The Emergence of the Socialist Movement in the Maritimes, 1899-1916." *Labour/Le Travailleur*, no. 4 (1979), pp. 84-114.

Harvey, F., éd.
Aspects historiques du mouvement ouvrier au Québec. Etudes d'histoire du Québec no. 6. Montréal: Boréal Express, 1973.

Heron, Craig
"Labourism and the Canadian Working Class." *Labour/Le Travail*, no. 13 (Spring 1984), pp. 45-76.

Kealey, Gregory S.
Toronto Workers Respond to Industrial Capitalism, 1867-1892. Toronto: University of Toronto Press, 1980.

"The Working Class in Recent Canadian Historical Writing." *Acadiensis* 7 (Spring 1978): 116-35.

Working Class Toronto at the Turn of the Century. Toronto: New Hogtown Press, 1975.

Kealey, Gregory, and Warrian, Peter, eds.
Essays in Canadian Working Class History. Toronto: McClelland and Stewart, 1976.

Keddie, Vincent
"Class Identification and Party Preference Among Manual Workers: The Influence of Community Union Membership and Kinship." *Canadian Review of Sociology and Anthropology* 17 (February 1980): 24-36.

Langdon, Steven
The Emergence of the Canadian Working-Class Movement, 1845-75. Toronto: New Hogtown Press, 1973.

LeBlanc, A., and Thwaites, James
Le Monde ouvrier au Québec: bibliographie rétrospective. Collection histoire des travailleurs québécois, no. 1. Montréal: Presses de l'Université du Québec, 1973.

Marchak, Patricia

"Labour in a Staples Economy." *Studies in Political Economy*, no. 2 (Autumn 1979), pp. 7-35.

McCormack, A. Ross

Reformers, Rebels, and Revolutionaries: The Western Canadian Radical Movement, 1899-1919. Toronto: University of Toronto Press, 1977.

Palmer, Bryan D.

Working-Class Experience: The Rise and Reconstitution of Canadian Labour, 1800-1980. Toronto: Butterworth, 1983.

"The Culture of Control." *Readings in Canadian Social History*, vol. 3: *Canada's Age of Industry, 1849-1896*. Edited by Michael S. Cross and Gregory S. Kealey. Toronto: McClelland and Stewart, 1982.

Phillips, Paul

"The National Policy and the Development of the Western Canadian Labour Movement." *Prairie Perspectives 2: Selected Papers of the Western Canadian Studies Conferences [Calgary], 1970, 1971*, pp. 41-62. Edited by A.W. Rasporich and H.C. Klassen. Toronto: Holt, Rinehart & Winston, 1973.

Piva, Michael J.

The Condition of the Working Class in Toronto, 1900-1921. Ottawa: University of Ottawa Press, 1979.

Rouillard, Jacques

"Le Militantisme des travailleurs au Québec et en Ontario, niveau de syndicalisation et mouvement de grève (1900-1980)." *Revue d'histoire de l'Amérique française* 37 (septembre 1983): 201-25.

"L'Action politique ouvrière, 1899-1915." *Idéologies au Canada français, 1900-1929*, pp. 267-312. Sous la direction de Fernand Dumont et al. Québec: Presses de l'Université Laval, 1974.

Traves, Tom

"Class and Culture: Dimensions of Canada's Labour Past, Montreal, March 1980." *Labour/Le Travailleur*, no. 6 (Autumn 1980), pp. 171-7. (A "review" of the McGill Conference on Class and Culture: Dimensions of Canada's Labour Past, 7-8 March 1980.)

Watt, F.W.

"The National Policy, the Workingman and Proletarian Ideas in Victorian Canada." *Canadian Historical Review* 40 (March 1959): 1-26.

C. INDEPENDENT COMMODITY PRODUCTION

Brym, Robert J.

"Regional Social Structure and Agrarian Radicalism in Canada: Alberta, Saskatchewan and New Brunswick." *Canadian Review of Sociology and Anthropology* 15 (August 1978): 339-51.

Conway, J.F.

"Populism in the United States, Russia, and Canada: Explaining the Roots of Canada's Third Parties." *Class, State, Ideology and Change: Marxist Perspectives on Canada*, pp. 305-22. Edited by J. Paul Grayson. Toronto: Holt, Rinehart & Winston, 1980. (Reprinted from the *Canadian Journal of Political Science* 9 [March 1978]: 99-124.)

Fowke, Vernon
The National Policy and the Wheat Economy. Toronto: University of Toronto Press, 1957.

Gagan, David
Hopeful Travellers: Families, Land and Social Change in Mid-Victorian Peel County, Canada West. Toronto: University of Toronto Press, 1981.

Irvine, William
The Farmers in Politics. Toronto: McClelland and Stewart, 1976. (First published 1920.)

Irving, John
The Social Credit Movement in Alberta. Toronto: University of Toronto Press, 1959.

Johnson, Leo A.
"Independent Commodity Production: Mode of Production or Capitalist Class Formation?" *Studies in Political Economy*, no. 6 (Autumn 1981), pp. 93-112.

Lipset, S.M.
Agrarian Socialism: The Cooperative Commonwealth Federation in Saskatchewan: A Study in Political Sociology. Rev. ed. Berkeley: University of California Press, 1971. (First published 1950.)

Macpherson, C.B.
Democracy in Alberta: Social Credit and the Party System. 2nd ed. Toronto: University of Toronto Press, 1968. (First edition 1953.)

McCallum, John
Unequal Beginnings in Quebec and Ontario until 1870: Agricultural and Economic Development. Toronto: University of Toronto Press, 1980.

Morton, W.L.
"The Western Progressive Movement, 1919-1921." *Prophecy and Protest: Social Movements in Twentieth-Century Canada*, pp. 115-29. Edited by Samuel D. Clark, J. Paul Grayson, and Linda M. Grayson. Toronto: Gage, 1975. (Reprinted from the Canadian Historical Association's *Annual Report*, 1946.)

Sacouman, R.J.
"Semi-Proletarianization and Rural Underdevelopment in the Maritimes." *Canadian Review of Sociology and Anthropology* 17 (August 1980): 232-45.

Sharp, Paul F.
The Agrarian Revolt in Western Canada: A Survey Showing American Parallels. Minneapolis: University of Minnesota Press, 1948.

Sinclair, P.R.
"Class Structure and Populist Protest: The Case of Western Canada." *Canadian Journal of Sociology* 1 (Spring 1975): 1-17.

Wood, Louis Aubrey
A History of Farmers' Movements in Canada. Toronto: University of Toronto Press, 1975. (First published 1924.)

D. CAPITALIST

Acheson, T.W.
"The Great Merchant and Economic Development in Saint John 1820-1850." *Acadiensis* 8 (Spring 1979): 3-27.

"Changing Social Origins of the Canadian Industrial Elite, 1880-1910." *Business History Review* 47 (Summer 1973): 189-217.

"The National Policy and the Industrialization of the Maritimes, 1880-1910." *Acadiensis* 1 (Spring 1972).

"The Social Origins of Canadian Industrialization: A Study of Entrepreneurship." Ph.D. dissertation, University of Toronto, 1972.

"The Social Origins of the Canadian Industrial Elite, 1880-1885." *Canadian Business History: Selected Studies, 1497-1971*, pp. 144-74. Edited by D.S. Macmillan. Toronto: McClelland and Stewart, 1972.

Betke, Carl
"The Original City of Edmonton: A Derivative Prairie Urban Community." *Town and City: Aspects of Western Canadian Urban Development*, pp. 309-46. Edited by Alan F.J. Artibise. Regina: Canadian Plains Research Centre, University of Regina, 1981.

Bliss, Michael
A Living Profit: Studies in the Social History of Canadian Business, 1883-1911. Toronto: McClelland and Stewart, 1974.

Clark, S.D.
The Canadian Manufacturers' Association: A Study in Collective Bargaining and Political Pressure. Toronto: University of Toronto Press, 1939.

Clement, Wallace
"The Corporate Elite, the Capitalist Class and the Canadian State." *The Canadian State: Political Economy and Political Power*, pp. 225-48. Edited by Leo Panitch. Toronto: University of Toronto Press, 1977.

The Canadian Corporate Elite: An Analysis of Economic Power. The Carleton Library, no. 89. Toronto: McClelland and Stewart, 1975.

"Inequality of Access: Characteristics of the Canadian Corporate Elite." *Canadian Review of Sociology and Anthropology* 12 (February 1975): 33-52.

Creighton, D.G.
The Commercial Empire of the St. Lawrence, 1760-1850. Toronto: Ryerson, for the Carnegie Endowment for International Peace, 1937. (Republished in 1956 under the title *The Empire of the St. Lawrence.*)

Fischer, L.R., and Sager, Eric W., eds.
The Enterprising Canadians: Entrepreneurs and Economic Development in Eastern Canada, 1820-1914: Proceedings of the Second Conference of the Atlantic Canada Shipping Project, March 30-April 1, 1978. St. John's: Maritime History Group, Memorial University of Newfoundland, 1979.

Katz, Michael B.
"The Entrepreneurial Class in a Canadian City: The Mid-Nineteenth Century." *Journal of Social History* 8 (Winter 1975): 1-29.

Linteau, Paul-André
   "Quelques réflexions autour de la bourgeoisie québécoise 1850-1914." *Revue d'histoire de l'Amérique française* 30 (juin 1976): 55-66.

Macdonald, Larry
   "Merchants Against Industry: An Idea and Its Origins." *Canadian Historical Review* 56 (September 1975): 263-81.

Myers, Gustavus
   A History of Canadian Wealth. 1st Canadian ed. Toronto: James Lorimer, 1972. (First published 1914.)

Naylor, R.T.
   The History of Canadian Business, 1867-1914. 2 vols. Toronto: James Lorimer, 1975.

   "The Rise and Fall of the Third Commercial Empire of the St. Lawrence." *Capitalism and the National Question in Canada*, pp. 1-41. Edited by G. Teeple. Toronto: University of Toronto Press, 1972.

Neis, Barbara
   "Competitive Merchants and Class Struggle in Newfoundland." *Studies in Political Economy*, no. 5 (Spring 1981), pp. 127-43.

Niosi, Jorge
   "The Canadian Bourgeoisie: Towards a Synthetical Approach." *Canadian Journal of Political and Social Theory* (Special Issue: "Beyond Dependency") 7 (Fall 1983): 128-49.

   "The New French-Canadian Bourgeoisie." *Studies in Political Economy*, no. 1 (Spring 1979), pp. 113-61.

Selwood, H.J., and Baril, Evelyn
   "The Hudson's Bay Company and Prairie Town Development, 1870-1888." *Town and City: Aspects of Western Canadian Urban Development*, pp. 61-94. Edited by Alan F.J. Artibise. Regina: Canadian Plains Research Centre, University of Regina, 1981.

Stelter, G.A.
   "Community Development in Toronto's Commercial Empire: The Industrial Towns of the Nickel Belt, 1883-1931." *Laurentian University Review* 6 (June 1974): 3-53.

Tulchinsky, Gerald J.J.
   The River Barons: Montreal Businessmen and the Growth of Industry and Transportation, 1837-53. Toronto: University of Toronto Press, 1977.

   "The Montreal Business Community, 1837-1853." *Canadian Business History: Selected Studies, 1497-1971*, pp. 125-43. Edited by D.S. Macmillan. Toronto: McClelland and Stewart, 1972.

4

Quebec

DANIEL LATOUCHE

Translated by David Homel

It has become increasingly difficult to evaluate present theoretical currents in and research on Quebec society. An exhaustive bibliography now being prepared on Quebec society, politics, culture and economy already includes some 10,000 titles. In Quebec universities, research centres and institutes alone, more than 700 individuals have chosen Quebec as their field of work. And, indeed, even the fact that Quebec is considered on its own in this Canadian bibliography is, perhaps, misleading. Most of the categories in this guide are equally applicable to Quebec as a distinct national community.

Quebec social scientists have adopted many different theoretical and methodological perspectives to examine Quebec society. And while in the past there was much rivalry and sharp debate between the different schools of theorists, today these divisions are much less evident. Indeed, the groups now appear to coexist with some semblance of peace and harmony. Perhaps the reason for this is that criticism in Quebec has evolved into something dynamic, fluid and capable of responding to Quebec's rapidly changing politics. The period when only a handful of sociologists, most trained in French or American universities, whould dare to make analytical statements about the nature of Quebec society is long behind us. However, it was, nonetheless, an important period in the development of Quebec social science, a tranquil time when Laval researchers such as Dumont could debate with their Montreal counterparts Rioux and Rocher about the nature of Quebec society. The period was followed by the radical questioning of a younger generation raised on Marxist analytical methods (Bourque, Laurin-Frenette) who began to probe the character and goals of Quebec nationalism, which up until then had been perceived in essentially non-class terms.

In the 1968-75 period, Quebec's national "specificity" was examined in minute detail through the optic of class relations. But the unexpected election of the Parti Québécois posed a fundamental challenge to the orthodox view of many Marxist social scientists who stressed the elite, middle-class character of Quebec nationalism. What must be realized is that the PQ's electoral success was only made possible by massive support from the working class. With the 1976 election, more attention was given to politics as an explanatory variable than to the workings of the economic infrastructure.

The defeat of the referendum in 1980 and the growing economic problems between 1982 and 1984 provoked yet more critical analyses of the PQ's electoral support and its policies. This new track ran parallel to the ongoing debate about Quebec class structure, its place in the Canadian scene, its internal workings and the political ambitions of its various splinter groups.

In addition to this dynamic and responsive political analysis, and quite independent of it, is another tradition of Quebec thought that focuses on culture. This *cultural approach*, so dominant from 1958 to 1969, continues to analyze Quebec in the light of its unique cultural and ideological character that has helped it to maintain its identity within an ever-homogenizing North America (Rioux, Dion, Bergeron, Dumont).

There are few theorists still willing to defend the traditional Marxist approach, since it gives no priority to the national question. However, there are several theorists, such as Laurin-Frenette and Mascotto, who accord more importance to the national question than do others, such as Bourque, Boismenu and Légaré. Ironically, it is precisely the national question to which the methodologies that hope to explain the Quebec nation and its society must respond.

However, the national question no longer takes centre stage. Today, there are other developing fields of research: the economic policies of a social democratic government, the corporatist behaviour of unions that continue to call themselves progressive, attempts to create alternatives to the reigning social model, and, above all else, the women's movement in Quebec society.

Archibald, Clinton
   Un Québec corporatiste? Corporatisme et néo-corporatisme: du passage d'une idéologie corporatiste sociale à une idéologie corporatiste politique: le Québec de 1930 à nos jours. Hull, Qué: Editions Asticou, 1983.

Armstrong, Elizabeth
   Crisis in Quebec, 1914-18. The Carleton Library, no. 74. Toronto: McClelland and Stewart, 1974. (First published 1937.)

Arnaud, Nicole, and Dofny, Jacques
   Nationalism and the National Question. Montreal: Black Rose Books, 1977.

Association canadienne des sociologues et anthropologues de langue française
   La Transformation du pouvoir au Québec: actes du colloque. Laval, Qué: Editions coopératives Albert Saint-Martin, 1980.

Audet, Louis-Philippe
   Histoire de l'enseignement au Québec. Montréal: Holt, Rinehart & Winston, 1971.

Beattie, Christopher
   Minority Men in a Majority Setting: Middle-Level Francophones in the Canadian Public Service. The Carleton Library, no. 92. Toronto: McClelland and Stewart, 1975.

Bergeron, Gérard, et Pelletier, Réjean, éds.
   L'Etat du Québec en devenir. Montréal: Boréal Express, 1980.

Bergeron, Léandre
   The History of Quebec: A Patriote's Handbook. Rev. ed. Toronto: NC Press, 1971.

Bernard, André
   What Does Quebec Want? Toronto: James Lorimer, 1978.

La Politique au Canada et au Québec. 2e. éd. Montréal: Presses de l'Université du Québec, 1977.

Bernard, Jean-Paul, éd.
Les Rébellions de 1837-1838: les patriotes du Bas-Canada dans la memoire collective et chez les historiens. Montréal: Boréal Express, 1983.

Bernier, Bernard
"The Penetration of Capitalism in Quebec Agriculture." *Canadian Review of Sociology and Anthropology* 13 (November 1976): 422-34.

Black, Conrad
Duplessis. Toronto: McClelland and Stewart, 1976.

Blais, André, et McRoberts, Kenneth
"Dynamique et contraintes des finances publiques au Québec." *Politique* 3 (hiver 1983): 27-62.

Boismenu, Gérard
Le Duplessisme: politique économique et rapports de force, 1944-1960. Montréal: Presses de l'Université de Montréal, 1981.

Boismenu, Gérard, et al.
Espace régional et nation: pour un nouveau débat sur le Québec. Montréal: Boréal Express, 1983.

Bourque, Gilles
Classes sociales et question nationale au Québec (1760-1840). Montréal: Parti Pris, 1970.

Bourque, Gilles, et Laurin-Frenette, Nicole
"Social Classes and Nationalist Ideologies in Quebec, 1760-1970." *Capitalism and the National Question in Canada*, pp. 185-210. Edited by G. Teeple. Toronto: University of Toronto Press, 1972.

Bourque, Gilles, et Légaré, Anne
Le Québec: la question nationale. Paris: François Maspero, 1979.

Brazeau, Jacques
"Quebec's Emerging Middle Class." *French Canadian Society*, pp. 319-27. Edited by Marcel Rioux and Yves Martin. Toronto: McClelland and Stewart, 1964.

Brunelle, Dorval
L'Etat solide: sociologie du fédéralisme au Canada et au Québec. Montréal: Editions Select, 1982.

La Désillusion tranquille. Montréal: Hurtubise HMH, 1978.

Brunet, Michel
"The British Conquest: Canadian Social Scientists and the Fate of the *Canadiens*." *Canadian Historical Review* 40 (June 1959): 93-107.

Cahiers de l'Université du Québec
Economie québécoise. Montréal: Presses de l'Université du Québec, 1970.

Caldwell, Gary, et Waddell, Eric, éds.
Les Anglophones du Québec: de majoritaires à minoritaires. Identité et changements culturels, no. 1. Québec: Institut québécois de recherche sur la culture, 1982.

Canada. Royal Commission on Bilingualism and Biculturalism
Report. 3 vols. Ottawa: Information Canada, 1969.

Centre de formation populaire
Au-delà du Parti québécois: lutte nationale et classes populaires. Montréal: Nouvelle optique, 1982.

Clift, Dominique
Le Déclin du nationalisme au Québec. Montréal: Libre Expression, 1981.

Cohen, Yolande, éd.
Femmes et politique. Montréal: Le Jour, 1981.

Collectif Clio
L'Histoire des femmes au Québec depuis quatre siècles. Par Micheline Dumont-Johnson et al. Montréal: Les Quinze, 1982.

Comeau, Paul-André
Le Bloc populaire: 1942-1948. Montréal: Québec-Amérique, 1982.

Cook, Ramsay
Canada and the French-Canadian Question. Toronto: Macmillan, 1966.

Cook, Ramsay, ed.
French-Canadian Nationalism: An Anthology. Toronto: Macmillan, 1969.

Craig, Gerald M., ed.
Lord Durham's Report. The Carleton Library, no. 1. Toronto: McClelland and Stewart, 1963.

Cuneo, Carl J., and Curtis, James E.
"Quebec Separatism: An Analysis of Determinants Within Social-Class Levels." *Canadian Review of Sociology and Anthropology* 11 (February 1974): 1-29.

Desbarats, Peter
René: A Canadian in Search of a Country. Toronto: McClelland and Stewart, 1976.

Denis, Roch
Luttes de classes et question nationale au Québec (1948-1968). Montréal: Presses socialistes internationales, 1979.

DesRochers, Monique Frappier; Morgan, Alison; et St-Onge, Alain
Evolution de la répartition des revenues au Québec 1961-1976: quelques facteurs explicatifs. Québec: Office de planification et de développement du Québec, 1979.

Dion, Leon
La Prochaine Revolution. Montréal: Leméac, 1973. English edition: *Quebec: The Unfinished Revolution.* Montreal: McGill-Queen's University Press, 1976.

Nationalismes et politique au Québec. Montréal: Hurtubise HMH, 1975.

"Quebec and the Future of Canada." *Quebec Society and Politics: Views From the Inside*, pp. 251-62. Edited by D.C. Thomson. Toronto: McClelland and Stewart, 1973.

"Towards a Self-Determined Consciousness." *Quebec Society and Politics: Views From the Inside*, pp. 26-38. Edited by D.C. Thomson. Toronto: McClelland and Stewart, 1973.

Drache, Daniel, ed.
Quebec — Only the Beginning: The Manifestoes of the Common Front. Toronto: New Press, 1972.

Drouilly, Pierre
Le Paradoxe canadien: le Québec et les élections fédérales. Montréal: Parti Pris, 1979.

Dumas, Evelyn
The Bitter Thirties in Quebec. Montreal: Black Rose Books, 1975.

Dumont, Fernand; Hamelin, Jean; et Montminy, Jean-Paul, éds.
Idéologies au Canada français, 1940-1976. 2 vols. Québec: Presses de l'Université Laval, 1981.

Dumont, Fernand, et Montminy, Jean-Paul, éds.
Le Pouvoir dans la société canadienne-française. Québec: Presses de l'Université Laval, 1966.

En collaboration
Québec: un pays incertain: réflexions sur le Québec post-référendaire. Montréal: Québec-Amérique, 1980.

Faucher, Albert
Québec en Amerique au XIXe siècle. Histoire économique et sociale du Canada français. Montréal: Fides, 1973.

Faucher, Albert, and Lamontagne, M.
"History of Industrial Development." *French Canadian Society*, vol. 1, pp. 257-71. Edited by M. Rioux and Y. Martin. Toronto: McClelland and Stewart, 1964.

Fournier, Louis
F.L.Q.: histoire d'un movement clandestin. Montréal: Québec-Amérique, 1982.

Fournier, Marcel
Communisme et anticommunisme au Québec: 1920-1950. Montréal: Editions coopératives Albert Saint-Martin, 1979.

Fournier, Pierre
Les Sociétés d'état et les objectifs économiques du Québec: un évolution préliminaire. Collection études et dossiers, no. 1. Québec: Office de planification et de développement du Québec, 1979.

The Quebec Establishment: The Ruling Class and the State. Montreal: Black Rose Books, 1976.

Fournier, Pierre, éd.
Le Capitalisme et politique au Québec: un bilan critique du Parti québécois au pouvoir. Laval, Qué.: Editions coopérative Albert Saint-Martin, 1981.

Fréchette, Pierre; Jouandet-Bernadat, R.; and Vézina, J.-P.
L'Economie du Québec. 2e éd. Montréal: Editions HRW, 1979.

Gagnon, Alain G., ed.
Quebec: State and Society. Toronto: Methuen, 1984.

Gagnon, Charles
"Classe et conscience de classe." *Socialisme* 69 (juillet-septembre 1969): 66-74.

Gémar, Jean-Claude
Les Trois Etats de la politique linguistique du Québec: d'une société traduite à une société d'expression. Dossiers du Conseil de la langue française. Etudes juridiques, no. 17. Québec: Conseil de la langue française, 1983.

Gérin-Lajoie, Jean
  Les Métallos, 1936-1981. Montréal: Boréal Express, 1982.

Godbout, Jacques
  La Participation contre la démocratie. Montréal: Editions coopératives Albert Saint-Martin, 1983.

Godin, Pierre
  Daniel Johnson. 2 vols. Montréal: Editions de l'Homme, 1980.

Granatstein, J.L., and Hitsman, J.M.
  Broken Promises: A History of Conscription in Canada. Toronto: Oxford University Press, 1977.

Guindon, Hubert
  "The Modernization of Quebec and the Legitimacy of the Canadian State." *Modernization and the Canadian State*, pp. 212-46. Edited by D. Glenday, A. Turowetz, and H. Guindon. Toronto: Macmillan, 1977.

  "Two Cultures: An Essay on Nationalism, Class, and Ethnic Tension." *Contemporary Canada*, pp. 33-59. Edited by Richard H. Leach. Toronto: University of Toronto Press, 1968.

  "Social Unrest, Social Class and Quebec's Bureaucratic Revolution." *Queen's Quarterly* 71:2 (1964).

Haggart, Ron, and Golden, Aubrey E.
  Rumours of War. Toronto: James Lorimer, 1979.

Hamel, Pierre; Léonard, Jean-François; et Mayer, Robert, éds.
  Les Mobilisations populaires urbaines. Montréal: Nouvelle optique, 1982.

Harvey, F., éd.
  Aspects historiques du mouvement ouvrier au Québec. Montréal: Boréal Express, 1973.

Hughes, E.C.
  French Canada in Transition. Chicago: University of Chicago Press, 1963. (First published 1943.)

Jacobs, Jane
  Canadian Cities and Sovereignty Association. Toronto: Canadian Broadcasting Association, 1980.

Johnson, Daniel
  Egalité ou indépendance. Montréal: Editions Renaissance, 1965.

Jones, Richard
  Community in Crisis: French-Canadian Nationalism in Perspective. The Carleton Library, no. 59. Toronto: McClelland and Stewart, 1972.

Joy, Richard J.
  Languages in Conflict: The Canadian Experience. The Carleton Library, no. 61. Toronto: McClelland and Stewart, 1972.

Kwavnik, David, ed.
  The Tremblay Report: Report of the Royal Commission of Inquiry on Constitutional Problems. The Carleton Library, no. 64. Toronto: McClelland and Stewart, 1973.

Lacroix, Robert, et Vaillancourt, François
  Les Révenus et la langue au Québec, 1970-1978. Dossiers du Conseil de la

langue française. Etudes et recherches, no. 8. Québec: Conseil de la langue française, 1981.

Lapalme, Georges-Emile
Le Paradis du pouvoir. Collections vies et mémoires. Montréal: Leméac, 1973.

LaRochelle, Louis
En flagrant délit de pouvoir: chronique des événements politiques de Maurice Duplessis à René Lévesque. Montréal: Boréal Express, 1982.

Latouche, Daniel
Une société de l'ambiguité: libération et récupération dans le Québec actuel. Montréal: Boréal Express, 1979.

    "La Vrai Nature de...la révolution tranquille." *Canadian Journal of Political Science* 7 (September 1974): 525-36.

Laurendeau, André
Witness for Quebec. Toronto: Macmillan, 1973.

Laurendeau, Marc
Les Québécois violents: un ouvrage sur les causes et la rentabilité de la violence d'inspiration politique au Québec. Rev. éd. Montréal: Boréal Express, 1974.

Laurin-Frenette, Nicole, et Léonard, Jean-François, éds.
L'Impasse: enjeux et perspectives de l'après-référendum. Montréal: Nouvelle optique, 1980.

Lavigne, Marie, et Pinard, Yolande, éds.
Travailleuses et féministes: les femmes dans la société québécoise. Etudes d'histoire du Québec, no. 13. Montréal: Boréal Express, 1983.

Légaré, Anne
    "Heures et promesses d'un débat: les analyses des classes au Québec (1960-1980)." *Cahiers du socialisme*, no. 5 (printemps 1980), pp. 60-84 + .

Lemieux, Vincent, éd.
Personnel et partis politiques au Québec: aspects historiques. Montréal: Boréal Express, 1982.

Lesemann, Frédéric
Du pain et des services: la réforme de la santé et des services sociaux au Québec. Laval, Qué.: Editions coopératives Albert Saint-Martin, 1981.

Lévesque, René
An Option for Quebec. Toronto: McClelland and Stewart, 1968.

Levitt, Joseph
Henri Bourassa and the Golden Calf: The Social Programme of the Nationalists of Quebec (1900-1914). Ottawa: Editions de l'Université d'Ottawa, 1969.

Levitt, Kari
    "Towards Decolonization: Canada and Quebec." *Canadian Forum* 51 (March 1972).

Lewis, David
The Good Fight: Political Memoirs, 1909-1958. Toronto: Macmillan, 1981.

Linteau, Paul-André; Durocher, René; and Robert, Jean-Claude
Quebec: A History, 1867-1929. Toronto: James Lorimer, 1983.

Major, Robert
Parti pris: idéologies et littérature. LaSalle, Qué: Hurtibise HMH, 1979.

Mascotto, Jacques, and Soucy, Pierre-Yves
Sociologie politique de la question nationale. Montréal: Editions coopérative Albert Saint-Martin, 1979.

McCallum, John
Unequal Beginnings: Agriculture and Economic Development in Quebec and Ontario Until 1870. Toronto: University of Toronto Press, 1980.

McGraw, Donald
Le Développement des groupes populaires à Montréal, 1963-1973. Montréal: Editions coopératives Albert Saint-Martin, 1978.

McKenna, Brian, and Purcell, Susan
Drapeau. Toronto: Clarke, Irwin, 1980.

McRoberts, Kenneth, and Posgate, Dale
Quebec: Social Change and Political Crisis. Rev. ed. Toronto: McClelland and Stewart, 1980.

McWhinney, Edward
Quebec and the Constitution, 1960-1978. Toronto: University of Toronto Presss, 1979.

Milner, Henry
Politics in the New Quebec. Toronto: McClelland and Stewart, 1978.

"The Decline and Fall of the Quebec Liberal Regime: Contradictions in the Modern Quebec State." *The Canadian State: Political Economy and Political Power*, pp. 101-32. Edited by Leo Panitch. Toronto: University of Toronto Press, 1977.

Milner, Sheilagh Hodgins, and Milner, Henry
The Decolonization of Quebec. Toronto: McClelland and Stewart, 1973.

Monière, Denis
André Laurendeau et le destin d'un peuple. Montréal: Québec-Amérique, 1983.

Le Développement des idéologies au Québec: des origines à nos jours. Montréal: Editions Québec-Amérique, 1977.

Morin, Claude
Quebec vs. Ottawa: The Struggle for Self-Government, 1960-72. Toronto: University of Toronto Press, 1976.

Ouellet, Fernand
Histoire économique et sociale du Québec, 1760-1850: structures et conjoncture. Montréal: Fides, 1966.

Parti libéral du Canada (Québec)
Une nouvelle fédération canadienne. Montréal: Parti libéral du Québec, 1980.

Parti québécois
Prochaine étape…quand nous serons vraiment chez nous. Montréal: Editions du Parti québécois, 1972.

Qui controle l'économie du Québec? Le Citoyen, no. 3. Montréal: Editions du Parti québécois, 1969.

Pinard, Maurice
"Working Class Politics: An Interpretation of the Quebec Case." *Canadian Review of Sociology and Anthropology* 7:2 (1970): 87-109.

Piotte, Jean-Marc
Un parti pris politique: essais. Montréal: V.L.B., 1979.
"A Question of Strategy." *Canadian Dimension* 10 (March 1975).

Piotte, Jean-Marc; Ethier, D.; and Reynolds, J.
Les Travailleurs contre l'état bourgeois. Montréal: L'Aurore, 1975.

Politique
"Femmes et pouvoir." (Special Issue) 5 (1984).

Proulx, Serge, and Vallières, Pierre, éds.
Changer de société. Montréal: Québec-Amérique, 1982.

Québec (Province). Conseil exécutif
La Nouvelle Entente Québec-Canada: proposition du gouvernement du Québec pour une entente d'égal à égal: la souveraineté-association. Québec: Editeur officiel, 1979.

Québec (Province). Ministre d'Etat du développement culturel
La Politique quebecoise du developpement culturel. 2 vols. Québec: Editeur officiel, 1978.

Québec (Province). Ministre d'Etat au développement économique
Le Virage technologique: bâtir le Québec, phase 2: programme d'action économique 1982-1986. Québec: Gouvernement du Québec, Développement économique, 1982.

Bâtir le Québec: énoncé de politique économique. Québec: Développement eéonomique, 1979.

Quinn, Herbert, F.
The Union nationale: Quebec Nationalism from Duplessis to Lévesque. 2nd enl. ed. Toronto: University of Toronto Press, 1979.

Raboy, Marc
Libérer la communication: médias et mouvements sociaux au Québec, 1960-1980. Montréal: Nouvelle optique, 1983.

Reid, M.
The Shouting Signpainters: A Literary and Political Account of Quebec Revolutionary Nationalism. Toronto: McClelland and Stewart, 1968.

Rémillard, Gil
Le Fédéralisme canadien. 2e éd. rev., corr. et augm. Montréal: Québec-Amérique, 1983.

Renaud, Gilbert
A l'ombre du rationalisme: la société québécoise de sa dépendance à sa quotidienneté. Montréal: Editions coopératives Albert Saint-Martin, 1984.

Rioux, Marcel
Quebec in Question. 2nd ed. Toronto: James Lorimer, 1978. (Originally published 1969.)

French-Canadian Society. Vol. 1. The Carleton Library, no. 18. Toronto: McClelland and Stewart, 1964.

Rotstein, A., ed.
Power Corrupted: The October Crisis and the Repression of Quebec. Toronto: New Press, 1971.

Roy, Jean-Louis
Le Choix d'un pays: le débat constitutionnel Québec-Canada, 1960-1976. Montréal: Leméac, 1978.

La Marche des Québécois: le temps des ruptures, 1945-1960. Montréal: Leméac, 1976.

Ryan, W.F.
The Clergy and Economic Growth in Quebec (1896-1914). Québec: Presses de l'Université Laval, 1966.

Ryerson, Stanley B.
"Quebec: Concepts of Class and Nation." *Capitalism and the National Question in Canada,* pp. 211-27. Edited by G. Teeple. Toronto: University of Toronto Press, 1972.

Unequal Union. Toronto: Progress Books, 1968.

French Canada. Toronto: Progress Books, 1953.

Saint-Germain, M.
Une économie à libérer: le Québec analysé dans ses structures économiques. Montréal: Presses de l'Université de Montréal, 1973.

Sales, Arnaud
La Bourgeoisie industrielle au Québec. Montréal: Presses de l'Université de Montréal, 1979.

Saywell, John
The Rise of the Parti Quebecois. Toronto: University of Toronto Press, 1977.

Siegfried, André
The Race Question in Canada. The Carleton Library, no. 29. Edited by F.H. Underhill. Toronto: McClelland and Stewart, 1966.

Silver, A.I.
The French-Canadian Idea of Confederation, 1864-1900. Toronto: University of Toronto Press, 1982.

Simard, Jean-Jacques
La Longue Marche des technocrates. Laval, Qué.: Editions coopératives Albert Saint-Martin, 1979.

Taylor, Norman W.
"French Canadians as Industrial Entrepreneurs." *Journal of Political Economy* 68 (February 1969).

Thompson, Dale, ed.
Quebec Society and Politics: Views from the Inside. Toronto: McClelland and Stewart, 1973.

Tremblay, Louis-Marie
Le Syndicalisme québécois: idéologies de la C.S.N. et de la F.T.Q., 1940-1970. Montréal: Presses de l'Université de Montréal, 1970.

Trofimenkoff, Susan Mann
The Dream of Nation: A Social and Intellectual History of Quebec. Toronto: Macmillan, 1982.

Trudeau, Pierre Elliott
Federalism and the French Canadians. Toronto: Macmillan, 1968.

Trudeau, Pierre Elliott, ed.
The Asbestos Strike. Toronto: James Lorimer, 1974. (First published 1956).

Vaillancourt, Jean-Guy
Mouvement écologiste, énergie et environnement: essais d'écosociologie. Montréal: Editions coopératives Albert Saint-Martin, 1982.

Vallières, Pierre
Choose. Toronto: New Press, 1972.

White Niggers of America. Toronto: McClelland and Stewart, 1971.

Vincenthier, Georges, éd.
Histoire des idées au Québec: des troubles de 1837 au référendum de 1980. Montréal: V.L.B., 1983.

Wade, Mason
The French Canadians, 1760-1967. Rev. ed. 2 vols. Toronto: Macmillan, 1968.

The French-Canadian Outlook: A Brief Account of the Unknown North Americans. The Carleton Library, no. 14. Toronto: McClelland and Stewart, 1964.

5

Women

PAT ARMSTRONG and HUGH ARMSTRONG

When the first edition of this guide was compiled, the problem was to find enough material focusing on or including women. Many of the entries bore scant relation to the concerns of political economy. Today, the problem is what to omit. The literature in the field has grown enormously, much of it taking a broadly defined political economy perspective or indicating why such a perspective is inadequate.

Early theoretical contributions concentrated on work and on fitting women into Marxist categories, particularly those of class, productive labour and value. Canadians have figured prominently in an international controversy of increasing theoretical sophistication: the domestic labour debate. Marxist analysis is being approached critically and the categories of political economy re-examined as the debate moves beyond the question of the relationship between household and formal economy to involve a range of issues, including sexuality, resistance and power. While some have argued that the basic assumptions of political economy preclude an analysis of women, and some have held that two distinct explanatory frameworks — one for "reproduction" and one for production — are necessary, others have maintained that the political economy approach has to be stretched, not by adding women to it or by focusing exclusively on women, but by making the theory in general more sex-conscious. At what level, in what form and through what means this transcending, complementing or developing of political economy should take place is still very much a matter of debate. Thus, some would argue that the very existence here of a special bibliographic section on women is, in itself, an indication that political economy has so far failed to take sex differences into account, while others would contend that not only different research topics and theory but also different methods are essential for an understanding of women's position.

Empirical examination of the segregated labour market, of the sexual divisions in domestic labour and of their interrelationship, as well as investigations of such issues as demography, physiology and technology, have further extended the theoretical debate. Additional questions about what should be included in political economy, about the adequacy of any explanations limited to the formal economy, and about the ability of the political economy perspective to explain class differences among women and between women and men have been raised. There seems now to be a shift towards getting on with it, towards finding out how useful the theory is in explaining the actual historical and contemporary experiences of women in the various regions and classes of Canada.

Because the literature is so extensive, anthologies have had to be listed here rather than the important individual articles within them. The same is true of special issues of journals. The focus is on material that takes a broadly defined political economy perspective or is explicitly critical of such an approach. For the most part, strictly descriptive publications, historical documents and government publications have been excluded. Publications by Canadians who have concentrated on the experiences of women in other countries have also been left out. What remains is, of necessity, selective.

The reader is referred as well to section 7, on labour conflict and working-class organization.

Acton, Janice, et al., eds.
Women at Work: Ontario 1850-1930. Toronto: Canadian Women's Educational Press, 1974.

Alternate Routes
"Feminism." 6 (1983).

Armstrong, Pat
Labour Pains: Women's Work in Crisis. Toronto: Women's Press, 1984.

"Marxism and Feminism." *Atlantis* 4 (Spring 1979): 125-32.

Armstrong, Pat, and Armstrong, Hugh
The Double Ghetto: Canadian Women and Their Segregated Work. Rev. ed. Toronto: McClelland and Stewart, 1984.

"Beyond Sexless Class and Classless Sex: Towards Feminist Marxism." *Studies in Political Economy*, no. 10 (Winter 1983), pp. 7-43.

A Working Majority: What Women Must Do For Pay. Ottawa: Canadian Advisory Council on the Status of Women, 1983.

Arnopoulos, Sheila McLeod
Problems of Immigrant Women in the Canadian Labour Force. Ottawa: Canadian Advisory Council on the Status of Women, 1979.

Atlantis
"Domestic Labour and Wage Labour." 7 (Fall 1981). (Whole issue.)

Bank Book Collective, Vancouver, B.C.
An Account to Settle: The Story of the United Bank Workers (SORWUC). Vancouver: Press Gang, 1979.

Barry, Francine
Le Travail de la femme au Québec: l'évolution de 1940 à 1970. Montréal: Presses de l'Université du Québec, 1977.

Benston, Margaret
"For Women, the Chips Are Down." *The Technological Woman: Interfacing with Tomorrow*, pp. 44-54. Edited by Jan Zimmerman. New York: Praeger, 1983.

"The Political Economy of Women's Liberation." *Monthly Review* 21 (September 1969): 13-27.

Bourgeault, Ron G.
"The Indian, the Métis and the Fur Trade: Class, Sexism and Racism in the Transition From 'Communism' To Capitalism." *Studies in Political Economy*, no. 12 (Fall 1983), pp. 45-80.

Briskin, Linda, and Yantz, Lynda, eds.
Union Sisters: Women in the Labour Movement. Toronto: Women's Press, 1983.

Brown, Jennifer S.H.
Strangers in Blood: Fur Trade Company Families in Indian Country. Vancouver: University of British Columbia Press, 1980.

Burstyn, Varda
"Economy, Sexuality, Politics: Engels and the Sexual Division of Labour." *Socialist Studies*, 1983. (Published by the Society for Socialist Studies, Winnipeg.)

"Masculine Dominance and the State." *The Socialist Register 1983*, pp. 45-89. Edited by Ralph Miliband and John Saville. London: Merlin Press, 1983.

Cameron, Barbara
"The Sexual Division of Labour and Class Struggle." *Socialist Studies*, 1983, pp. 40-50. (Published by the Society for Socialist Studies, Winnipeg.)

Canada. Commission of Inquiry Into Part-Time Work
Part-Time Work in Canada: Report. Ottawa: Labour Canada, 1983.

Canada. Royal Commission on the Status of Women
Report. Ottawa: Information Canada, 1970.

Canada. Task Force on Micro-Electronics and Employment
In the Chips: Opportunities, People, Partnerships: Report of the Labour Canada Task Force on Micro-Electronics and Employment. Ottawa: Labour Canada, 1982.

Canadian Advisory Council on the Status of Women
Working Together: Women and Unions. Ottawa: The Council, 1981.

Canadian Research Institute for the Advancement of Women
Women and Work: An Inventory of Research. Ottawa: The Institute, 1978.

Canadian Review of Sociology and Anthropology
"Women and the Canadian Social Structure." 12 (November 1975). (Whole issue.)

Canadian Woman Studies
"Women and the Economy." 3 (Summer 1982). (Whole issue.)

Chénier, Nancy Miller
Reproductive Hazards at Work: Men, Women and the Fertility Gamble. Ottawa: Canadian Advisory Council on the Status of Women, 1982.

Clark, Susan, and Harvey, Andrew S.
"The Sexual Division of Labour: The Use of Time." *Atlantis* 2 (Fall 1976): 46-66.

Clark, Susan, and Stephenson, M.
"Housework as Real Work." *Work in the Canadian Context: Continuity Despite Change*, pp. 73-92. Edited by Katherine Lundy and Barbara Warme. Toronto: Butterworth, 1981.

Cleverdon, Catherine Lyle
The Woman Suffrage Movement in Canada. 2nd ed. Toronto: University of Toronto Press, 1974. (First edition 1950.)

Collectif Clio
Histoire des femmes au Québec depuis quatre siècles. Par Micheline Dumont-Johnson et al. Montréal: Les Quinze, 1982.

Collins, Kevin
Women and Pensions. Ottawa: Canadian Council on Social Development, 1978.

Connelly, M. Patricia
"Women's Work and the Family Wage in Canada." *Women and the World of Work*, pp. 223-38. Proceedings of a NATO Symposium on Women and the World of Work held August 4-8, 1980, in Lisbon, Portugal. Edited by Anne Hoiberg. New York: Plenum Press in cooperation with the NATO Scientific Affairs Division, 1982.

"The Economic Context of Women's Labour Force Participation in Canada." *Economy, Class and Social Reality*, pp. 206-23. Edited by John Allan Fry. Toronto: Butterworth, 1979.

"Female Labour Force Participation: Choice or Necessity." *Atlantis* 3:2, pt. 1 (Spring 1978): 40-53.

Last Hired, First Fired: Women and the Canadian Work Force. Toronto: Women's Press, 1978.

Connelly, M. Patricia, and MacDonald, Martha
"Women's Work: Domestic and Wage Labour in a Nova Scotia Community." *Studies in Political Economy*, no. 10 (Winter 1983), pp. 45-72.

Cook, Gail, ed.
Opportunity for Choice: A Goal for Women in Canada. Ottawa: Statistics Canada, 1976.

Descarries-Bélanger, Francine
L'Ecole rose...et les cols roses: la réproduction de la division sociale des sexes. Laval, Qué.: Editions coopératives Albert Saint-Martin, 1980.

Edelson, Miriam
"Breaking Down the Barriers! Women and the Nature of Union Work." *Our Generation* 15 (Fall 1982): 26-35.

Eichler, Margrit
The Double Standard: a Feminist Critique of the Social Sciences. London: Croom Helm, 1980.

"Social Policy Concerning Women." *Canadian Social Policy*, pp. 133-46. Edited by Shankar A. Yelaja. Waterloo, Ont.: Wilfrid Laurier University Press, 1978.

"Women's Unpaid Labour." *Atlantis* 3:2, pt. 2 (Spring 1978): 52-62.

Fitzgerald, Maureen; Guberman, Connie; and Wolfe, Margie, eds.
Still Ain't Satisfied! Toronto: Women's Press, 1982.

Fox, Bonnie J., and Fox, John
"Effects of Women's Employment on Wages." *The Canadian Journal of Sociology* 8 (Summer 1983): 319-28.

Fox, Bonnie J., ed.
Hidden in the Household: Women's Domestic Labour Under Capitalism. Toronto: Women's Press, 1980.

Gagnon, Mona Josée
  *Les Femmes vues par le Québec des hommes: 30 ans d'histoire des idéologies,
  1940-1970.* Montréal: Editions du Jour, 1974.

Gaskell, Jane
  "Conceptions of Skill and the Work of Women: Some Historical and Political
  Issues." *Atlantis* 8 (Spring 1983): 11-25.

Guettel, Charnie
  Marxism & Feminism. Toronto: Women's Press, 1974.

Hersom, Naomi, and Smith, Dorothy E., eds.
  Women and the Canadian Labour Force. Ottawa: Social Sciences and Humanities Research Council of Canada, 1982.

Jamieson, Kathleen
  "Sisters Under the Skin: An Exploration of the Implications of Feminist-
  Materialist Perspective Research." *Canadian Ethnic Studies* 13:1 (1981): 130-
  43.

  Indian Women and the Law in Canada: Citizens Minus. Ottawa: Advisory
  Council on the Status of Women, 1978.

Johnson, Laura Climenko, and Johnson, Robert E.
  The Seam Allowance: Industrial Home Sewing in Canada. Toronto: Women's
  Press, 1982.

Kealey, Linda, ed.
  A Not Unreasonable Claim: Women and Reform in Canada, 1880s-1920s.
  Toronto: Women's Press, 1979.

Kuyek, Joan Newman
  The Phone Book: Working at the Bell. Kitchener, Ont.: Between the Lines,
  1979.

Lavigne, Marie, and Stoddart, Jennifer
  "Les Travailleuses Montréalaises entre les deux guerres." *Labour/Le Travailleur,* no. 2 (1977), pp. 170-83.

Light, Beth, and Strong-Boag, Veronica
  *True Daughters of the North: Canadian Women's History: An Annotated Bibli-
  ography.* Toronto: OISE Press, 1980.

Lipsig-Mummé, Carla
  "La Renaissance du travail à domicile dans les économies développées."
  Sociologie du travail, no. 3 (juillet-août-septembre 1983), pp. 313-35.

Lord, Stella
  "The Struggle for Equal Pay for Work of Equal Value: A Case Study."
  Alternate Routes, no. 4 (1980), pp. 21-52.

Lowe, Graham S.
  "Women, Work and the Office: The Feminization of Clerical Occupations
  in Canada, 1901-1931." *Canadian Journal of Sociology* 5 (Fall 1980): 361-
  81.

Luxton, Meg
  "Two Hands for the Clock: Changing Patterns in the Gendered Division of
  Labour in the Home." *Studies in Political Economy,* no. 12 (Fall 1983), pp.
  27-44.

"Taking on the Double Day: Housewives as a Reserve Army of Labour." *Atlantis* 7 (Fall 1981): 12-22.

More Than a Labour of Love: Three Generations of Women's Work in the Home. Toronto: Women's Educational Press, 1980.

Marchak, M. Patricia, ed.
The Working Sexes: Symposium Papers on the Effects of Sex on Women at Work, Delivered October 15-16, 1976 at the University of British Columbia. Vancouver: Institute of Industrial Relations, University of British Columbia, 1977.

Maroney, Heather Jon
"Feminism at Work." *New Left Review*, no. 141 (September-October 1983), pp. 51-71.

McClain, Janet
Women and Housing: Changing Needs and the Failure of Policy. Edited by Brigitta Arnotti and Mary Crawford. Ottawa: Canadian Council on Social Development, 1984.

McClung, Nellie
In Times Like These. Edited by V. Strong-Boag. Toronto: University of Toronto Press, 1972. (First published 1915.)

McCormack, Thelma
"Toward a Nonsexist Perspective on Social and Political Change." *Another Voice: Feminist Perspectives on Social Life and Social Science*, pp. 1-33. Edited by Marcia Millman and Rosabeth Moss Kanter. Garden City, N.Y.: Anchor Press, 1975.

McFarland, Joan
"Economics and Women: A Critique of the Scope of Traditional Analysis and Research." *Atlantis* 1 (Spring 1976): 26-41.

Menzies, Heather
Computers on the Job: Surviving Canada's Microcomputer Revolution. Toronto: James Lorimer, 1982.

Women and the Chip: Case Studies of the Effects of Informatics on Employment in Canada. Montreal: Institute for Research on Public Policy, 1981.

Miles, Angela R., and Finn, Geraldine, eds.
Feminism in Canada: From Pressure to Politics. Montreal: Black Rose Books, 1982.

Mitchell, Elizabeth Buchanan
In Western Canada Before the War: Impressions of Early Twentieth Century Prairie Communities. Saskatoon: Western Producer Prairie Books, 1981. (First published 1915.)

Mossman, Mary Jane, and Jai, Julie Ramona
"Women and Work and the Canadian Human Rights Acts." *Resources for Feminist Research* (Special Issue: "(Unequal) Pay: Canadian and International Perspectives." Guest editor Ceta Ramkhalawansingh) 7 (Fall 1979): 1-12.

Ng, Roxana, and Ramirez, Judith
Immigrant Housewives in Canada: A Report. Toronto: Immigrant Women's Center, 1981.

O'Brien, Mary
"Reproductive Labour and the Creation of Value." *Atlantis* 8 (Spring 1983): 1-10.

The Politics of Reproduction. London: Routledge & Kegan Paul, 1981.

"Reproducing Marxist Man." *The Sexism of Social and Political Theory: Women and Reproduction from Plato to Nietzsche*, pp. 99-116. Edited by Lorenne M.G. Clark and Lynda Lange. Toronto: University of Toronto Press, 1979.

Pelletier, Jacqueline, in collaboration with The Women & Technology Committee
"The Future is Now": Women and the Impact of Microtechnology. Ottawa: Women and Technology Committee, 1983.

Penney, Jennifer, ed.
Hard Earned Wages: Women Fighting for Better Work. Toronto: Women's Press, 1983.

Phillips, Paul, and Phillips, Erin
Women and Work: Inequality in the Labour Market. Toronto: James Lorimer, 1983.

Proulx, Monique
Women and Work: Five Million Women: A Study of the Canadian Housewife. Ottawa: Advisory Council on the Status of Women, 1978.

Québec. Conseil du statut de la femme
Pour les Québécoises: égalité et indépendance. Québec: Conseil du statut de la femme, Gouvernement du Québec, 1978.

Resources for Feminist Research
"Women and Education I." 12 (November 1983). (Whole issue, guest editors Somer Brodribb and Mary O'Brien.)

"Women and Agricultural Production." 11 (March 1982). (Whole issue, guest editors E.A. [Nora] Cebotarev and Frances M. Shaver.)

"Women and Trade Unions." 10 (July 1981). (Whole issue, guest editors Linda Briskin and Lynda Yanz.)

Roberts, Wayne
Honest Womanhood: Feminism, Femininity and Class Consciousness Among Toronto Working Women, 1896-1914. Toronto: New Hogtown Press, 1977.

Saunders, Eileen
"Women in Canadian Society." *Social Issues: Sociological Views of Canada*, pp. 211-57. Edited by Dennis Forcese and Stephen Richer. Scarborough, Ont.: Prentice-Hall, 1982.

"Implications of the Domestic Role of Women." *Alternate Routes*, no. 1 (1977), pp. 142-57.

Seccombe, Wally
"Marxism and Demography." *New Left Review*, no. 137 (January-February 1983), pp. 22-47.

"Domestic Labour — Reply to Critics." *New Left Review*, no. 94 (November-December 1975), pp. 85-96.

"The Housewife and Her Labour Under Capitalism." *New Left Review*, no. 83 (January-February 1974), pp. 3-24.

Smith, Dorothy E.
"Women, Class and Family." *The Socialist Register 1983*, pp. 1-44. Edited by Ralph Miliband and John Saville. London: Merlin Press, 1983.

Feminism and Marxism: A Place to Begin, a Way to Go. Vancouver: New Star Books, 1977.

Sociologie et sociétés
"Women in Sociology." 13 (octobre 1981). (Whole issue.)

"Femme, travail, syndicalisme." 6 (mai 1974). (Whole issue, guest editor Nicole Laurin-Frenette.)

Stephenson, Marylee, ed.
Women in Canada. Rev. ed. Don Mills, Ont.: General Publishing, 1977. (First edition 1973.)

Strong-Boag, Veronica
"Working Women and the State: The Case of Canada, 1889-1945." *Atlantis* 6 (Spring 1981): 1-9.

"Canada's Early Experience with Income Supplements: The Introduction of Mothers' Allowances." *Atlantis* 4:2, pt. 2 (Spring 1979): 35-43.

Sugiman, Pamela H.
"The Sales Clerks: Worker Discontent and Obstacles to its Collective Expression." *Atlantis* 8 (Fall 1982): 13-33.

Trofimenkoff, Susan Mann, and Prentice, Alison, eds.
The Neglected Majority: Essays in Canadian Women's History. Toronto: McClelland and Stewart, 1977.

Université du Québec à Montréal. Laboratoire sur la répartition de la sécurité du revenu, pour le Conseil du statut de la femme
La Condition économique des femmes au Québec. Vol. 1: *L'Exposé de la question.* Vol. 2: *L'Evaluation de la réponse apportée par l'Etat.* Québec: Editeur officiel du Québec, 1978.

Vinet, Alain
La Condition féminine en milieu ouvrier: une inquête auprès des travailleuses de cinq usines de la région de Québec. Québec: Institut de recherche sur la culture, 1982.

White, Julie
Women and Part-Time Work. Ottawa: Canadian Advisory Council on the Status of Women, 1983.

Wilson, Susannah Jane Foster
Women, the Family and the Economy: The Sociology of Women in Canada. Toronto: McGraw-Hill Ryerson, 1982.

6

The Capitalist Class

JORGE NIOSI

Aside from the pioneering studies done on the Canadian bourgeoisie by Gustav Myers and several other Canadian economic historians prior to 1945, it has only been during the last twenty years that this class has been subjected to much critical study and debate.

In the postwar period, the landmark Marxist analysis of Frank and Libbie Park was followed by many other Marxist studies, including those by W. Carroll, S. Moore and D. Wells, and J. Niosi. The more sociological works of John Porter inspired a spate of new critiques, for example, those by T.W. Acheson and W. Clement. Historians, such as Michael Bliss, Tom Naylor and Stanley Ryerson, have made perhaps the most prolific contribution to the subject. The best journalistic accounts of the Canadian establishment are those by Peter Newman.

The main themes being discussed include the capitalist class, its links to the state and the political system, the special characteristics of the Canadian bourgeoisie in the dependent economy, its ethnic composition and its regional divisions. Most authors consider the core of the Canadian bourgeoisie to be composed of owners and controllers of large private corporations, while the position of salaried managers, hired consultants and other non-propertied groups is less clear. Several studies show the Canadian bourgeoisie to be heavily represented on the boards of crown corporations, but there is less of a consensus on their links to other parts of the state apparatus. There is, however, broad agreement on the extent to which Canadian business is involved in finance, resource extraction, transportation and commerce. However, the role of Canadian industrial capitalists vis-à-vis Canadian development is much debated. The rise of a French-speaking bourgeoisie has been widely accepted, but its political orientation (federalist or separatist) has provoked debate, particularly in Quebec. Provincialism and regionalism have been perceived either as the result of the growth of regional bourgeoisies or as the result of the development fostered by foreign multinationals in the resource sector of the Canadian economy.

Several aspects of this topic remain to be studied: the social and political links between different factions of the capitalist class; the relationship between the capitalist class and the subordinated classes; the links between the two major political parties and the capitalist class; and the strategic responses of Canadian business to the new technology. What follows are some of the main contributions to the study of the Canadian capitalist class.

Acheson, T.W.
"Changing Social Origins of the Canadian Industrial Elite, 1880-1910." *Business History Review* 47 (Summer 1973): 189-217.

"The Social Origins of the Canadian Industrial Elite, 1880-1885." *Canadian Business History, Selected Studies, 1497-1971*, pp. 144-74. Edited by D.S. Macmillan. Toronto: McClelland and Stewart, 1972.

Ashley, Charles Allen
"Concentration of Economic Power." *Canadian Journal of Economics and Political Science* 23 (February 1957): 105-8.

Bliss, Michael
A Living Profit: Studies in the Social History of Canadian Business, 1883-1911. Toronto: McClelland and Stewart, 1974.

" 'Dyspepsia of the Mind': The Canadian Businessman and His Enemies, 1880-1914." *Canadian Business History, Selected Studies, 1497-1971*, pp. 175-91. Edited by D.S. Macmillan. Toronto: McClelland and Stewart, 1972.

"Canadianizing American Business: The Roots of the Branch Plant." *Close the 49th Parallel Etc.: The Americanization of Canada*, pp. 27-42. Edited by Ian Lumsden. Toronto: University of Toronto Press, 1970.

Brunelle, Dorval
La Désillusion tranquille. Montréal: Hurtubise HMH, 1978.

Canada. Royal Commission on Corporate Concentration.
Report. Ottawa: Royal Commission on Corporate Concentration, 1978.

Canada. Royal Commission on Price Spreads
Report. Ottawa: J.O. Patenaude, printer to the King, 1935.

Canada. Statistics Canada.
Annual Report of the Minister of Supply and Services Canada under the Corporations and Labour Unions Return Act. Part 1: Corporations. Ottawa: Supply and Services Canada, annual. (First issue 1970.)

Inter-Corporate Ownership, 1967. Occasional. Ottawa: Supply and Services Canada, 1967.

Inter-Corporate Ownership, 1965. Occasional. Ottawa: Supply and Services Canada, 1965.

Carroll, William K.
"The Canadian Corporate Elite: Financiers or Finance Capitalists?" *Studies in Political Economy*, no. 8 (Summer 1982), pp. 89-114.

Chodos, R., and Murphy, R., eds.
Let Us Prey. Toronto: James Lorimer, 1974.

Clark, S.D.
The Developing Canadian Community. Toronto: University of Toronto Press, 1962.

Clement, Wallace
Class, Power and Property: Essays on Canadian Society. Toronto: Methuen, 1983.

Continental Corporate Power: Economic Elite Linkages Between Canada and the United States. Toronto: McClelland and Stewart, 1977.

"Inside 'The Canadian Establishment': Trivia or Tempest?" *This Magazine* 10 (April-May 1976): 30-32.

Clement, Wallace (con'd)
The Canadian Corporate Elite: An Analysis of Economic Power. The Carleton Library, no. 89. Toronto: McClelland and Stewart, 1975.

Connelly, Patricia
"Capital and the State in Canada: Critical Questions in Carroll's Finance Capitalists." *Studies in Political Economy*, no. 12 (Fall 1983), pp. 163-8.

Creighton, Donald G.
"The Commercial Class in Canadian Politics, 1792-1840." *Towards the Discovery of Canada: Selected Essays*, pp. 84-102. Toronto: Macmillan, 1972.

The Empire of the St. Lawrence. Toronto: Macmillan, 1956. (First published 1937.)

Cuneo, Carl
"The Controlled Entry of Canadian Managers to the United States." *International Journal of Comparative Sociology* 18 (March-June 1977): 81-101.

Dhingra, Harbans L.
"Patterns of Ownership and Control in Canadian Industry: A Study of Large Non-Financial Private Corporations." *Canadian Journal of Sociology* 8 (Winter 1983): 21-44.

Drache, Daniel
"Staple-ization: A Theory of Canadian Capitalist Development." *Imperialism, Nationalism and Canada: Essays From the Marxist Institute of Toronto*, pp. 15-33. Edited by Craig Heron. Toronto: New Hogtown Press, 1977.

"The Canadian Bourgeoisie and Its National Consciousness." *Close the 49th Parallel Etc.: The Americanization of Canada*, pp. 3-25. Edited by Ian Lumsden. Toronto: University of Toronto Press, 1970.

Foster, Peter
The Blue-Eyed Sheiks: The Canadian Oil Establishment. Don Mills, Ont.: Collins, 1979.

Fournier, Pierre
"The New Parameters of the Quebec Bourgeoisie." *Studies in Political Economy*, no. 3 (Spring 1980), pp. 67-92.

The Québec Establishment: The Ruling Class and the State. Montreal: Black Rose Books, 1976.

Goff, Colin H., and Reasons, Charles E.
Corporate Crime in Canada: A Critical Analysis of Anti-Combines Legislation. Scarborough, Ont.: Prentice-Hall, 1978.

Goldenberg, Susan
Men of Property: The Canadian Developers Who Are Buying America. Toronto: Personal Library, 1981.

Gorecki, Paul K., and Stanbury, W.T., eds.
Perspectives on the Royal Commission on Corporate Concentration. Toronto: Butterworth, for the Institute for Research on Public Policy, 1979.

Heap, James L., ed.
Everybody's Canada: The Vertical Mosaic Reviewed and Reexamined. Toronto: Burns & MacEachern, 1974.

Hutcheson, John
Dominance and Dependency: Liberalism and National Policies in the North

Atlantic Triangle. Toronto: McClelland and Stewart, 1978.

Johnson, Leo A.
"The Development of Class in Canada in the Twentieth Century." *Capitalism and the National Question in Canada*, pp. 141-84. Edited by G. Teeple. Toronto: University of Toronto Press, 1972.

Katz, Michael B.
"The Entrepreneurial Class in a Canadian City: The Mid-Nineteenth Century." *Journal of Social History* 8 (Winter 1975): 1-29.

Laxer, Robert, ed.
(Canada) Ltd. The Political Economy of Dependency. Toronto: McClelland and Stewart, 1973.

Levitt, Kari
Silent Surrender: The Multinational Corporation in Canada. Toronto: Macmillan, 1970.

Macdonald, L.R.
"Merchants Against Industry: An Idea and Its Origins." *Canadian Historical Review* 56 (September 1975): 263-81.

Marchak, M. Patricia
In Whose Interests: An Essay on Multinational Corporations in a Canadian Context. Toronto: McClelland and Stewart, 1979.

McCullum, Watt Hugh
Who Owns Canada? An Examination of the Facts Concerning the Concentration of Ownership and Control of the Means of Production, Distribution and Exchange in Canada. 2nd ed. Ottawa: Woodsworth House, 1947.

McDougall, W.J., and Fogelbert, G.
Corporate Boards in Canada: How 64 Directorates Function. The School of Business Administration Research Series. London, Ont.: University of Western Ontario, 1968.

Moore, Steve, and Wells, Debbi
Imperialism and the National Question in Canada. Toronto: Moore, 1975.

Myers, Gustavus
A History of Canadian Wealth. 1st Canadian ed. Toronto: James Lorimer, 1972. (First published 1914.)

Naylor, R.T.
"Dominion of Capital: Canada and International Investment." *Domination*, pp. 33-56. Edited by A. Kontos. Toronto: University of Toronto Press, 1975.
The History of Canadian Business, 1867-1914. 2 vols. Toronto: James Lorimer, 1975.

Newman, Peter C.
The Establishment Man: A Portrait of Power. Toronto: McClelland and Stewart, 1982.
The Canadian Establishment. Vol. 2: *The Acquisitors*. Toronto: McClelland and Stewart, 1981.
Bronfman Dynasty: The Rothschilds of the New World. Toronto: McClelland and Stewart, 1978.
The Canadian Establishment. Vol. 1. Toronto: McClelland and Stewart, 1975.

Niosi, Jorge
   "The Canadian Bourgeoisie: Towards a Synthetical Approach." *Canadian Journal of Political and Social Theory* 7 (Fall 1983): 128-49.
   "La Multinationalisation des firmes canadiennes-françaises." *Recherches sociographiques* 24 (janvier 1983): 55-73.
   Les Multinationales canadiennes. Montréal: Boréal Express, 1982.
   Canadian Capitalism: A Study of Power in the Canadian Business Establishment. Toronto: James Lorimer, 1981.
   "The New French-Canadian Bourgeoisie." *Studies in Political Economy*, no. 1 (Spring 1979), pp. 113-61.
   The Economy of Canada: A Study of Ownership and Control. Montreal: Black Rose Books, 1978.

Ornstein, Michael D.
   "The Boards and Executives of the Largest Canadian Corporations: Size, Composition and Interlocks." *Canadian Journal of Sociology* 1 (Winter 1976): 411-37.

Park, Frank, and Park, Libbie
   Anatomy of Big Business. Toronto: James Lorimer, 1973. (First published 1962.)

Peterson, Susan
   Canadian Directorship Practices: A Critical Self-Examination. Canadian Studies, no. 48. Ottawa: Conference Board of Canada, 1977.

Piédalue, Gilles
   "Les Groupes financiers au Canada, 1900-1930." *Revue d'histoire de l'Amérique française* 30 (juin 1976): 3-34.

Porter, Glen, and Cuff, Robert, eds.
   Enterprise and National Development: Essays in Canadian Business and Economic History. Toronto: Hakkert, 1973.

Porter, John
   The Vertical Mosaic: An Analysis of Social Class and Power in Canada. Toronto: University of Toronto Press, 1965.

Raynauld, André
   La Propriété des entreprises au Québec; les années 60. Montréal: Presses de l'Université de Montréal, 1974.

Resnick, Philip
   "The Maturing of Canadian Capitalism." *Our Generation* 15 (Fall 1982): 11-24.

Rohmer, Richard H.
   E.P. Taylor: The Biography of Edward Plunket Taylor. Toronto: McClelland and Stewart, 1978.

Ryerson, Stanley
   "Who's Looking After Business? A Review." *This Magazine* 10 (November-December 1976): 41-46.
   Unequal Union: Roots of Crisis in the Canadas, 1815-1873. 2nd ed. Toronto: Progress Books, 1973.

Sales, Arnaud
La Bourgeoisie industrielle au Québec. Montréal: Presses de l'Université de Montréal, 1979.

Starowicz, Mark, and Murphy, Rae, eds.
Corporate Canada: 14 Probes Into the Workings of a Branch-Plant Economy. A Last Post Special. Toronto: James Lorimer, 1972.

Taylor, A.J.P.
Beaverbrook. London: Hamish Hamilton, 1972.

Taylor, Norman W.
"The French-Canadian Industrial Entrepreneur and His Social Environment." *French-Canadian Society*, vol. 1, pp. 271-95. Edited by Marcel Rioux and Yves Martin. The Carleton Library, no. 18. Toronto: McClelland and Stewart, 1964.

Tulchinsky, Gerald J.J.
The River Barons: Montreal Businessmen and the Growth of Industry and Transportation, 1937-53. Toronto: University of Toronto Press, 1977.

"The Montreal Business Community, 1837-1853." *Canadian Business History: Selected Studies, 1497-1971*, pp. 125-43. Edited by D.S. Macmillan. Toronto: McClelland and Stewart, 1972.

Wilson, Alan
John Northway: A Blue Serge Canadian. Toronto: Burns & MacEachern, 1965.

Wise, S.F.
"Upper Canada and the Conservative Tradition." *Profiles of a Province: Studies in the History of Ontario*, pp. 20-33. Toronto: Ontario Historical Society, 1967.

Young, Bert
"Corporate Interests and the State: Anti-Combine Activity in Canada — 1900 to 1970." *Our Generation* 10 (Winter/Spring 1974): 70-83.

7

Labour Conflict and Working-Class Organization

CRAIG HERON and GREG KEALEY

Probably no branch of Canadian political economy has grown as quickly and as massively as the study of the working class. Until the early 1970s, this field was largely the domain of a small number of left-wing and labour movement journalists, a scattering of antiquarians, and the staid fraternity of institutional labour economists who had created their own narrow discipline of ''industrial relations.'' In the past fifteen years, however, scores of researchers and writers have been producing a wealth of more sophisticated literature on the Canadian working-class experience, both past and present.

To point to an explosion of new work is not to suggest conceptual or theoretical consensus. In the first place, the older practitioners in the field have remained largely oblivious to the work of the newcomers. Industrial relations texts, for example, continue to exude the functionalist odour of the 1950s social sciences. Second, communication between the many writers and researchers studying the Canadian working class continues to be hampered by the solid walls surrounding not only the various social sciences but also the specialized fields within each discipline (e.g., women's history, urban history, immigration history, business history, as well as labour history). More important, however, is the unfortunately rigid line of demarcation between social democrats and Marxists. The former continue to be more interested in the political and economic institutions of the mainstream labour movement and to snip at the Marxist writers for their allegedly ''romantic'' fixation on a unified class culture and on overt class conflict; see, in particular, the pot shots from D.J. Bercuson, Kenneth McNaught and Desmond Morton, listed in subsection A of this section's bibliography. Their left-wing critics have generally stressed larger social and economic forces within the evolving capitalist system that inevitably generate conflict at all levels of society, from the shop floor to national politics. Their writing has highlighted both capitalist and state aggression and the ingenuity and toughness of working-class resistance, without losing sight of the material and ideological factors that have frequently elicited workers' ''consent'' to their own subordination. The debate between these two camps has occasionally become acerbic, but on the whole, the polite antagonism has forced all students of the Canadian working class to clarify their assumptions and sharpen their analytical tools.

The working-class experience in Canada is being investigated by writers of varying perspectives. One avenue into workers lives has been the study of immigration patterns, race and ethnicity, which has broadened our understanding of the formation of working-class communities and the cultural diversity which resulted. Unfortunately, too many writers in the field of "multiculturalism" ignore the fact that the majority of newcomers to Canada in the past 150 years became wage earners for at least part of their lives. Subsection B contains several titles that consider class formation. Growing numbers of historians and sociologists have been studying the restructuring of the work force through transformations in the labour process. Their work is noted in subsections B, C, and E. Feminist writers have contributed some of the most vibrant and stimulating additions to working-class studies through their exploration of women workers' unique combination of unpaid domestic labour and waged work outside the home. This writing on women, listed in subsection C, has been extremely important in forcing a redefinition of the working-class experience so as to encompass the household and the process of reproduction. In an area of related research, light is now being shed on the material conditions of working-class communities. Subsection D includes assessments of poverty among Canadian workers from the 1820s to the 1980s, as well as recent studies of the social welfare institutions and social security legislation that spawned our rapidly unravelling patchwork of a "welfare state."

Central to recent studies of the Canadian working class has been the attention given to industrial conflict. As subsection E indicates, the major strikes across the country in the past 150 years are finally being chronicled. The unions that waged many of these battles have been receiving more attention as class organizations within the specific contexts of class relationships and evolving labour processes, rather than merely as isolated institutions, which was how they were perceived in the older industrial relations tradition. Similarly, studies of working-class political activity (subsection F) have proliferated, although there has been greater emphasis on Communists and less interest in social-democratic workers or in working-class Liberals and Conservatives. Somewhat less intellectual energy has gone into analyzing the role of the state in workers' lives, although some important new books and articles have pushed the conceptual horizons beyond the persistently blinkered "public policy" orientation of industrial relations writers (see subsection G).

For further reading (including a myriad of unpublished theses), the most useful bibliographic guides are Douglas Vaisey, comp., *The Labour Companion: A Bibliography of Canadian Labour History Based on Materials Printed from 1950 to 1975* (Halifax: Committee on Canadian Labour History, 1980); Peter Weinrich, comp., *Social Protest from the Left in Canada, 1870-1970* (Toronto: University of Toronto Press, 1982); and the bibliographies published in *Labour/ Le Travail* and *Relations Industrielles/Industrial Relations*. A number of Canadian periodicals carry regular commentary and analysis on contemporary labour issues; see especially *Briarpatch, Canadian Dimension, Canadian Forum, New Maritimes, Our Generation, Our Times* and *This Magazine*.

A. GENERAL

Abella, Irving, and Millar, David, eds.
The Canadian Worker in the Twentieth Century. Toronto: Oxford University Press, 1978.

Anderson, John, and Gunderson, Morley, eds.
Union-Management Relations in Canada. Don Mills, Ont.: Addison-Wesley, 1982.

Bercuson, David J.
"Through the Looking Glass of Culture: An Essay on the New Labour History and Working-Class Culture in Recent Canadian Historical Writing." *Labour/ Le Travailleur*, no. 7 (Spring 1981), pp. 95-112.

Craig, Alton W.J.
The System of Industrial Relations in Canada. Scarborough, Ont.: Prentice-Hall, 1983.

Cross, Michael
The Workingman in the Nineteenth Century. Toronto: Oxford University Press, 1974.

Hameed, S.M.A., ed.
Canadian Industrial Relations: A Book of Readings. Toronto: Butterworth, 1975.

Hann, Russell, G., et al.
Primary Sources in Canadian Working Class History, 1860-1930. Kitchener, Ont.: Dumont Press, 1973.

Industrial Relations Centre, Queen's University
Current Industrial Relations Scene in Canada. Kingston, Ont.: Industrial Relations Centre, Queen's University, vol. 1-   (1973-   ).

Innis, Harold A.
"Labour in Canadian Economic History." *Essays in Canadian Economic History*, pp. 176-99. Edited by Mary Q. Innis. Toronto: University of Toronto Press, 1956.

Innis, Harold A., ed.
Labour in Canadian-American Relations. New York: Russell & Russell, 1970. (First published 1937.)

Isbester, Fraser, and Miller, Richard, eds.
Canadian Labour in Transition. Scarborough, Ont.: Prentice-Hall, 1971.

Jamieson, Stuart Marshall
Industrial Relations in Canada. 2nd ed. Toronto: Macmillan, 1973. (First edition 1957.)

Kealey, Gregory S.
"Labour and Working-Class History in Canada: Prospects in the 1980s." *Labour/Le Travailleur*, no. 7 (Spring 1981), pp. 67-94.

"H.C. Pentland and Working Class Studies." *Canadian Journal of Political and Social Theory* 3 (Spring-Summer 1979): 79-94.

Kealey, Gregory S., and Warrian, Peter, eds.
Essays in Canadian Working Class History. Toronto: McClelland and Stewart, 1976.

LeBlanc, A., and Thwaites, James
Le Monde ouvrier au Québec: bibliographie rétrospective. Montréal: Presses de l'Université du Québec, 1973.

McNaught, Kenneth
"E.P. Thompson vs. Harold Logan: Writing About Labour and the Left in the 1970s." *Canadian Historical Review* 62 (June 1981): 141-68.

Morton, Desmond
"E.P. Thompson dans les arpents de neige: les historiens canadiens-anglais et la classe ouvrière." *Revue d'histoire de l'Amérique française* 37 (septembre 1983): 165-84.

Morton, Desmond, and Copp, Terry
Working People. Ottawa: Deneau & Greenberg, 1980.

Ostry, Sylvia, and Zaidi, Mahmood A.
Labour Economics in Canada. 3rd ed. Toronto: Macmillan, 1979.

Palmer, Bryan D.
Working-Class Experience: The Rise and Reconstitution of Canadian Labour, 1800-1980. Toronto: Butterworth, 1983.

"Working-Class Canada: Recent Historical Writing." *Queen's Quarterly* 86 (1979/80): 594-616.

Pentland, H. Clare
Labour and Capital in Canada, 1650-1860. Edited by Paul Phillips. Toronto: James Lorimer, 1981.

"The Canadian Industrial Relations System: Some Formative Factors." *Labour/ Le Travailleur*, no. 4 (1979), pp. 9-23.

A Study of the Changing Social, Economic and Political Background of the Canadian System of Industrial Relations. Ottawa: Task Force on Labour Relations, Privy Council Office, 1968.

Seymour, Edward
An Illustrated History of Canadian Labour, 1800-1974. Ottawa: Canadian Labour Congress, 1976.

B. THE WORKERS AND THEIR JOBS

Avery, Donald
"Dangerous Foreigners": European Immigrant Workers and Labour Radicalism in Canada, 1896-1932. Toronto: McClelland and Stewart, 1979.

Bélanger, Noël, et al.
Les Travailleurs québécois, 1851-1896. Montréal: Presses de l'Université du Québec, 1973.

Bercuson, David J.
"Tragedy at Bellevue: Anatomy of a Mine Disaster." *Labour/Le Travailleur*, no. 3 (1978), pp. 221-32.

Bird, Richard M., et al.
The Growth of Public Employment in Canada. The I.R.P.P. Series on Public Sector Employment in Canada, vol. 3. Montreal: Institute for Research on Public Policy; distributed by Butterworth, 1979.

Bradwin, Edmund W.
The Bunkhouse Man: A Study of Work and Pay in the Camps of Canada, 1903-1914. Toronto: University of Toronto Press, 1972. (First published 1928.)

Brown, Cassie
Death on the Ice: The Great Newfoundland Sealing Disaster of 1914. Toronto: Doubleday, 1974.

Burgess, Joanne
"L'Industrie de la chaussure à Montréal, 1840-1870: le passage de l'artisanat à la fabrique." *Revue d'histoire de l'Amérique française* 31 (septembre 1977): 187-210.

Chan, Anthony B.
"Chinese Bachelor Workers in Nineteenth-Century Canada." *Ethnic and Racial Studies* 5 (October 1982): 513-34.

Chanteloup, Robert, ed.
Labour in Atlantic Canada. Saint John: Division of Social Science, University of New Brunswick at Saint John, 1981.

Clement, Wallace
Hardrock Mining: Industrial Relations and Technological Changes at INCO. Toronto: McClelland and Stewart, 1981.

"The Subordination of Labour in Canadian Mining." *Labour/Le Travailleur*, no. 5 (Spring 1980), pp. 133-48.

Conference of the Atlantic Canada Shipping Project
Working Men Who Got Wet: Proceedings of the Fourth Conference of the Atlantic Canada Shipping Project, July 24-July 26, 1980. Edited by Rosemary Ommer and Gerald Panting. St. John's: Maritime History Group, Memorial University of Newfoundland, 1980.

Cuneo, Carl
"Surplus Labour in Staple Commodities Merchant and Early Industrial Capitalism." *Studies in Political Economy*, no. 7 (Winter 1982), pp. 61-87.

Dahlie, Jorgen, and Fernando, Tissa, eds.
Ethnicity, Power and Politics in Canada. Canadian Ethnic Studies Association Series, vol. 8. Toronto: Methuen, 1981.

Duncan, Kenneth
"Irish Famine Immigration and the Social Structure of Canada West." *Studies in Canadian Social History*, pp. 140-63. Edited by Michiel Horn and Ronald Sabourin. Toronto: McClelland and Stewart, 1974. (Reprinted from *Canadian Review of Sociology and Anthropology* 2 [February 1965]: 19-40.)

Fingard, Judith
Jack in Port: Sailortowns of Eastern Canada. Toronto: University of Toronto Press, 1982.

Greer, Allan
"Fur-Trade Labour and Lower Canadian Agrarian Structures." Canadian Historical Association. *Historical Papers: A Selection From the Papers Presented at the Annual Meeting Held at Halifax* (1981), pp. 197-214.

Hardy, Jean-Pierre, and Ruddell, David Thierry
Les Apprentis artisans à Québec, 1660-1815. Montréal: Presses de l'Université du Québec, 1977.

Harney, Robert F.
"Montreal's King of Italian Labour: A Case Study of Padronism." *Labour/ Le Travailleur*, no. 4 (1979), pp. 57-84.

"The Commerce of Migration." *Canadian Ethnic Studies* 9:1 (1977): 42-53.

Harney, Robert F., and Troper, Harold
Immigrants: A Portrait of the Urban Experience, 1890-1930. Toronto: Van Nostrand Reinhold, 1975.

Harvey, Fernand
Révolution industrielle et travailleurs: une enquête sur les rapports entre le capital et le travail au Québec à la fin du 19e siècle. Montréal: Boréal Express, 1978.

"Technologie et organisation du travail à la fin du XIXe siècle: le cas du Québec." *Recherches sociographiques* 18 (septembre-décembre 1977): 397-414.

Heron, Craig
"Hamilton's Steelworkers and the Rise of Mass Production." Canadian Historical Association. *Historical Papers: A Selection From the Papers Presented at the Annual Meeting Held at Ottawa* (1982), pp. 103-31.

"The Crisis of the Craftsman: Hamilton's Metal Workers in the Early Twentieth Century." *Labour/Le Travailleur*, no. 6 (Autumn 1980), pp. 7-48.

Igartua, José E., et Fréminville, Marine de
"Les Origines des travailleurs de l'Alcan au Saguenay, 1925-1939." *Revue d'histoire de l'Amérique française* 37 (septembre 1983): 291-308.

Johnson, Leo A.
"The Development of Class in Canada in the Twentieth Century." *Capitalism and the National Question in Canada*, pp. 141-83. Edited by G. Teeple. Toronto: University of Toronto Press, 1972.

Johnson, Walter, ed.
Working in Canada. Montreal: Black Rose Books, 1976.

Judd, Carol M.
"Native Labour and Stratification in the Hudson's Bay Company's Northern Department, 1770-1870." *Canadian Review of Sociology and Anthropology* 17 (November 1980): 305-14.

Katz, Michael B.; Doucet, Michael J.; and Stern, Mark J.
The Social Organization of Early Industrial Capitalism. Cambridge, Mass.: Harvard University Press, 1982.

Kealey, Gregory S., ed.
Canada Investigates Industrialism: The Royal Commission on the Relations of Labour and Capital 1889. Toronto: University of Toronto Press, 1973.

Leyton, Elliott
Dying Hard: The Ravages of Industrial Carnage. Toronto: McClelland and Stewart, 1975.

Lindstrom-Best, Varpu
The Finnish Immigrant Community of Toronto, 1887-1913. Occasional Papers in Ethnic and Immigration Studies, no. 79-8. Toronto: Multicultural History Society of Ontario, 1979.

Lundy, Katherina, and Warme, Barbara
Work in the Canadian Context: Continuity Despite Change. Toronto: Butterworth, 1981.

MacKay, Donald
The Lumberjacks. Toronto: McGraw-Hill Ryerson, 1978.

Makahonuk, Glen
"The Working and Living Conditions of the Saskatchewan Deep Seam Coal Miners, 1930-1939." *Saskatchewan History* 33 (Spring 1980): 41-55.

Marchak, M. Patricia
Green Gold: The Forestry Industry in British Columbia. Vancouver: University of British Columbia Press, 1983.

"Labour in a Staples Economy." *Studies in Political Economy*, no. 2 (Autumn 1979), pp. 7-36.

Mather, Boris; Stinson, Jane; and Warskett, George
The Implications of Microelectronics for Canadian Workers: A Discussion Paper. Inaugural Conference Proceedings, Publication no. 2. Ottawa: Canadian Centre for Policy Alternatives, 1981.

McKay, Ian
"Capital and Labour in the Halifax Baking and Confectionery Industry During the Last Half of the Nineteenth Century." *Labour/Le Travailleur*, no. 3 (1978), pp. 63-108.

Menzies, Heather
Computers on the Job: Surviving Canada's Microcomputer Revolution. Toronto: James Lorimer, 1982.

Moogk, Peter N.
Building a House in New France: An Account of the Perplexities of Client and Craftsmen in Early Canada. Toronto: McClelland and Stewart, 1977.

Morrison, Jean
"Ethnicity and Class Consciousness: British, Finnish and South European Workers at the Canadian Lakehead Before World War I." *Lakehead University Review* 9 (Spring 1976): 41-54.

Neary, Peter
"Canada Immigration Policy and the Newfoundlanders, 1912-1939." *Acadiensis* 11 (Spring 1982): 69-83.

"Canada and the Newfoundland Labour Market, 1939-49." *Canadian Historical Review* 62 (December 1981): 470-95.

Neis, Barbara
"Competitive Merchants and Class Struggle in Newfoundland." *Studies in Political Economy*, no. 5 (Spring 1981), pp. 127-43.

O'Neill, Brian
Work and Technological Change: Case Studies of Longshoremen and Postal Workers in St. John's. St. John's, Nfld.: NAFE-Ten Days Committee; Jesperson Press, 1981.

Palmer, Bryan D.
"Most Uncommon Common Men: Craft and Culture in Historical Perspective." *Labour/Le Travailleur*, no. 1 (1976), pp. 5-31.

Parr, Joy
Labouring Children: British Immigrant Apprentices to Canada, 1869-1924.
Montreal: McGill-Queen's University Press, 1980.

Peitchinis, Stephen G.
The Canadian Labour Market. Toronto: Oxford University Press, 1975.

Pentland, H. Clare
"The Development of a Capitalist Labour Market in Canada." *Canadian Journal of Economics and Political Science* 25 (November 1959): 450-61.

Phillips, Paul
"Divide and Conquer: Class and Consciousness in Canadian Trade Unionism." *Socialist Studies* 2 (May 1980): 43-62. (Published by the Society for Socialist Studies, Winnipeg.)

"Clare Pentland and the Labour Process." *Canadian Journal of Political and Social Theory* 3 (Spring-Summer 1979): 45-52.

Radforth, Ian
"Woodsworkers and the Mechanization of the Pulpwood Logging Industry of Northern Ontario, 1950-1970." Canadian Historical Association. *Historical Papers: A Selection From the Papers Presented at the Annual Meeting Held at Ottawa* (1982), pp. 71-102.

"Finnish Lumber Workers in Ontario, 1919-46." *Polyphony: The Bulletin of the Multicultural History Society of Ontario* 3 (Fall 1981): 23-34.

Ramirez, Bruno, and Del Balso, Michael
The Italians of Montreal: From Sojourning to Settlement, 1900-1921. Montreal: Associazione di Cultura Popolare Italo-Quebecchese; Editions du Courant, 1980.

Reasons, Charles E.; Ross, Lois L.; and Paterson, Craig
Assault on the Worker: Occupational Health and Safety in Canada. Toronto: Butterworth, 1981.

Rinehart, James W.
"Contradictions of Work-Related Attitudes and Behaviour: An Interpretation." *Canadian Review of Sociology and Anthropology* 15 (February 1978): 1-15.

The Tyranny of Work. Don Mills, Ont.: Longmans, 1975.

Roberts, Wayne
"Toronto Metal Workers and the Second Industrial Revolution, 1889-1914." *Labour/Le Travailleur*, no. 6 (Autumn 1980), pp. 49-72.

Russell, Peter A.
"Wage Labour Rates in Upper Canada, 1818-1840." *Histoire sociale/Social History* 16 (May 1983): 61-80.

Shedden, Leslie, et al.
Mining Photographs and Other Pictures, 1948-1968: A Selection From the Negative Archives of Shedden Studio, Glace Bay, Cape Breton. Photographs by Leslie Shedden; essays by Don Macgillivray and Allan Sekula; edited by Benjamin H.D. Buchloch and Robert Wilkie. Halifax: Press of the Nova Scotia College of Art and Design, and the University College of Cape Breton Press, 1983.

Thompson, John Herd
"Bringing In the Sheaves: The Harvest Excursionists, 1890-1929." *Canadian Historical Review* 59 (December 1978): 467-89.

Thompson, John Herd, and Seager, Allen
"Workers, Growers and Monopolists: The 'Labour Problem' in the Alberta Beet Sugar Industry During the 1930s." *Labour/Le Travailleur*, no. 3 (1978), pp. 153-74.

Tremblay, Robert
"La Formation matérielle de la classe ouvrière à Montréal entre 1790 et 1830." *Revue d'histoire de l'Amérique française* 33 (juin 1979): 39-50.

C. WOMEN AT WORK

Backhouse, Constance, and Cohen, Leah
The Secret Oppression: Sexual Harassment of Working Women. Toronto: Macmillan, 1978.

Baker, Maureen, and Robertson, Mary-Ann
"Trade Union Reactions to Women Workers and Their Concerns." *Canadian Journal of Sociology* 6 (Winter 1981): 19-31.

Barber, Marilyn
"The Women Ontario Welcomed: Immigrant Domestics for Ontario Homes, 1870-1930." *Ontario History* 72 (September 1980): 148-72.

Brandt, Gail Cuthbert
" 'Pigeon-Holed and Forgotten': The Work of the Subcommittee on the Post-War Problems of Women, 1943." *Histoire sociale/Social History* 15 (May 1982): 239-59.

" 'Weaving It Together': Life Cycle and the Industrial Experience of Female Cotton Workers in Quebec, 1910-1950." *Labour/Le Travailleur*, no. 7 (Spring 1981), pp. 113-25.

Danylewycz, Marta; Light, Beth; and Prentice, Alison
"The Evolution of the Sexual Division of Labour in Teaching: A Nineteenth-Century Ontario and Quebec Case Study." *Histoire sociale/Social History* 16 (May 1983): 81-109.

Knight, Rolf, and Knight, Phyllis
A Very Ordinary Life. Vancouver: New Star Books, 1974.

Lacelle, Claudette
"Les Domestiques dans les villes canadiennes au XIXe siècle: effectifs et conditions de vie." *Histoire sociale/Social History* 15 (mai 1982): 181-207.

Lowe, Graham S.
"Class, Job and Gender in the Canadian Office." *Labour/Le Travailleur*, no. 10 (Autumn 1982), pp. 11-37.

"Causes of Unionization in Canadian Banks." *Relations industrielles/Industrial Relations* 36:4 (1981): 865-93.

"Women, Work and the Office: The Feminization of Clerical Occupations in Canada, 1901-1931." *Canadian Journal of Sociology* 5 (Fall 1980): 363-81.

Marchak, M. Patricia
"Women Workers and White-Collar Unions." *Canadian Review of Sociology and Anthropology* 10 (May 1974): 134-47.

Pierson, Ruth Roach
Canadian Women and the Second World War. Canadian Historical Association. Historical Booklet no. 37. Ottawa: Canadian Historical Association, 1983.

"Women's Emancipation and the Recruitment of Women into the Canadian Labour Force in World War II." Canadian Historical Association. *Historical Papers 1976: A Selection from the Papers Presented at the 1976 Annual Meeting Held at Quebec City* (1976), pp. 141-74.

Pierson, Ruth Roach, and Cohen, Marjorie
"Educating Women for Work: Government Training Programs for Women Before, During, and After World War II." *Readings in Canadian Social History*, vol. 5: *The Emergence of the Welfare State, 1930-1981.* Edited by Michael S. Cross and Gregory S. Kealey. Toronto: McClelland and Stewart, 1984.

Roberts, Wayne
Honest Womanhood: Feminism, Femininity and Class Consciousness Among Toronto Working Women, 1893-1914. Toronto: New Hogtown Press, 1976.

Rosenthal, Star
"Union Maids: Organized Women Workers in Vancouver 1900-1915." *BC Studies*, no. 41 (Spring 1979), pp. 36-55.

Sangster, Joan
"Finnish Women in Ontario, 1890-1930." *Polyphony: The Bulletin of the Multicultural Society of Ontario* 3 (Fall 1981): 46-54.

"The 1907 Bell Telephone Strike: Organizing Women Workers." *Labour/ Le Travailleur*, no. 3 (1978), pp. 109-30.

Silvera, Makeda
Silenced: Makeda Silvera Talks with Working Class West Indian Women About Their Lives and Struggles as Domestic Workers in Canada. Toronto: Williams-Wallace, 1983.

Strong-Boag, Veronica
"The Girl of the New Day: Canadian Working Women in the 1920s." *Labour/ Le Travailleur*, no. 4 (1979), pp. 131-64.

Trofimenkoff, Susan Mann
"One Hundred and Two Muffled Voices: Canada's Industrial Women in the 1880s." *Atlantis* 3 (Autumn 1977): 66-83.

Vance, Catharine
Not by Gods But by People: The Story of Bella Hall Gauld. Toronto: Progress Books, 1968.

Van Kirk, Sylvia
"Many Tender Ties": Women in Fur-Trade Society in Western Canada, 1670-1870. Winnipeg: Watson & Dwyer, 1980.

Wade, Susan
"Helena Gutteridge: Votes for Women and Trade Unions." *"In Her Own Right": Selected Essays on Women's History in B.C.*, pp. 187-204. Edited by Barbara Latham and Cathy Kess. Victoria, B.C.: Camosun College, 1980.

Watson, Louise
She Was Never Afraid: The Biography of Annie Buller. Toronto: Progress Books, 1976.

D. MATERIAL CONDITIONS AND CULTURE

Adams, Ian
The Real Poverty Report. Edmonton: Hurtig, 1971.

Ames, H.B.
The City Below the Hill: A Sociological Study of a Portion of the City of Montreal, Canada. Toronto: University of Toronto Press, 1972. (First published 1897.)

Baker, Melvin; Cuff, Robert; and Gillespie, Bill
Workingmen's St. John's: Aspects of Social History in the Early 1900s. St. John's, Nfld.: Cuff Publications, 1982.

Baldwin, Doug
"The Life of the Silver Miner in Northern Ontario." *Labour/Le Travailleur*, no. 2 (1977), pp. 79-107.

Bartlett, Eleanor, A.
"Real Wages and the Standard of Living in Vancouver, 1901-1929." *BC Studies*, no. 51 (Autumn 1981), pp. 3-62.

Black, Errol, and Black, Tom
"The Making of the East End Community Club." *Labour/Le Travailleur*, no. 12 (Autumn 1983), pp. 155-72.

Bonville, Jean de
Jean-Baptiste Gagnepetit: les travailleurs Montréalais à la fin du XIXe siècle. Montréal: Editions de l'Aurore, 1975.

Broadfoot, Barry
Ten Lost Years, 1929-1939: Memories of Canadians Who Survived the Depression. Toronto: Doubleday, 1973.

Copp, Terry
The Anatomy of Poverty: The Condition of the Working Class in Montreal, 1897-1929. Toronto: McClelland and Stewart, 1974.

Darroch, A. Gordon
"Early Industrialization and Inequality in Toronto, 1861-1905." *Labour/Le Travailleur*, no. 11 (Spring 1983), pp. 31-62.

DeLottinville, Peter
"Joe Beef of Montreal: Working Class Culture and the Tavern, 1869-1889." *Labour/Le Travailleur*, no. 8/9 (Autumn/Spring 1981/1982), pp. 9-40.

Fingard, Judith
"The Winter's Tale: Contours of Pre-Industrial Poverty in British America, 1815-1860." Canadian Historical Association. *Historical Papers 1974: A Selection from the Papers Presented at the 1974 Annual Meeting Held at Toronto, Ontario* (1974), pp. 65-94.

Guest, Dennis
The Emergence of Social Security in Canada. Vancouver: University of British Columbia Press, 1979.

Hamilton, Richard, and Pinard, Maurice
"Poverty in Canada: Illusion and Reality." *Canadian Review of Sociology and Anthropology* 14 (May 1977): 247-52.

Harney, Robert F.
"Boarding and Belonging: Thoughts on Sojourner Institutions." *Urban History Review* 2-78 (October 1978): 8-37.

Horn, Michiel, ed.
The Dirty Thirties: Canadians in the Great Depression. Toronto: Copp Clark, 1972.

Hutcheson, Sydney
Depression Stories. Vancouver: New Star Books, 1976.

Lamonde, Yvan
La Culture ouvrière à Montréal (1880-1920): bilan historiographie. Québec: Institut québécois de recherche sur la culture, 1982.

Larocque, Paul
"Aperçu de la condition ouvrière à Québec, 1896-1914." *Labour/Le Travailleur*, no. 1 (1976), pp. 122-38.

Lorimer, James, and Phillips, Myfanwy
Working People: Life in a Downtown City Neighbourhood. Toronto: James Lorimer, 1971.

Lucas, Rex
Minetown, Milltown, Railtown: Life in Canadian Communities of a Single Industry. Toronto: University of Toronto Press, 1971.

Moscovitch, Allan
The Welfare State in Canada: A Selected Bibliography, 1840 to 1978. Waterloo, Ont.: Wilfrid Laurier University Press, 1983.

Moscovitch, Allan, and Drover, Glenn, eds.
Inequality: Essays on the Political Economy of Social Welfare. Toronto: University of Toronto Press, 1981.

Piva, Michael J.
"Urban Working Class Incomes and Real Incomes in 1921: A Comparative Analysis." *Histoire social/Social History* 16 (May 1983): 145-65.

The Condition of the Working Class in Toronto, 1900-1921. Ottawa: University of Ottawa Press, 1979.

Ross, David P.
The Working Poor: Wage Earners and the Failure of Income Security Policies. Toronto: James Lorimer in association with the Canadian Institute for Economic Policy, 1981.

Watt, F.W.
"Literature of Protest." *Literary History of Canada: Canadian Literature in English*, 2nd ed., vol. 1, pp. 473-89. Edited by C.F. Klinck. Toronto: University of Toronto Press, 1976.

Wylie, William N.T.
"Poverty, Distress, and Disease: Labour and the Construction of the Rideau Canal, 1826-1832." *Labour/Le Travailleur*, no. 11 (Spring 1983), pp. 7-29.

E. UNIONS AND INDUSTRIAL CONFLICT

Abella, Irving M.
The Canadian Labour Movement, 1902-1960. Canadian Historical Association. Historical Booklet no. 28. Ottawa: Canadian Historical Association, 1975.

Nationalism, Communism and Canadian Labour: The C.I.O., the Communist Party and the Canadian Congress of Labour, 1935-1956. Toronto: University of Toronto Press, 1973.

Abella, Irving M., ed.
On Strike: Six Key Labour Struggles in Canada, 1919-1949. Toronto: James Lorimer, 1975.

Babcock, Robert
Gompers in Canada: A Study in American Continentalism Before the First World War. Toronto: University of Toronto Press, 1974.

Baillargeon, Denise
"La Grève de Lachute (1947)." Revue d'histoire de l'Amérique française 37 (septembre 1983): 271-90.

Battye, John
"The Nine-Hour Pioneers: The Genesis of the Canadian Labour Movement." *Labour/Le Travailleur*, no. 4 (1979), pp. 25-56.

Bélanger, Guy
"La Grève de Murdochville (1957)." *Labour/Le Travailleur*, no. 8/9 (Autumn/Spring 1981/1982), pp. 103-35.

Bennett, Arnold
"Red Baiting — Trade Union Style: Cold-War Factionalism in the Canadian Trade Union Movement." *Our Generation* 13 (Spring 1979): 31-49.

Bercuson, David J.
Fools and Wise Men: The Rise and Fall of the One Big Union. Toronto: McGraw-Hill Ryerson, 1978.

Confrontation at Winnipeg: Labour, Industrial Relations and the General Strike. Montreal: McGill-Queen's University Press, 1974.

Bergren, Myrtle Woodward
Tough Timber: The Loggers of B.C. — Their Story. 2nd rev. ed. Toronto: Progress Books, 1967.

Bernard, Elaine
The Long Distance Feeling: A History of the Telecommunications Workers Union. Vancouver: New Star Books, 1982.

Bleasdale, Ruth
"Class Conflict on the Canals of Upper Canada in the 1840s." *Labour/Le Travailleur*, no. 7 (Spring 1981), pp. 9-40.

Bowen, Lynne
Boss Whistle: The Coal Miners of Vancouver Island Remember. Lantzville, B.C.: Oolichan Books, 1982.

Bradbury, J.H.
"Class Structures and Class Conflicts in 'Instant' Resource Towns in British Columbia — 1965-1972." *BC Studies*, no. 37 (Spring 1978), pp. 3-18.

Brodie, Steve
Bloody Sunday, Vancouver 1938. Vancouver: Young Communist League, 1974.

Cameron, Silver Donald
The Education of Everett Richardson: The Nova Scotia Fishermen's Strike, 1970-71. Toronto: McClelland and Stewart, 1977.

Caragata, Warren
Alberta Labour: A Heritage Untold. Toronto: James Lorimer, 1979.

Charpentier, Alfred
Les Mémoires d'Alfred Charpentier. Présenté par Gérard Dion. Québec: Presses de l'Université Laval, 1971.

"La Grève du textile dans le Québec en 1937." *Relations industrielles* 20 (janvier 1965): 86-127.

Comeau, Robert
"La Canadian Seamen's Union (1936-1949): un chapitre de l'histoire mouvement ouvrier canadien." *Revue d'histoire de l'Amérique française* 29 (mars 1976): 503-38.

Cooper, J.I.
"The Quebec Ship Labourers' Benevolent Society." *Canadian Historical Review* 30 (December 1949): 336-43.

Copp, Terry
"The Rise of Industrial Unions in Montreal, 1935-1945." *Relations industrielles/Industrial Relations* 37:4 (1982): 843-75.

The I.U.E. in Canada. Elora, Ont.: Cumnock Press, 1980.

Copp, Terry, ed.
Industrial Unionism in Kitchener, 1937-1947. Elora, Ont.: Cumnock Press, 1976.

Crispo, John H.G., and Arthurs, H.W.
"Industrial Unrest in Canada: A Diagnosis of Recent Experience." *Relations industrielles/Industrial Relations* 23 (April 1968): 237-64.

Cross, Michael
"Violence and Authority: The Case of Bytown." *Law and Society in Canada in Historical Perspective*, pp. 5-22. Edited by D.J. Bercuson and L.A. Knafla. Studies in History, no. 2. Calgary: University of Calgary, 1979.

"The Shiners' War: Social Violence in the Ottawa Valley in the 1930s." *Canadian Historical Review* 54 (March 1973): 1-26.

Davidson, Joe, and Deverell, John
Joe Davidson. Toronto: James Lorimer, 1978.

Desrochers, Luc
"Les Facteurs d'apparition du syndicalisme catholique dans l'imprimérie et les déterminants de la stratégie syndicale, 1921-1945." *Revue d'histoire de l'Amérique française* 37 (septembre 1983): 241-70.

Desrosiers, Richard, et Héroux, Denis
Le Travailleur québécois et le syndicalisme. 2e éd. Montréal: Presses de l'Université du Québec, 1973.

Deverell, John
"The Ontario Hospital Dispute, 1980-81." *Studies in Political Economy*, no. 9 (Fall 1982), pp. 179-90.

Drache, Daniel, ed.
Quebec — Only the Beginning: The Manifestoes of the Common Front. Toronto: New Press, 1972.

Dumas, Evelyn
The Bitter Thirties in Quebec. Montreal: Black Rose Books, 1975.

Faber, Seymour
"Working Class Organisation." *Our Generation* 11 (Summer 1976): 13-26.

Ferris, John, ed.
50 Years of Labour in Algoma: Essays on Aspects of Algoma's Working-Class History. Sault Ste. Marie, Ont.: Algoma University College, 1978.

Forsey, Eugene
Trade Unions in Canada 1812-1902. Toronto: University of Toronto Press, 1981.
The Canadian Labour Movement 1812-1902. Historical Booklet no. 27. Ottawa: Canadian Historical Association, 1974.

Fowke, Edith
"Labor and Industrial Protest Songs in Canada." *Journal of American Folk-Lore* 82 (January-March 1969): 34-50.

Frank, J.A.
"The 'Ingredients' in Violent Labour Conflict: Patterns in Four Case Studies." *Labour/Le Travailleur*, no. 12 (Autumn 1983), pp. 87-112.

Freeman, Bill
1005: Political Life in a Union Local. Toronto: James Lorimer, 1982.

Gérin-Lajoie, Jean
Les Métallos, 1936-1981. Montréal: Boréal Express, 1982.

Hamelin, Jean, et Bélanger, Noël
Les Travailleurs québécois, 1851-1896. Montréal: Presses de l'Université du Québec, 1973.

Hamelin, Jean, et Harvey, Fernand, éds.
Les Travailleurs québécois, 1941-1971: dossier. Québec: Institute Supérieur des Science Humaines, Université Laval, 1976.

Hamelin, Jean; Larocque, Paul; et Rouillard, Jacques
Répertoire des grèves dans la province de Québec au XIXe siècle. Montréal: Presses de l'Ecole des hautes études commerciales, 1971.

Harvey, Fernand, éd.
Le Mouvement ouvrier au Québec: aspects historiques. Montréal: Boréal Express, 1980.
Aspects historiques du mouvement ouvrier au Québec. Montréal: Boréal Express, 1973.

Hébert, Gérard, and Fraser, C.R.P., et al.
Research Publications. Vol. 5: *Labour Relations in the Newspaper Industry*. Ottawa: Royal Commission on Newspapers, 1981. (The Kent Commission.)

Hennessy, Peter H.
Schools in Jeopardy: Collective Bargaining in Education. Toronto: McClelland and Stewart, 1979.

Heron, Craig, et al.
All that Our Hands Have Done: A Pictorial History of the Hamilton Workers. Oakville, Ont.: Mosaic Press in association with the Office of Labour Studies, McMaster University, 1981.

Heron, Craig, and Palmer, Bryan D.
"Through the Prism of the Strike: Industrial Conflict in Southern Ontario, 1901-14." *Canadian Historical Review* 58 (December 1977): 423-58.

Hogan, Brian F.
Cobalt: Year of the Strike 1919. Cobalt, Ont.: Highway Book Shop, 1978.

Jamieson, Stuart
Times of Trouble: Labour Unrest and Industrial Conflict in Canada, 1900-1966. Study no. 22. Ottawa: Task Force on Labour Relations, 1968.

Jamieson, Stuart, and Gladstone, Percy
"Unionism in the Fishing Industry of British Columbia." *Canadian Journal of Economics and Political Science* 16 (May 1950): 146-71.

Kealey, Gregory S.
Toronto Workers Respond to Industrial Capitalism, 1867-1892. Toronto: University of Toronto Press, 1980.

Kealey, Gregory S., and Palmer, Bryan D.
Dreaming of What Might Be: The Knights of Labor in Ontario, 1880-1900. Cambridge, Eng.: Cambridge University Press, 1982.

"The Bonds of Unity: The Knights of Labor in Ontario, 1880-1900." *Histoire sociale/Social History* 14 (November 1981): 369-411.

Knight, Rolf, and Koizuini, Maya
A Man of Our Times: The Life-History of a Japanese-Canadian Fisherman. Vancouver: New Star Books, 1976.

Kwavnick, David
Organized Labour and Pressure Politics: The Canadian Labour Congress, 1956-1968. Montreal: McGill-Queen's University Press, 1972.

Lang, John
"The Million Dollar Question: The CLC and Canadian Unions." *This Magazine* 7 (August 1973): 19-22.

Larivière, Claude
Histoire des travailleurs de Beauharnois et Valleyfield. Montréal: Editions coopératives Albert Saint-Martin, 1974.

Laxer, Robert
Canada's Unions. Toronto: James Lorimer, 1976.

Lembcke, Jerry
"The International Woodworkers of America in British Columbia, 1942-1952." *Labour/Le Travailleur*, no. 6 (Autumn 1980), pp. 113-48.

Lemelin, Maurice
The Public Service Alliance of Canada: A Look at a Union in the Public Sector. Los Angeles: Institute of Industrial Relations, University of California, 1978.

Levant, Victor
   Capital & Labour: Partners? Two Classes — Two Views. Toronto: Steel Rail
   Educational, 1977.

Lipton, Charles
   The Trade Union Movement of Canada, 1827-1959. 3rd ed. Toronto: NC
   Press, 1973.

Logan, H.A.
   Trade Unions in Canada: Their Development and Functioning. Toronto:
   Macmillan, 1948.

Macdonald, David A.
   *Power Begins at the Cod End: The Newfoundland Trawlermen's Strike, 1974-
   75*. St. John's: Institute of Social and Economic Research, Memorial University of Newfoundland, 1980.

MacDowell, G.F.
   The Brandon Packers' Strike: A Tragedy of Errors. Toronto: McClelland and
   Stewart, 1971.

MacDowell, Laurel Sefton
   *Remember Kirkland Lake: The History and Effects of the Kirkland Lake Gold
   Miners' Strike, 1941-42*. Toronto: University of Toronto Press, 1983.

   "The 1943 Steel Strike Against Wartime Wage Controls." *Labour/Le Travailleur*, no. 10 (Autumn 1982), pp. 65-86.

MacPherson, Ian
   *Each For All: A History of the Co-operative Movement in English Canada,
   1900-1945*. The Carleton Library, no. 116. Toronto: Macmillan, 1979.

Mahon, Rianne
   "Canadian Labour in the Battle of the Eighties." *Studies in Political Economy*, no. 11 (Summer 1983), pp. 149-75.

Makahonuk, Glen
   "Trade Unions in the Saskatchewan Coal Industry, 1907-1945." *Saskatchewan History* 31 (Spring 1978): 51-68.

Malles, Paul
   Canadian Industrial Conflict in International Perspective. Ottawa: Infor-
   metrica, 1977.

Masters, Donald Campbell
   The Winnipeg General Strike. Toronto: University of Toronto Press, 1973.
   (First published 1950.)

McNaught, Kenneth, and Bercuson, David J.
   The Winnipeg Strike, 1919. Don Mills, Ont.: Longmans, 1974.

Miner, Bob
   *Miner's Life: Bob Miner and Union Organizing in Timmins, Kirkland Lake
   and Sudbury*. Edited by Wayne Roberts. Hamilton, Ont.: Labour Studies
   Programme, McMaster University, 1979.

Montero, Gloria
   *We Stood Together: First-Hand Accounts of Dramatic Events in Canada's
   Labour Past*. Toronto: James Lorimer, 1979.

Moogk, Peter N.
"In the Darkness of a Basement: Craftsmen's Associations in Early French Canada." *Canadian Historical Review* 57 (December 1976): 399-439.

Morton, Desmond
"Taking on the Grand Trunk: The Locomotive Engineers Strike of 1876-7." *Labour/Le Travailleur*, no. 2 (1977), pp. 5-34.

Nightingale, Donald V.
Workplace Democracy: An Inquiry into Employee Participation in Canadian Work Organizations. Toronto: University of Toronto Press, 1982.

Osborne, Kenneth W.
R.B. Russell and the Labour Movement. Agincourt, Ont.: Book Society of Canada, 1978.

Palmer, Bryan D.
A Culture in Conflict: Skilled Workers and Industrial Capitalism in Hamilton, Ontario, 1860-1914. Montreal: McGill-Queen's University Press, 1979.

"Discordant Music: Charivaris and Whitecapping in Nineteenth-Century North America." *Labour/Le Travailleur*, no. 3 (1978), pp. 5-62.

Pendergest, James A.
"The Attempt at Unionization in the Automobile Industry in Canada, 1928." *Ontario History* 70 (December 1978): 245-62.

Penner, Norman, ed.
Winnipeg 1919: The Strikers' Own History of the Winnipeg General Strike. Toronto: James Lorimer, 1973.

"The Lachine Strike of 1843." *Canadian Historical Review* 29 (September 1948): 255-77.

Peterson, Larry
"The One Big Union in International Perspective: Revolutionary Industrial Unionism, 1900-1925." *Labour/Le Travailleur*, no. 7 (Spring 1981), pp. 41-66.

Phillips, Paul A.
"Canadian Labour and the New Industrial State." *Nationalism, Technology and the Future of Canada*, pp. 123-45. Edited by Wallace Gagne. Toronto: Macmillan, 1976.

"The National Policy and the Development of the Western Canadian Labour Movement." *Prairie Perspectives 2*, pp. 41-62. Edited by A.W. Rasporich and H.C. Klassen. Toronto: Holt, Rinehart & Winston, 1973.

Piotte, Jean-Marc; Ethier, D.; et Reynolds, J.
Les Travailleurs contre l'état bourgeois. Montréal: L'Aurore, 1975.

Pratt, Michel
La Grève de la United Aircraft. Québec: Presses de l'Université du Québec, 1980.

Radforth, Ian, and Sangster, Joan
"'A Link Between Labour and Learning': The Workers Educational Association in Ontario, 1917-1951." *Labour/Le Travailleur*, no. 8/9 (Autumn/Spring 1981/1982), pp. 41-78.

Ready, Alf
Organizing Westinghouse: Alf Ready's Story. Edited by Wayne Roberts. Hamilton, Ont.: McMaster University, 1979.

Repo, Satu
"Rosvall and Voutilainen: Two Union Men Who Never Died." *Labour/Le Travailleur,* no. 8/9 (Autumn/Spring 1981/1982), p. 79-102.

Roberts, Wayne
"Artisans, Aristocrats, and Handymen: Politics and Unionism Among Toronto Skilled Building Trades Workers, 1896-1914." *Labour/Le Travailleur,* no. 1 (1976), pp. 92-121.

Roberts, Wayne, and Bullen, John
"A Heritage of Hope and Struggle: Workers, Unions, and Politics in Canada, 1930-1982." *Readings in Canadian Social History,* vol. 5: *The Emergence of the Welfare State, 1930-1981,* pp. 105-43. Edited by Michael S. Cross and Gregory S. Kealey. Toronto: McClelland and Stewart, 1984.

Roberts, Wayne, ed.
Baptism of a Union: Stelco Strike of 1946. Hamilton, Ont.: Labour Studies Programme, McMaster University, 1981.

Rose, Joseph B.
Public Policy, Bargaining Structure and the Construction Industry. Toronto: Butterworth, 1980.

Rouillard, Jacques
"Le Militantisme des travailleurs au Québec et en Ontario, niveau de syndicalisation et mouvement de grève (1900-1980)." *Revue d'histoire de l'Amérique française* 37 (septembre 1983): 201-25.

"Implantation et expansion de l'Union internationale des travailleurs en chaussures au Québec de 1900 à 1940." *Revue d'histoire de l'Amérique française* 36 (juin 1982): 75-105.

Histoire de la CSN, 1921-1981. Montréal: Boréal Express, 1981.

Les Syndicats nationaux au Québec de 1900 à 1930. Québec: Presses de l'Université Laval, 1979.

Les Travailleurs du coton au Québec, 1900-1915. Montréal: Presses de l'Université du Québec, 1974.

Scott, Bruce
" 'A Place in the Sun': The Industrial Council at Massey-Harris, 1919-1929." *Labour/Le Travailleur,* no. 1 (1976), pp. 158-92.

Scott, Jack
Canadian Workers, American Unions. Vancouver: New Star Books, 1978.

Plunderbund and Proletariat. Vancouver: New Star Books, 1975.

Sweat and Struggle: Working Class Struggles in Canada. Vol. 1: *1789-1899.* Vancouver: New Star Books, 1974.

Scott, Stanley
"A Profusion of Issues: Immigrant Labour, the World War, and the Cominco Strike of 1917." *Labour/Le Travailleur,* no. 2 (1977), pp. 54-78.

Seager, Allen
"Finnish Canadians and the Ontario Miners' Movement." *Polyphony: The Bulletin of the Multicultural History Society of Ontario* 3 (Fall 1981): 35-45.

Siemiatycki, Myer
"Munitions and Labour Militancy: The 1916 Hamilton Machinists' Strike."
Labour/Le Travailleur, no. 3 (1978), pp. 131-51.

Stanton, John
Life and Death of a Union: The Canadian Seamen's Union, 1936-1949.
Toronto: Steel Rail Educational, 1978.

Storey, Robert
"Unionization Versus Corporate Welfare: The 'Dofasco Way'." *Labour/Le Travailleur*, no. 12 (Autumn 1983), pp. 7-42.

Sufrin, Eileen
The Eaton Drive: The Campaign to Organize Canada's Largest Department Store, 1948 to 1952. Toronto: Fitzhenry & Whiteside, 1982.

Sullivan, John Alan (Pat)
Red Sails on the Great Lakes. Toronto: Macmillan, 1955.

Swartz, Donald
"New Forms of Worker Participation: A Critique of Quality of Working Life." *Studies in Political Economy*, no. 5 (Spring 1981), pp. 55-78.

Thompson, Mark, and Blum, Albert A.
"International Unionism in Canada: The Move to Local Control." *Industrial Relations* (Berkeley, Calif.) 22 (Winter 1983): 71-86.

Thomson, Anthony
"The Nova Scotia Civil Service Association, 1956-1967." *Acadiensis* 12 (Spring 1983): 81-105.

" 'The Large and Generous View': The Debate on Labour Affiliation in the Canadian Civil Service, 1918-1928." *Labour/Le Travailleur*, no. 2 (1977), pp. 108-36.

Tremblay, Robert
"La Grève des ouvriers de la construction navale à Québec (1840)." *Revue d'histoire de l'Amérique française* 37 (septembre 1983): 227-40.

Trudeau, Pierre Elliott, ed.
The Asbestos Strike. Toronto: James Lorimer, 1974. (First published 1956.)

Tuck, J.H.
"The United Brotherhood of Railway Employees in Western Canada, 1898-1905." *Labour/Le Travailleur*, no. 11 (Spring 1983), pp. 63-88.

"Canadian Railways and Unions in the Running Trades, 1865-1914." *Relations industrielles/Industrial Relations* 36:1 (1981): 106-31.

Turk, James L.
"Surviving the Cold War: A Study of the United Electrical Workers in Canada." *Canadian Oral History Association Journal* 4:2 (1980): 6-28.

Vance, C.
"1837, Labor and the Democratic Tradition." *Marxist Quarterly* 12 (Winter 1965): 29-42.

"Early Trade Unionism in Quebec: 1833-1834: The Carpenters' and Joiners' General Strike in Montreal." *Marxist Quarterly* 3 (Autumn 1962): 26-42.

Zerker, Sally F.
The Rise and Fall of the Toronto Typographical Union, 1832-1972: A Case Study of Foreign Domination. Toronto: University of Toronto Press, 1981.

Zwelling, Marc
The Strikebreakers: The Report of the Strikebreaking Committee of the Ontario Federation of Labour and the Labour Council of Metropolitan Toronto. Toronto: New Press, 1972.

F. POLITICS AND IDEOLOGY

Angus, Ian
Canadian Bolsheviks: An Early History of the Communist Party of Canada. Montreal: Vanguard, 1981.

Avakumovic, Ivan
Socialism in Canada: A Study of the CCF-NDP in Federal and Provincial Politics. Toronto: McClelland and Stewart, 1978.

Avery, Donald H.
"British-born 'Radicals' in North America, 1900-1941: The Case of Sam Scarlett." *Canadian Ethnic Studies* 10:2 (1978): 65-85.

Bercuson, David J.
"Labour Radicalism and the Western Industrial Frontier: 1897-1919." *Canadian Historical Review* 58 (June 1977): 154-75.

Betcherman, Lita-Rose
The Little Band: The Clashes Between the Communists and the Political and Legal Establishments in Canada, 1928-1932. Ottawa: Deneau, 1982.

Buck, Tim
Yours in the Struggle: Reminiscences of Tim Buck. Edited by William Beeching and Phyllis Clarke. Toronto: NC Press, 1977.

Comeau, Robert, and Dionne, Bernard
Les Communistes du Québec, 1936-1956: sur le Parti communiste du Canada, Parti ouvrier-progressiste. Montréal: Presses de l'Unité, 1981.

[Communist Party of Canada]
Canada's Party of Socialism: History of the Communist Party of Canada, 1921-1976. Toronto: Progress Books, 1982.

Denis, Roch
Luttes des classes et question national au Québec, 1948-1968. Montréal: Presses socialistes internationales, 1979.

Frank, David
"Company Town/Labour Town: Local Government in the Cape Breton Coal Towns, 1917-1926." *Histoire social/Social History* 14 (May 1981): 177-96.

Frank, David, and Reilly, Nolan
"The Emergence of the Socialist Movement in the Maritimes, 1899-1916." *Labour/Le Travailleur,* no. 4 (1979), pp. 85-113.

Friesen, Gerald
" 'Yours in Revolt': Regionalism, Socialism, and the Western Canadian Labour Movement." *Labour/Le Travailleur,* no. 1 (1976), 139-57.

Gauvin, Bernard
Les Communistes et la question nationale au Québec: sur le Parti communiste du Canada, de 1921 à 1938. Montréal: Presses de l'Unité, 1981.

Germain, Annick
"L'Emergence d'une scène politique: mouvement ouvrier et mouvements de réforme urbaine à Montréal au tournant du siècle — essai d'interpretation." *Revue d'histoire de l'Amérique française* 37 (septembre 1983): 185-99.

Hoar, Victor
The Mackenzie-Papineau Battalion: Canadian Participation in the Spanish Civil War. Toronto: Copp Clark, 1969.

Homel, Gene Howard
"'Fading Beams of the Nineteenth Century': Radicalism and Early Socialism in Canada's 1890s." *Labour/Le Travailleur*, no. 5 (Spring 1980), pp. 7-32.

Horn, Michiel
The League for Social Reconstruction: Intellectual Origins of the Democratic Left in Canada, 1930-1942. Toronto: University of Toronto Press, 1980.

Johnston, William, and Ornstein, Michael D.
"Class, Work and Politics." *Canadian Review of Sociology and Anthropology* 19 (May 1982): 196-214.

Kealey, Gregory S.
"Stanley Bréhaut Ryerson: Canadian Revolutionary Intellectual." *Studies in Political Economy*, no. 9 (Fall 1982), pp. 103-31.

"Stanley Bréhaut Ryerson: Marxist Historian." *Studies in Political Economy*, no. 9 (Fall 1982), pp. 133-70.

Keddie, Vincent
"Class Identification and Party Preference Among Manual Workers: The Influence of Community, Union Membership and Kinship." *Canadian Review of Sociology and Anthropology* 17 (February 1980): 24-36.

Kolasky, John
The Shattered Illusion: The History of Ukrainian Pro-Communist Organizations in Canada. Toronto: PMA Books, 1979.

Krawchuk, Peter
The Ukrainian Socialist Movement in Canada (1907-1918). Toronto: Progress Books, 1979.

Larivière, Claude
Albert Saint-Martin, militant d'avant-garde, 1865-1947. Laval, Qué.: Editions coopératives Albert Saint-Martin, 1979.

Mardiros, Anthony
William Irvine: The Life of a Prairie Radical. Toronto: James Lorimer, 1979.

Martynowych, Orest T.
"The Ukrainian Socialist Movement in Canada, 1900-1918." *Journal of Ukrainian Graduate Studies* 1 (Fall 1976): 27-44; 2 (Spring 1977): 22-31.

McCormack, A. Ross
"British Working-Class Immigrants and Canadian Radicalism: The Case of Arthur Puttee." *Canadian Ethnic Studies* 10:2 (1978): 22-37.

McDonald, Ian
"W.F. Coaker and the Balance of Power Strategy: The Fishermen's Protective Union in Newfoundland." *Newfoundland in the Nineteenth and Twentieth Centuries: Essays in Interpretation*, pp. 148-80. Edited by James Hiller and Peter Neary. Toronto: University of Toronto Press, 1980.

McEwen, Tom
The Forge Glows Red: From Blacksmith to Revolutionary. Toronto: Progress Books, 1974.

Mills, Allen
"Single Tax, Socialism, and the Independent Labour Party of Manitoba: The Political Ideas of F.J. Dixon and S.J. Farmer." *Labour/Le Travailleur*, no. 5 (Spring 1980), pp. 33-56.

Morton, Desmond
NDP: The Dream of Power. Toronto: Hakkert, 1974.

Munn, Edwidge
"L'Action politique partisane à la FTQ (1957-76)." *Labour/Le Travailleur*, no. 12 (automne 1983), pp. 43-62.

Ostry, Bernard
"Conservatives, Liberals and Labour in the 1880's." *Canadian Journal of Economics and Political Science* 27 (May 1961): 141-61.

Petryshn, J.
" 'Class Conflict and Civil Liberties': The Origins and Activities of the Canadian Labour Defense League, 1925-1940." *Labour/Le Travailleur*, no. 10 (Autumn 1982), pp. 39-64.

"R.B. Bennett and the Communists, 1930-1935." *Journal of Canadian Studies* 9 (November 1974): 43-55.

Pinard, Maurice
"Working Class Politics: An Interpretation of the Quebec Case." *Canadian Review of Sociology and Anthropology* 7 (May 1970): 87-109.

Piva, Michael J.
"The Toronto District Labour Council and Independent Political Action: Factionalism and Frustration, 1900-1921." *Labour/Le Travailleur*, no. 4 (1979), pp. 115-30.

"Workers and Tories: The Collapse of the Conservative Party in Urban Ontario, 1908-1919." *Urban History Review* 3-76 (February 1977): 23-39.

Pryke, Ken
"Labour and Politics: Nova Scotia at Confederation." *Histoire sociale/Social History* 6 (November 1970): 33-55.

Rawlyk, G.A., ed.
"The Farmer-Labour Movement and the Failure of Socialism in Nova Scotia." *Essays on the Left*, pp. 3-41. Edited by L. Lapierre et al. Toronto: McClelland and Stewart, 1971.

Rodney, William
Soldiers of the International: A History of the Communist Party of Canada, 1919-1929. Toronto: University of Toronto Press, 1968.

Ryan, Oscar
Tim Buck: A Conscience for Canada. Toronto: Progress Books, 1975.

Schulz, Patricia V.
The East York Workers' Association: A Response to the Great Depression. Toronto: New Hogtown Press, 1975.

Schwantes, Carlos A.
Radical Heritage: Labor, Socialism, and Reform in Washington and British Columbia, 1885-1917. Seattle: University of Washington Press, 1979.

Smith, Albert Edward
All My Life: An Autobiography. Toronto: Progess Books, 1977. (First published 1949.)

Steeves, Dorothy G.
The Compassionate Rebel: Ernest Winch and the Growth of Socialism in Western Canada. Vancouver: J.J. Douglas, 1977. (First published 1960.)

Stevenson, Paul
"Class and Left-Wing Radicalism." *Canadian Review of Sociology and Anthropology* 14 (August 1977): 269-84.

Thompson, Thomas Phillips
The Politics of Labour. Toronto: University of Toronto Press, 1975. (First published 1887.)

Tremblay, Louis-Marie
Le Syndicalisme québécois: idéologies de la C.S.N. et de la F.T.Q., 1940-1970. Montréal: Presses de l'Université de Montréal, 1970.

Usiskin, Roz
"The Winnipeg Jewish Community: Its Radical Elements 1905-1918." *Historical and Scientific Society of Manitoba Transactions.* Series 3, no. 33 (1976-77), pp. 5-33.

Watt, Frank W.
"Literature of Protest." *Literary History of Canada: Canadian Literature in English*, pp. 457-73. Edited by Carl F. Klinck. Toronto: University of Toronto Press, 1965.

"The National Policy, the Workingman and Proletarian Ideas in Victorian Canada." *Canadian Historical Review* 40 (March 1959): 1-26.

Weinrich, Peter, comp.
Social Protest From the Left in Canada 1870-1970: A Bibliography. Toronto: University of Toronto Press, 1982.

Whitaker, Reginald
"The Liberal Corporatist Ideas of Mackenzie King." *Labour/Le Travailleur*, no. 2 (1977), pp. 137-69.

G. LABOUR AND THE STATE

Adams, Roy J.
"The Federal Government and Tripartism." *Relations industrielles/Industrial Relations* 37:3 (1982): 606-17.

Arthurs, H.W.; Carter, D.D.; and Glasbeek, H.J.
Labour Law and Industrial Relations in Canada. 2nd ed. Toronto: Butterworth, 1984.

Auld, D.A.L., et al.
"The Impact of the Anti-Inflation Board on Negotiated Wage Settlements." *Canadian Journal of Economics* 12 (May 1979): 195-213.

Baker, William M.
"The Miners and the Mediator: The 1906 Lethbridge Strike and Mackenzie King." *Labour/Le Travailleur*, no. 11 (Spring 1983), pp. 89-118.

Canada. Task Force on Labour Relations
Canadian Industrial Relations: The Report. Ottawa: Privy Council Office, 1968.

Carrothers, Alfred W.R.
Collective Bargaining Law in Canada. Toronto: Butterworth, 1965.

Downie, Bryan M.
Collective Bargaining and Conflict Resolution in Education: The Evolution of Public Policy in Ontario. Kingston, Ont.: Industrial Relations Centre, Queen's University, 1978.

Hodgetts, John Edwin, and Dwivedi, O.P.
Provincial Governments as Employers: A Survey of Public Personnel Administration in Canada's Provinces. Montreal: McGill-Queen's University Press, 1974.

Horrall, S.W.
"The Royal North-West Mounted Police and Labour Unrest in Western Canada, 1919." *Canadian Historical Review* 61 (June 1980): 169-90.

Jamieson, Stuart
"Some Reflections on Violence and the Law in Industrial Relations." *Law and Society in Canada in Historical Perspective*, pp. 141-56. Edited by D.J. Bercuson and L.A. Knafla. Calgary: University of Calgary, 1979.

Johnson, Walter
Trade Unions and the State. Montreal: Black Rose Books, 1978.

King, W.L. Mackenzie
Industry and Humanity: A Study in the Principles Underlying Industrial Reconstruction. Toronto: University of Toronto Press, 1973. (First published 1918.)

Lipsig-Mummé, Carla
"Quebec Unions and the State: Conflict and Dependence." *Studies in Political Economy*, no. 3 (Spring 1980), pp. 119-46.

Logan, H.A.
State Intervention and Assistance in Collective Bargaining: The Canadian Experience, 1943-1954. Toronto: University of Toronto Press, 1956.

Macgillivray, Don
"Military Aid to the Civil Power: The Cape Breton Experience in the 1920's." *Acadiensis* 3 (Spring 1974): 45-65.

Morton, Desmond
"Aid to the Civil Power: The Canadian Militia in Support of Social Order, 1867-1914." *Studies in Canadian Social History*, pp. 417-434. Edited by Michiel Horn and Ronald Sabourin. Toronto: McClelland and Stewart, 1974. (Reprinted from *Canadian Historical Review* 51 [December 1970]: 407-25.)

Piva, Michael J.
"The Workingmen's Compensation Movement in Ontario." *Ontario History* 67 (March 1975): 39-56.

Reid, Frank

"The Effect of Controls on the Rate of Wage Change in Canada." *Canadian Journal of Economics* 12 (May 1979): 214-27.

Rinehart, James W.

"Wage Controls, Unions and Class Conflict in Canada." *Our Generation* 11 (Summer 1976): 27-34.

Sautter, Udo

"Measuring Unemployment in Canada: Federal Efforts Before World War II." *Histoire sociale/Social History* 15 (November 1982): 475-87.

"The Origins of the Unemployment Service of Canada, 1900-1920." *Labour/ Le Travailleur*, no. 6 (Autumn 1980), pp. 89-112.

Tremblay, Robert

"Un aspect de la consolidation du pouvoir d'Etat de la bourgeoisie coloniale: la législation anti-ouvrière dans le Bas-Canada, 1800-50." *Labour/Le Travailleur*, no. 8/9 (automne/printemps 1981/1982), pp. 243-52.

Tucker, Eric

"The Determination of Occupational Health and Safety Standards in Ontario, 1860-1982: From the Market to Politics to...?" *McGill Law Journal* 29 (March 1984): 260-311.

Walters, Vivienne

"Occupational Health and Safety Legislation in Ontario: An Analysis of its Origins and Content." *Canadian Review of Sociology and Anthropology* 20 (November 1983): 423-34.

Weiler, Paul

Reconcilable Differences: New Directions in Canadian Labour Law. Toronto: Carswell, 1980.

Willes, John A.

The Ontario Labour Court, 1943-1944. Kingston, Ont.: Industrial Relations Centre, Queen's University, 1979.

8

The Economic Crisis

CY GONICK

The current crisis of world capitalism began in the late 1960s, although it was only recognized as such in 1974. Marxist scholars were the first to realize that this was indeed "a crisis" and not merely another in the series of business cycles that have characterized the postwar world. By the end of the 1970s, the discipline of economics was in total disarray: Keynesianism was declared dead, and the postwar consensus was replaced by a range of contending theories that variously interpreted the origins of the crisis and offered diverse methods for its resolution. Interestingly enough, the crisis in economic theory has precipitated the revival of political economy, as competing theorists all, in their various ways, focus on the role of the state in economic life.

Subsection A below lists works that have charted the crisis. Subsection B examines the major Marxist interpretations of the crisis, including the effects of the falling rate of profit, profit-squeeze, underconsumption and the social structures of accumulation. Subsection C lists some of the major contributions of the monetarists, supply-side economists and post-Keynesians.

A. CHARTING THE CRISIS

Aaronovitch, Sam
The Road From Thatcherism: Alternative Economic Strategy. London: Lawrence & Wishart, 1981.

Aglietta, Michel
"World Capitalism in the Eighties." *New Left Review*, no. 136 (November/December 1982), pp. 5-41.

A Theory of Capitalist Regulation: The U.S. Experience. New York: New Left Books; distributed by Schocken, 1979.

Amin, Samir
"The World Crisis of the 1980s." *Monthly Review* 33 (June 1981): 33-42.

Apple, Nixon
"The Rise and Fall of Full Employment Capitalism." *Studies in Political Economy*, no. 4 (Autumn 1980), pp. 5-40.

Armstrong, Pat, and Armstrong, Hugh
"Job Creation and Unemployment for Canadian Women." *Women and the World of Work*, pp. 129-152. Edited by Anne Hoiberg. NATO Conference Series III. Human Factors: vol. 18. New York: Plenum Press, 1982.

Bacon, Robert, and Eltis, W.A.
Britain's Economic Problem. London: Macmillan, 1978.

Block, Fred L.
The Origins of the International Economic Disorder: A Study of United States International Monetary Policy from World War Two to the Present. Berkeley: University of California Press, 1977.

Bowles, Samuel, and Gintis, Herbert
"The Crisis of Liberal Democratic Capitalism: The Case of the United States." *Politics & Society* 11:1 (1982): 51-94.

Calvert, John
Government Limited: The Corporate Take-Over of the Public Sector in Canada. Ottawa: Canadian Centre for Policy Alternatives, 1984.

Cameron, Duncan
"Order and Disorder in the World Economy." *Studies in Political Economy*, no. 11 (Summer 1983), pp. 105-26.

Campen, James T., and MacEwen, Arthur
"Crisis, Contradictions, and Conservative Controversies in Contemporary U.S. Capitalism." *Review of Radical Political Economy* 14 (Fall 1982): 1-22.

Clarkson, Stephen
Canada and the Reagan Challenge: Crisis in the Canadian-American Relationship. Toronto: James Lorimer in association with the Canadian Institute for Economic Policy, 1982.

Crozier, Michel, et al.
The Crisis of Democracy: Report on the Governability of Democracies to the Trilateral Commission. New York: New York University Press, 1975.

Currie, Elliott; Dunn, Robert; and Fogarty, David
"The New Immiseration: Stagflation, Inequality and the Working Class." *Socialist Review*, no. 54 (November-December 1980), pp. 7-32.

Frank, Andre Gunder
Reflections on the World Economic Crisis. New York: Monthly Review Press, 1981.

Frobel, F., et al.
The New International Division of Labour: Structural Unemployment in Industrialised Countries and Industrialisation in Developing Countries. Cambridge, Eng.: Cambridge University Press, 1980.

Glyn, Andrew, and Harrison, John
The British Economic Disaster. London: Pluto Press, 1980.

Gonick, Cy
"The Concessions Con Job." *Canadian Dimension* 16 (October/November 1982): 13-15.

"Notes on the New Economic Crisis." *Canadian Dimension* 14 (February-March 1980): 9-13.

Gordon, David
"Stages of Accumulation and Long Economic Cycles." *Processes of the World-System*. Edited by Terence K. Hopkins and Immanuel Wallerstein. Political Economy of the World-System Annals, vol.3. Beverly Hills, Calif.: Sage Publications, 1980.

Gorz, André
Farewell to the Working Class. London: Pluto Press, 1982.

Heilbroner, Robert Louis
"Inflationary Capitalism." *New Yorker* 55 (October 8, 1979): 121-2, 124-30, 133-41.

Beyond Boom and Crash. New York: W.W. Norton, 1978.

Hotson, John H.; Habibagahi, Hamid; and Lermer, George
Stagflation and the Bastard Keynesians. Waterloo, Ont.: University of Waterloo Press, 1976.

Hyman, R.
"André Gorz and His Disappearing Proletariat." *Socialist Register 1983.* Edited by R. Miliband and J. Saville. London: Merlin Press, 1983.

Kaldor, Nicholas
"Inflation and Recession in the World Economy." *Economic Journal* 86 (December 1976): 703-14.

Lipietz, Alain
"Towards a Global Fordism?" *New Left Review*, no. 132 (March-April 1982), pp. 48-58.

MacEwan, Arthur
"International Economic Crisis and the Limits of Macropolicy." *Socialist Review*, no. 59 (September-October 1981), pp. 113-38.

Magdoff, Harry, and Sweezy, Paul M.
The Deepening Crisis of U.S. Capitalism. New York: Monthly Review Press, 1981.

The End of Prosperity: The American Economy in the 1970s. New York: Monthly Review Press, 1977.

Mandel, Ernest
The Second Slump: A Marxist Analysis of Recession in the Seventies. New York: New Left Books; distributed by Schocken, 1979.

Late Capitalism. London: New Left Books, 1975.

Miliband, Ralph
Capitalist Democracy in Britain. Oxford: Oxford University Press, 1982.

Parboni, Ricardo
The Dollar and Its Rivals: Recession, Inflation, and International Finance. London: New Left Books, 1981.

Przeworski, Adam, and Wallerstein, M.
"Democratic Capitalism at the Crossroads." *Democracy* 2 (July 1982): 52-68.

Rada, Juan
The Impact of Microelectronics: A Tentative Appraisal of Information Technology. London: International Labour Office, 1980.

Ross, George, and Jensen, Jane
"Crisis and France's 'Third Way'." *Studies in Political Economy*, no. 11 (Summer 1983), pp. 71-104.

Sutcliffe, Bob
Hard Times: World Economy in Turmoil. London: Pluto Press, 1983.

Sweezy, Paul M.
"What's Wrong with the American Economy?" *Monthly Review* 36 (May 1984): 1-10.

"The Present Stage of the Global Crisis of Capitalism." *Monthly Review* 29 (April 1978): 1-13.

Sweezy, Paul M., and Magdoff, Harry
"Full Recovery or Stagnation." *Monthly Review* 35 (September 1983): 1-12.

"Unemployment: The Failure of Private Enterprise." *Monthly Review* 35 (June 1983): 1-9.

"Production and Finance." *Monthly Review* 35 (May 1983): 1-13.

"Listen, Keynesians!" *Monthly Review* 34 (January 1983): 1-11.

Tarshis, Lorie
World Economy in Crisis: Unemployment, Inflation and International Debt. Toronto: James Lorimer in association with the Canadian Institute for Economic Policy, 1984.

Weisskopf, Thomas
"The Current Economic Crisis in Historical Perspective." *Socialist Review,* no. 57 (May-June 1981), pp. 9-54.

B. DEBATES WITHIN MARXISM

Bowles, Samuel
"The Post-Keynesian Capital-Labour Stalemate." *Socialist Review,* no. 65 (September-October 1982), pp. 45-72.

Bowles, Samuel; Gordon, David M.; and Weisskopf, Thomas E.
Beyond the Waste Land: A Democratic Alternative to Economic Decline. Garden City, N.Y.: Anchor Books, 1984.

Bruegel, Irene
"Women as a Reserve Army of Labour: A Note on the Recent British Experience." *Feminist Review,* no. 3 (1979), pp. 12-23.

Fine, Ben, and Harris, Laurence
"Surveying the Foundations." *Socialist Register 1977,* pp. 106-20. Edited by Ralph Miliband and John Saville. London: Merlin Press, 1977.

"Controversial Issues in Marxist Economic Theory." *Socialist Register 1976,* pp. 141-78. Edited by Ralph Miliband and John Saville. London: Merlin Press, 1976.

Glyn, Andrew, and Sutcliffe, Bob
British Capitalism: Workers and the Profits Squeeze. Harmondsworth: Penguin, 1972.

Gough, Ian
The Political Economy of the Welfare State. Atlantic Highlands, N.J.: Humanities Press, 1979.

Harrison, John
"State Expenditure and Capital." *Cambridge Journal of Economics* 4 (December 1980): 379-92.

Hirsch, Joachim
"The State Apparatus and Social Reproduction: Elements of a Theory of a Bourgeois State." *State and Capital: A Marxist Debate*, pp. 57-107. Edited by John Holloway and Sol Piociotto. Austin: University of Texas Press, 1978.

Hodgson, Geoff
"The Theory of the Falling Rate of Profit." *New Left Review*, no. 84 (March-April 1974), pp. 55-84.

Holloway, J, and Picciotto, S.
"Capital, Crisis and the State." *Capital and Class* [Summer 1977]

O'Connor, James R.
The Fiscal Crisis of the State. New York: St. Martin's Press, 1973.

Rowthorn, Bob
"Late Capitalism". *New Left Review*, no. 98 (July 1976), pp. 59-83.

Shaikh, Anwar
"An Introduction to the History of Crisis Theories." *U.S. Capitalism in Crisis*, pp. 219-40. Edited by Crisis Reader Editorial Collective. New York: Economics Education Project of the Union for Radical Political Economics, 1978.

Sherman, Howard
"A Marxist Theory of the Business Cycle." *Review of Radical Political Economics* 11 (Spring 1979): 1-23.

Steedman, Ian, et al.
The Value Controversy. London: Verso, 1981.

Weisskopf, Thomas
"Marxian Crisis Theory and the Rate of Profit in the Postwar U.S. Economy." *Cambridge Journal of Economics* 3 (December 1979): 341-78.

"Marxist Perspectives on Cyclical Crisis." *U.S. Capitalism in Crisis*, pp. 241-61. Edited by Crisis Reader Editorial Collective. New York: Economics Education Project of the Union for Radical Political Economics, 1978.

Wright, Erik Olin
"Alternative Perspectives in Marxist Theory of Accumulation and Crisis." *Insurgent Sociologist* 6 (Fall 1975): 5-39.

Yanz, Lynda, and Smith, David
"Women as a Reserve Army of Labour: A Critique." *Review of Radical Political Economics* 15 (Spring 1983): 92-106.

C. MONETARISM, SUPPLY-SIDE AND POST-KEYNESIAN POLICY ALTERNATIVES

Ackerman, Frank
Reaganomics: Rhetoric vs. Reality. Boston: South End Press, 1982.

Barber, Clarence, and McCallum, John C.P.
Controlling Inflation: Learning from Experience in Canada, Europe and Japan. Toronto: James Lorimer in association with the Canadian Institute for Economic Policy, 1982.

"The Failure of Monetarism in Theory and Policy." *Canadian Public Policy* 7 (April 1981 Supplement): 221-32.

Unemployment and Inflation: The Canadian Experience. Ottawa: Canadian Institute for Economic Policy, 1980.

Baum, Gregory, and Cameron, Duncan, eds.
Ethics and Economics: Canada's Catholic Bishops on the Economic Crisis. Toronto: James Lorimer, 1984.

Bell, Daniel, and Kristol, Irving, eds.
The Crisis in Economic Theory. New York: Basic Books, 1981.

Black, Errol, et al.
"Solidarity's Work: Far From Over." *Canadian Dimension* 18 (March 1984): 2 ("What Happened in B.C.")

Block, Walter E., and Olsen, Edgar O., eds.
Rent Control: Myths and Realities: International Evidence of the Effects of Rent Control in Six Countries. Rev. ed. Vancouver: Fraser Institute, 1981.

Britton, John N.H., and Gilmour, James M.
The Weakest Link: A Technological Perspective on Canadian Industrial Underdevelopment. Background Study no. 43. Ottawa: Science Council of Canada, 1978.

Business Week
"The Reindustrialization of America." (Special Issue) no. 2643 (June 30, 1980).

Campen, James T.
"Economic Crisis and Conservative Economic Policies: U.S. Capitalism in the 1980's." *Radical America* 15 (Spring 1981): 33-54.

Campen, James T., and MacEwan, Arthur
"Crisis, Contradictions and Conservative Controversies in Contemporary U.S. Capitalism." *Review of Radical Political Economics* 14 (Fall 1982): 1-22.

Canada. Science Council of Canada
Hard Times, Hard Choices: Technology and the Balance of Payments: A Statement. Ottawa: Science Council of Canada, 1981.

Forging the Links: A Technology Policy for Canada. Report no. 29. Ottawa: Science Council of Canada, 1979.

Uncertain Prospects - Canadian Manufacturing Industry 1971-1977. Ottawa: Science Council of Canada, 1977.

Cornwall, John
"Modern Capitalism and the Trend Towards De-industrialization." *Journal of Economic Issues* 14 (June 1980): 275-89.

Cornwall, John, and Maclean, Wendy
Economic Recovery for Canada. Toronto: James Lorimer in association with the Canadian Institute for Economic Policy, 1984.

Courchene, Thomas J.
"Recent Canadian Monetary Policy: 1975-81: Reflections of a Gradualist." *Monetarism: Panacea or Perfidy?* Edited by G. Mason. Winnipeg: Institute for Social and Economic Research, 1983.

Monetarism and Controls: The Inflation Fighters. Montreal: C.D. Howe Research Institute, 1976.

Money, Inflation and the Bank of Canada. 2 vols. Montreal: C.D. Howe Research Institute, 1976.

Crane, David, ed.
Beyond the Monetarists: Post-Keynesian Alternatives to Rampant Inflation, Low Growth and High Unemployment. Toronto: James Lorimer, 1981.

Fortin, Pierre
"Monetary Targets and Monetary Policy in Canada: A Critical Assessment." *Canadian Journal of Economics* 12 (November 1979): 625-46.

Friedman, Milton
Capitalism and Freedom: With a New Preface. Chicago: University of Chicago Press, 1981. (First published 1963.)

Tax Limitation, Inflation and the Role of Government. Dallas: Fisher Institute, 1978.

Friedman, Milton, and Friedman, Rose
Free to Choose: A Personal Statement. New York: Harcourt Brace Jovanovich, 1980.

Galbraith, J.K.
Economics and the Public Purpose. Scarborough, Ont.: New American Library, 1975.

Gilder, George
Wealth and Poverty. New York: Basic Books, 1981.

Gonick, Cy
The Great Economic Debate. Toronto: James Lorimer, forthcoming.

Gordon, Myron J.
The Post-Keynesian Debate: A Review of Three Recent Canadian Contributions. Toronto: James Lorimer in association with the Canadian Institute for Economic Policy, 1980.

"A World Scale National Corporation Industrial Strategy." *Canadian Public Policy* 4 (Winter 1978): 46-56.

Grubel, Herbert G., and Walker, Michael A., eds.
Unemployment Insurance: Global Evidence of its Effects on Unemployment. Vancouver: Fraser Institute, 1978.

Hayek, Friedrich August von
Full Employment at Any Price? Occasional Paper no. 45. London: Institute of Economic Affairs, 1975.

Heilbroner, Robert Louis
"The Demand for the Supply-Side." *New York Review of Books* 28 (June 11, 1981): 37-41.

Jenkin, Michael
The Challenge of Diversity: Industrial Policy in the Canadian Federation. Background Study no. 50. Ottawa: Science Council of Canada, 1983.

Kuen, Larry
"B.C. Teachers Strengthen the Labour Movement." *Canadian Dimension* 18 (March 1984): 9-12. ("What Happened in B.C.")

Laidler, David
"Inflation and Unemployment in an Open Economy: A Monetarist View." *Canadian Public Policy* 7 (April 1981 Supplement): 179-88.

Laidler, David, et al.
The Illusion of Wage and Price Controls: Essays on Inflation, Its Causes and Its Curses. Vancouver: Fraser Institute, 1976.

Larkin, Jackie
"The Generals Didn't Strike." *Canadian Dimension* 18 (March 1984): 3-4,6. ("What Happened in B.C.")

Laxer, James
Rethinking the Economy. Toronto: NC Press, 1984.

Lipsey, R.
"The Understanding and Control of Inflation: Is There a Crisis in Macro-Economics?" *Canadian Journal of Economics* 14 (November 1981): 545-76.

"Wage-Price Controls: How to Do a Lot of Harm by Trying to Do a Little Good." *Canadian Public Policy* 3 (Winter 1977): 1-13.

Lithwick, Harvey M., and Derlin, J.
"Economic Development Policy: A Case Study in Underdeveloped Policy Making." *How Ottawa Spends: The New Agenda, 1984.* Rev. ed. Edited by Allan Maslove. Toronto: Methuen, 1984.

McCallum, John
"A Critical Review of Monetarism in Canada." *Monetarism: Panacea or Perfidy?* Edited by G. Mason. Winnipeg: Institute for Social and Economic Research, 1983.

Meade, James Edward
Stagflation. Vol. 1: *Wage-Fixing.* London: Allen & Unwin, 1982.

Modigliani, Franco
"The Monetarist Controversy, or Should We Forsake Stabilization Policies." *American Economic Review* 67 (March 1977): 1-19.

Naylor, R.T.
"High Interest Rates Are a Lot of Bouey." *Policy Alternatives* (Spring 1982): 3-10.

Ohashi, T.M.; Roth, T.D.; and Spindler, Zane
Privatization: Theory and Practice: Distributing Shares in Private and Public Enterprises: BCRIC, PETROCAN, ESOPs, GSOPs. Vancouver: Fraser Institute, 1980.

Ontario. Ontario Economic Council
Deficits: How Big and How Bad? Special Research Report. Proceedings of a Conference held in Toronto, March 8-9, 1983. Edited by David W. Conkin and Thomas J. Courchene. Toronto: Ontario Economic Council, 1983.

Palda, Kristian S.
The Science Council's Weakest Link: A Critique of the Science Council's Technocratic Industrial Strategy for Canada. Vancouver: Fraser Institute, 1979.

Palmer, Bryan
"A Funny Thing Happened on the Way to Kelowna." *Canadian Dimension* 18 (March 1984): 13, 16. ("What Happened in B.C.")

Rankin, Harry
"Solidarity — Here to Stay." *Canadian Dimension* 18 (March 1984): 7-8. ("What Happened in B.C.")

Reich, Robert B.
The Next American Frontier. New York: Times Books, 1983.

Robinson, H. Lukin
"Standing Keynes on His Head." *Canadian Forum* 63 (October 1983): 10-15; (November 1983): 11-14.

Canada's Crippled Dollar: An Analysis of International Trade and Our Troubled Balance of Payments. Toronto: James Lorimer in association with the Canadian Institute for Economic Policy, 1980.

Rotstein, Abraham
Rebuilding From Within: Remedies for Canada's Ailing Economy. Toronto: James Lorimer in association with the Canadian Institute for Economic Policy, 1984.

Trevithick, James Anthony
Inflation: A Guide to the Crisis in Economics. Harmondsworth: Penguin, 1977.

Walker, Michael, ed.
Which Way Ahead? Canada After Wage and Price Control. Vancouver: Fraser Institute, 1977.

Watkins, Mel
"Laxer's Choice." *This Magazine* 18 (April 1984): 16-19, 36.

Wolfe, David
"The Rise and Demise of the Keynesian Era in Canada." *Modern Canada*. Readings in Canadian Social History Series, vol. 5. Edited by Michael Cross and Gregory Kealey. Toronto: McClelland and Stewart, 1984.

Yandle, Sharon
"The NDP in BC: Observing Their Friends on the Move." *Canadian Dimension* 18 (March 1984): 5, 8. ("What Happened in B.C.")

9

Imperialism and Dependency

JOHN SAUL

There is such a wide and varied literature on this topic that any selection of the most relevant titles must necessarily be considered rather arbitrary. Nevertheless, it can safely be asserted that Marx's own analyses of the (inevitably) expansive nature of the capitalist system that emerged out of European feudalism provide the best starting point for the subject.

The intellectual tradition that sprang from Marx's work very soon gave rise to spirited debates regarding the precise dynamics of capitalist imperialism and the nature of its impact on the world beyond Europe (see subsection A, below). Lenin brought the issue into sharp polemical focus by characterizing imperialism as "the highest stage of capitalism." Certainly, the determining influence of capitalism's monopolistic tendencies has been confirmed by the increasingly prominent role of the multinational corporation within the global capitalist system. Recent literature has emphasized this latter phenomenon, but simultaneously reveals real differences of opinion regarding the precise nature of the interplay between the "transnational" logic of such corporations, on the one hand, and the aggressive assertion of national capitalism (and national states), on the other. Some authors debate such issues as the extent of "inter-imperialist rivalry" and the degree of American hegemony within the imperial camp, while others specify more clearly the character of capitalist imperialism's belligerent confrontation with forces antagonistic to it on the global front, be they of a nationalist, a socialist or a "bureaucratic collectivist" character (subsection B).

The discussion of global capitalism's impact on its "periphery" has been even more marked by controversy. Many twentieth-century Marxists (Paul Baran being a seminal example) believe Marx himself tended to overstate European capitalism's ability to "develop" and transform the world in its own image. They prefer, instead, to emphasize the extent to which capitalist imperialism has frozen many countries and regions of the world into a subordinate, dependent and "underdeveloped" role, and they have sought, often with great effect, to explore the various mechanisms that produce this result (subsection C). In recent years, certain extreme statements of this "dependency" approach have given rise to sharp criticism. Of course, such criticism has sometimes produced extreme formulations of its own (for example, Warren's uncategorical evocation of the "progressive" and transforming role of global capitalism.)

Yet, in general, the ongoing debate and continuing attempts to synthesize differing emphases promise subtle and interesting work of both a theoretical and empirical nature. In fact, this promise has begun to be realized in recent studies of the strengths and weaknesses of various peripheral (and not so peripheral) capitalisms, of the role of diverse classes, gender, "modes of production" and state structures to be found in such settings, and of the prospects for mounting successful socialist alternatives (subsection D).

A. THE CLASSICAL TRADITION

Brewer, Anthony
Marxist Theories of Imperialism: A Critical Survey. London: Routledge & Kegan Paul, 1980. (See especially Part I: "Classical Marxist Theories of Capitalist Expansion" and Part II: "Classical Marxist Theories of Imperialism and Inter-Imperialist Rivalry.")

Kemp, Tom
Theories of Imperialism. London: Dennis Dobson, 1967.

Kiernan, E. Victor Gordon
Marxism and Imperialism. London: Edward Arnold, 1974.

Lenin, Vladimir Illich
The Lenin Anthology. Edited by Robert C. Tucker. New York: Norton, 1975. (Including "Imperialism, the Highest Stage of Capitalism: A Popular Outline" [first published 1917], and other related writings.)

Luxemburg, Rosa, and Bukharin, Nikolai I.
The Accumulation of Capital — An Anti-Critique. Imperialism and the Accumulation of Capital. With an Introduction by Kenneth J. Tarbuck. New York: Monthly Review Press, 1972.

Marx, Karl
Karl Marx on Colonialism and Modernization; His Despatches and Other Writings on China, India, Mexico, the Middle East and North Africa. Edited by Shlomo Avineri. Garden City: Doubleday, 1968.

Melotti, Umberto
Marx and the Third World. Atlantic Highlands, N.J.: Humanities Press, 1977.

Schram, Stuart R., and Carrère d'Encausse, Hélène, eds.
Marxism and Asia: An Introduction with Readings. New ed. London: Allen Lane, 1969.

Shanin, Teodor, ed.
Late Marx and the Russian Road: Marx and 'The Peripheries of Capitalism': A Case. New York: Monthly Review Press, 1983.

Sweezy, Paul M.
The Theory of Capitalist Development: Principles of Marxian Political Economy. New York: Monthly Review Press, 1972. (First published 1942.)

B. THE DYNAMICS OF IMPERIALISM

Baran, Paul A., and Sweezy, Paul M.
"Notes on the Theory of Imperialism." *Readings in U.S. Imperialism*, pp. 69-84. Edited by K.T. Fann and Donald C. Hodges. Boston: Porter Sargent, 1971.

Barnett, Richard J., and Muller, Ronald E.
Global Reach: The Power of the Multinational Corporations. New York: Simon and Schuster, 1974.

Barratt-Brown, Michael
The Economics of Imperialism. Harmondsworth: Penguin, 1974.

Chomsky, Noam, and Herman, Edward S.
The Political Economy of Human Rights. 1st ed. Vol. 1: *The Washington Connection and Third World Fascism.* Vol. 2: *After the Cataclysm: Postwar Indochina and the Construction of Imperial Ideology.* Boston: South End Press, 1979.

Davis, Mike
"The Political Economy of Late-Imperial America." *New Left Review,* no. 143 (January-February 1984), pp. 6-38.

Fann, K.T., and Hodges, Donald C., eds.
Readings in U.S. Imperialism. Boston: Porter Sargent, 1971.

Frieden, Jeff
"'The Dollar and Its Rivals'." *New Left Review,* no. 135 (September-October 1983), pp. 91-96.

Horowitz, David
From Yalta to Vietnam: American Foreign Policy in the Cold War. Rev. ed. Harmondsworth: Penguin, 1967.

Hudson, Michael
Super Imperialism: The Economic Strategy of American Empire. New York: Holt, Rinehart & Winston, 1972.

Hymer, Stephen
"The Multinational Corporation and the Law of Uneven Development." *International Firms and Modern Imperialism: Selected Readings.* Edited by Hugo Radice. Harmondsworth: Penguin, 1975.

LaFeber, Walter
Inevitable Revolutions: The United States in Central America. 1st ed. New York: Norton, 1983.
America, Russia, and the Cold War, 1945-1980. 4th ed. New York: Wiley, 1980.

Lipietz, Alain
"Towards Global Fordism?" *New Left Review,* no. 132 (March-April 1982), pp. 33-47.

Magdoff, Harry
The Age of Imperialism: The Economics of U.S. Foreign Policy. New York: Monthly Review Press, 1969.

Magdoff, Harry, and Sweezy, Paul M.
The End of Prosperity: The American Economy in the 1970s. New York: Monthly Review Press, 1977.

Mandel, Ernest
Late Capitalism. London: New Left Books, 1975.

Marxist Economic Theory. London: Merlin Press, 1968. (See especially chapters 12 and 13.)

Michalet, Charles Albert
Le Capitalisme mondiale. 1e éd. Paris: Presses universitaires de France, 1976.

Modelski, George, ed.
Transnational Corporations and World Order: Readings in International Political Economy. San Francisco: W.H. Freeman, 1979.

Palloix, Christian
L'Internationalisation du capital: éléments critiques. Economie et socialisme, no. 23. Paris: François Maspero, 1975.

Parboni, Riccardo
"Capital and the Nation-State — A Reply to Frieden." *New Left Review*, no. 137 (January-February 1983), pp. 87-96.

The Dollar and Its Rivals: Recession, Inflation, and International Finance. London: NLB, 1981.

Payer, Cheryl
The World Bank: A Critical Analysis. New York: Monthly Review Press, 1982.

The Debt Trap: The IMF and the Third World. Harmondsworth: Penguin, 1974.

Petras, James, and Rhodes, Robert
"The Reconsolidation of U.S. Hegemony." *New Left Review*, no. 97 (May-June 1976), pp. 37-53.

Poulantzas, Nicos
"The Internationalization of Capital Relations and the Nation State." *Classes in Contemporary Capitalism*, part 1, pp. 37-88. London: Verso, 1978.

Radice, Hugo, ed.
International Firms and Modern Imperialism: Selected Readings. Harmondsworth: Penguin, 1975.

Ray, Ellen, et al., eds.
Dirty Work 2: The CIA in Africa. 1st ed. Secaucus, N.J.: Lyle Stuart, 1979.

Said, Abdul Aziz, and Simmons, Luiz R., eds.
The New Sovereigns: Multinational Corporations as World Powers. Englewood Cliffs, N.J.: Prentice-Hall, 1975.

Schurmann, Franz
The Logic of World Power: An Inquiry into the Origins, Currents, and Contradictions of World Politics. New York: Pantheon, 1974.

Sklar, Holly, ed.
Trilateralism: the Trilateral Commission and Elite Planning For World Management. 1st ed. Montreal: Black Rose Books, 1980.

Swift, Richard, and Clarke, Robert, eds.
Ties that Bind: Canada and the Third World. Toronto: Between the Lines, 1982.

Torrie, Jill, ed.
Banking on Poverty: The Global Impact of the IMF and the World Bank. Toronto: Between the Lines, 1983.

Vernon, Raymond
Storm Over the Multinationals: The Real Issues. Cambridge, Mass.: Harvard University Press, 1977.

Wilkins, Myra
The Maturing of Multinational Enterprise: American Business Abroad From 1914 to 1970. Cambridge, Mass.: Harvard University Press, 1974.

The Emergence of Multinational Enterprise: Business Abroad From the Colonial Era to 1914. Cambridge, Mass.: Harvard University Press, 1970.

C. DEPENDENCY AND UNDERDEVELOPMENT

Amin, Samir
Unequal Development: An Essay in the Social Formations of Peripheral Capitalism. New York: Monthly Review Press, 1976.

"Accumulation and Development: A Theoretical Model." *Review of African Political Economy*, no. 1 (1974), pp. 9-26. (A useful synthesis of his argument in *Accumulation on a World Scale* listed below.)

Accumulation on a World Scale: A Critique of the Theory of Underdevelopment. 2 vols. New York: Monthly Review Press, 1974.

Arrighi, Giovanni, and Saul, John S.
Essays on the Political Economy of Africa. New York: Monthly Review Press, 1973.

Baran, Paul A.
The Political Economy of Growth: With an Introduction by R.B. Sutcliffe. Harmondsworth: Penguin, 1973. (First published 1957.)

Bernstein, Henry, ed.
Underdevelopment and Development: The Third World Today: Selected Readings. Harmondsworth: Penguin, 1973.

Brewer, Anthony
Marxist Theories of Imperialism: A Critical Survey. London: Routledge & Kegan Paul, 1980. (See especially "Modern Marxist Theories of Development and Underdevelopment.")

Caldwell, Malcolm
The Wealth of Some Nations. London: Zed Press, 1977.

Cardoso, Fernando Henrique, and Faletto, Enzo
Dependency and Development in Latin America. Berkeley: University of California Press, 1979.

Cockcroft, James D.; Frank, André Gunder; Johnson, Dale L.
Dependence and Underdevelopment: Latin America's Political Economy. (Including several important essays by André Gunder Frank: "The Development of Underdevelopment", pp. 3-18; "Sociology of Development and Underdevelopment of Sociology", pp. 321-98; and "Who Is the Immediate Enemy?", pp. 425-34.) New York: Doubleday, 1972.

Dos Santos, Theotonio
"The Structure of Dependence." *Readings in U.S. Imperialism*, pp. 225-36. Edited by K.T. Fann and Donald C. Hodges. Boston: Porter Sargent, 1971.

Ehrensaft, Philip
"Semi-Industrial Capitalism in the Third World." *Africa Today* 18 (January 1971): 40-67.

Emmanuel, Arghiri
"Myths of Development Versus Myths of Underdevelopment." *New Left Review*, no. 85 (May-June 1974), pp. 61-82.

Unequal Exchange: A Study of the Imperialism of Trade. New York: Monthly Review Press, 1972.

Frank, André Gunder
Dependent Accumulation and Underdevelopment. New York: Monthly Review Press, 1979.

Capitalism and Underdevelopment in Latin America: Historical Studies of Chile and Brazil. Rev. and enl. New York: Monthly Review Press, 1969.

Hayter, Teresa
The Creation of World Poverty. London: Pluto Press in association with Third World First, 1981.

Jalée, P.
The Pillage of the Third World. New York: Monthly Review Press, 1970.

Jenkins, Robin
Exploitation: The World Power Structure and the Inequality of Nations. London: Paladin, 1971.

Leys, Colin
Underdevelopment in Kenya: The Political Economy of Neo-Colonialism, 1964-1971. Berkeley: University of California Press, 1974.

Palma, Gabriel
"Dependency: A Formal Theory of Underdevelopment or a Methodology for the Analysis of Concrete Situations of Underdevelopment?" *World Development* 6 (July/August 1978): 881-924.

Rodney, Walter
How Europe Underdeveloped Africa. London: Boble-L'Ouverture, 1972.

Szentes, Tamás
The Political Economy of Underdevelopment. Budapest: Akadémiai Kiadó, 1971.

Thomas, Clive
Dependence and Transformation: The Economics of the Transition to Socialism. New York: Monthly Review Press, 1974.

Wilber, Charles K., ed.
The Political Economy of Development and Underdevelopment. 2nd ed. New York: Random House, 1973. (Including "On the Political Economy of Backwardness," pp. 91-102, by Paul Baran, among other important texts.)

D. DEPENDENCY DEBATED

Bernstein, Henry
"Sociology of Underdevelopment Versus Sociology of Development?" *Development Theory*, pp. 77-106. Edited by David Lehmann. London: Frank Cass, 1979.

Brenner, Robert
"The Origins of Capitalist Development: A Critique of Neo-Smithian Marx-

ism." *New Left Review*, no. 104 (July-August 1977), pp. 25-92.

Chilcote, Ronald H.
"Dependency: A Critical Synthesis of the Literature." *Latin American Perspectives* (Special Issue) 1 (Spring 1974): 4-29.

Elsenhans, Hartmut
"Rising Mass Incomes as a Condition of Capitalist Growth: Implications for Today's World Economy." *International Organization* 37 (Winter 1983): 1-39.

Evans, Peter
Dependent Development: The Alliance of Multinational, State, and Local Capital in Brazil. Princeton, N.J.: Princeton University Press, 1979.

Foster-Carter, Aidan
"The Modes of Production Controversy." *New Left Review*, no. 107 (January-February, 1978), pp. 47-77.

"Neo-Marxist Approaches to Development and Underdevelopment." *Sociology and Development*, pp. 67-105. Edited by Emmanuel De Kadt and Gavin Williams. London: Tavistock Publications, 1974.

Frank, André Gunder
"Dependence is Dead: Long Live Dependence and the Class Struggle: An Answer to Critics." *Latin American Perspectives* (Special Issue) 1 Spring 1974): 87-106.

Halliday, Jon
"Capitalism and Socialism in East Asia." *New Left Review*, no. 124 (November-December 1980), pp. 3-24.

Hamilton, Nora
The Limits of State Autonomy: Post-Revolutionary Mexico. Princeton, N.J.: Princeton University Press, 1982.

Kay, Geoffrey
Development and Underdevelopment: A Marxist Analysis. New York: St. Martin's Press, 1975.

Laclau, Ernesto
"Feudalism and Capitalism in Latin America." *New Left Review*, no. 67 (May-June 1971), pp. 19-38. (Reprinted as Chapter 1 in his *Politics and Ideology in Marxist Theory.* London: New Left Books, 1977.)

Leys, Colin
"Underdevelopment and Dependency: Critical Notes." *Neo-Marxist Theories of Development.* Edited by Peter Limqueco and Bruce McFarlane. London: Croom Helm, 1983.

"African Economic Development in Theory and Practice." *Daedalus* 111 (Spring 1982): 99-124.

Lipietz, Alain
"Marx or Rostow? (A Critique of Warren, 1980)." *New Left Review*, no. 132 (March-April 1982), pp. 48-58.

Lówy, Michael
The Politics of Combined and Uneven Development: The Theory of Permanent Revolution. London: NLB, 1981.

Marcussen, Henrik Secher, and Torp, Jens Erik
The Internationalization of Capital: The Prospects For the Third World.
London: Zed Press, 1982.

O'Brien, Philip J.
"A Critique of Latin American Theories of Dependency." *Beyond the Sociology of Development: Economy and Society in Latin America and Africa,*
pp. 7-27. Edited by Ivar Oxaal, Tony Barnett and David Booth. London:
Routledge & Kegan Paul, 1975.

Preston, P.W.
Theories of Development. London: Routledge & Kegan Paul, 1982.

Roxborough, Ian
Theories of Underdevelopment. London: Macmillan, 1979.

Review of African Political Economy (ROAPE)
"Women, Oppression and Liberation." 27/28 (February 1984). (Special issue,
various authors.)

"Facing the 1980s: New Directions in the Theory of Imperialism." 11 (Winter
1979). (Special issue, various authors.)

Saul, John S.
The State and Revolution in Eastern Africa: Essays. New York: Monthly
Review Press, 1979.

Stepan, Alfred C.
The State and Society: Peru in Comparative Perspective. Princeton, N.J.:
Princeton University Press, 1978.

Sutcliffe, Bob
"Imperialism and industrialization in the Third World." *Studies in the Theory
of Imperialism*, pp. 171-92. Edited by Roger Owen and Bob Sutcliffe. New
York: Longman, 1972.

Taylor, John G.
*From Modernization to Modes of Production: A Critique of the Sociologies
of Development and Underdevelopment.* London: Macmillan, 1979.

Veltmeyer, Henry
"Dependency and Underdevelopment: Some Questions and Problems."
Canadian Journal of Political and Social Theory 2 (Spring 1978): 55-72.

Warren, Bill
Imperialism: Pioneer of Capitalism. London: N.L.B., 1980.

"Imperialism and Capitalist Industrialization." *New Left Review*, no. 81
(September-October 1973), pp. 3-44.

Wolf, Eric Robert
Europe and the People Without History. Berkeley: University of California
Press, 1982.

Worsley, Peter
"One World or Three: A Critique of the World System of Immanuel Wallerstein." *Socialist Register 1980*, pp. 298-338. Edited by Ralph Miliband
and John Saville. London: Merlin Press, 1980.

10

Multinationals, Branch Plants and Canada-U.S. Relations

MEL WATKINS

Ask anyone who is even remotely in touch with the real world to cite the characteristic features of the political economy of Canada and the shortest of lists would surely include the high level of foreign ownership and the extraordinary extent to which things Canadian are integrated into things American; if both are not already included in the *Guinness Book of Records*, they should be. Since so much of the foreign ownership comes from the United States, and since the ownership of the means of production is a most significant form of integration, the two features are, as well, closely interrelated. Together they lie at the heart of Canada's peripheral, dependent status, which is, in turn, properly so central to the concerns of contemporary political economists.

The old political economy school of the interwar period, which formed around the leadership of Innis, was much concerned with the Canadian-American relationship and with the implications for Canada of joint occupation of the continent with the more dynamic and powerful United States; this is evident in Innis's own writings, as well as in those of Creighton, Brebner and others. Notwithstanding the wealth of detail in Marshall, Southard and Taylor's study of American investment in Canada, the issue of foreign ownership per se was thought unimportant; it is arguably the great lacuna in the *weltanschauung* of the old political economy.

In the post-Second World War period, the old political economy school withered in the face of a quantum leap in Americanization. But by the 1960s, foreign ownership and the attendant costs of dependency could no longer be ignored; Gordon, Rotstein, Hymer, Watkins and Levitt were key writers at this time. Their work culminated in the very important writings of Naylor and Clement on the roots of Canada's dependent industrialization. The so-called Naylor-Clement thesis became the central (albeit controversial) theme of the new, more class conscious, political economy that flourished in the 1970s. It is this work on foreign ownership that largely provides the bridge from the old to the new political economy.

In the 1970s much useful work was done, notably by the Science Council of Canada, on the nature of the truncated branch-plant economy and on the need for an industrial strategy to offset the costs of foreign ownership. In the 1980s, the consequent circumstances of a waning and truculent America are compelling a sharper focus on the Canadian-American relationship, beginning with the excellent study by Clarkson.

While the level of foreign ownership has fallen in recent years, one would be hard put to find much evidence in support of occasional allegations about greater Canadian maturity and autonomy. Rather, I sense a present consensus within the new political economy schools about Canada's dependent status as a staples-producing, semi-industrialized, branch-plant economy highly vulnerable to American whim.

The Canadian-American relationship, being pervasive, encompasses more than foreign ownership. Note must be made explicit of the role, though now declining, of the so-called international unions or American unions operating in Canada. Though well-documented historically, there is a need for research on this topic in the contemporary period from the political economy perspective.

Abella, Irving M.
Nationalism, Communism, and Canadian Labour: The CIO, the Communist Party, and the Canadian Congress of Labour 1935-1956. Toronto: University of Toronto Press, 1973.

Aitken, Hugh G.J.
American Capital and Canadian Resources. Cambridge, Mass.: Harvard University Press, 1961.

Aitken, Hugh G.J., et al., eds.
The American Economic Impact on Canada. Durham, N.C.: Duke University Press, 1959.

Axline, W.A.; Hyndman, J.E.; Lyon, P.; and Molot, M., eds.
Continental Community?: Independence and Integration in North America. Toronto: McClelland and Stewart, 1974.

Babcock, Robert H.
Gompers in Canada: A Study in American Continentalism Before the First World War. Toronto: University of Toronto Press, 1974.

Beigie, Carl E., and Stewart, James K.
New Pressures, Old Constraints: Canada-United States Relations in the 1980s. Behind the Headlines, vol. 40, no. 6. Toronto: Canadian Institute of International Affairs, 1983.

Blyth, C.D., and Carty, E.B.
"Non-Resident Ownership of Canadian Industry." *Canadian Journal of Economics and Political Science* 22 (November 1956): 449-60.

Bothwell, Robert, and Kilbourn, William
C.D. Howe: A Biography. Toronto: McClelland and Stewart, 1979.

Bourgault, Pierre, L.
Innovation and the Structure of Canadian Industry. Science Council of Canada. Special Study no. 23. Ottawa: Information Canada, 1972.

Brebner, John Bartlet
North Atlantic Triangle: The Interplay of Canada, the United States and Great Britain. The Carleton Library, no. 30. Toronto: McClelland and Stewart, 1966. (First published 1945.)

Brecher, Irving, and Reisman, S.S.
Canada-United States Economic Relations: Study for the Royal Commission on Canada's Economic Prospects. Ottawa: Queen's Printer, 1957.

Britton, John N.H.
"Locational Perspectives on Free Trade for Canada." *Canadian Public Policy* 4 (Winter 1978): 4-19.

Britton, John N.H., and Gilmour, James M.
The Weakest Link: A Technological Perspective on Canadian Industrial Underdevelopment. Background Study no. 43. Ottawa: Science Council of Canada, 1978.

Caloren, Fred; Chossudovsky, Michel; and Gingrich, Paul
Is the Canadian Economy Closing Down? Montreal: Black Rose Books, 1978.

Canada
Foreign Direct Investment in Canada. (The Gray Report.) Ottawa: Information Canada, 1972.

Canada. External Affairs
Canadian Trade Policy for the 1980s: A Discussion Paper. Ottawa: External Affairs, 1983.

A Review of Canadian Trade Policy: A Background Document to Canadian Trade Policy for the 1980s. Ottawa: External Affairs Canada, 1983.

Canada. Federal Task Force on the Canadian Motor Vehicle and Automotive Parts Industries
An Automotive Strategy for Canada: Report of the Federal Task Force on the Canadian Motor Vehicle and Automotive Parts Industries to Edward C. Lumley, Minister of Industry, Trade and Commerce and Regional Economic Expansion. Ottawa: The Task Force, 1983.

Canada. Foreign Investment Review Agency
Foreign Investment Review Act, Annual Report. Ottawa: Supply and Services Canada.

Canada. Privy Council
Foreign Ownership and the Structure of Canadian Industry: Report of the Task Force on the Structure of Canadian Industry. (The Watkins Report.) Ottawa: Queen's Printer, 1968.

Canada. Royal Commission on Canada's Economic Prospects
Final Report. (The Gordon Report.) Ottawa: Queen's Printer, 1958.

Canada. Royal Commission on Corporate Concentration
Report. Ottawa: Supply and Services, 1978.

Canada. Senate. Standing Committee on Foreign Affairs
Canada-United States Relations. Vol. 2: *Canada's Trade Relations with the United States.* Ottawa: Queen's Printer, 1978.

Canada. Standing Committee on External Affairs and National Defence
Report (11th) of the Committee Respecting Canada-U.S. Relations. (The Wahn Report.) Ottawa: Queen's Printer, 1970.

Canada. Statistics Canada
Annual Report of the Minister of Supply and Services Canada Under the Corporations and Labour Unions Returns Act. Part 1: *Corporations.* Ottawa: Statistics Canada, 1970- .

Canada. Statistics Canada (con'd)

Annual Report of the Minister of Supply and Services Canada Under the Corporations and Labour Unions Returns Act. Part 2: *Labour Unions*. Ottawa: Statistics Canada, 1970- .

Canada's International Investment Position: System of National Accounts. Ottawa: Statistics Canada. Annual. (First issue 1926-67.)

Canadian Imports by Domestic and Foreign Controlled Enterprises, 1978. Ottawa: Financial Flows and Multinational Enterprises Division, Statistics Canada, 1981.

Inter-Corporate Ownership. Ottawa: Statistics Canada. Occasional. (Published in 1965, 1967, 1969, 1972, 1978-9.)

Carroll, William K.

"The Canadian Corporate Elite: Financiers or Finance Capitalists?" *Studies in Political Economy*, no. 8 (Summer 1982), pp. 89-114.

Chodos, Robert

The Caribbean Connection. A Last Post Book. Toronto: James Lorimer, 1977.

Clarkson, Stephen

Canada and the Reagan Challenge: Crisis in the Canadian-American Relationship. Toronto: James Lorimer in association with the Canadian Institute for Economic Policy, 1982.

Clement, Wallace

"Uneven Development: A Mature Branch-Plant Society." *Class, Power and Property: Essays on Canadian Society*, pp. 55-84. Edited by Wallace Clement. Toronto: Methuen, 1983.

"Canada and Multinational Corporations: An Overview." *Modernization and the Canadian State*. Edited by D. Glenday, H. Guindon, and A. Turowetz. Toronto: Macmillan, 1978.

Continental Corporate Power: Economic Elite Linkages Between Canada and the United States. Toronto: McClelland and Stewart, 1977.

Cordell, Arthur, J.

The Multinational Firm, Foreign Direct Investment, and Canadian Science Policy. Science Council of Canada, Special Study, no. 22. Ottawa: Information Canada, 1971.

Crane, David

Controlling Interest: The Canadian Gas and Oil Stakes. Toronto: McClelland and Stewart, 1982.

Crean, Susan, and Rioux, Marcel

Two Nations: An Essay on the Culture and Politics of Canada and Quebec in a World of American Pre-Eminence. Toronto: James Lorimer, 1983.

Creighton, Donald Grant

The Forked Road: Canada 1939-1957. Toronto: McClelland and Stewart, 1976.

Canada's First Century, 1867-1967. Toronto: Macmillan, 1970.

Crispo, John H.G.

International Unionism: A Study in Canada-American Relations. Toronto: McGraw-Hill, 1967.

Cuff, R.D., and Granatstein, J.L.
American Dollars, Canadian Prosperity: Canadian-American Economic Relations, 1945-1950. Toronto: Samuel-Stevens, 1978.

Ties that Bind: Canadian-American Relations in Wartime, from the Great War to the Cold War. 2nd ed. Toronto: Hakkert, 1977.

Deverell, John, and the Latin American Working Group
Falconbridge: Portrait of a Canadian Mining Multinational. Toronto: James Lorimer, 1975.

Drache, Daniel, ed.
Debates and Controversies From This Magazine. Toronto: McClelland and Stewart, 1979.

Drouin, Marie-Josée, and Malmgren, Harald B.
"Canada, the United States and the World Economy." *Foreign Affairs* 60 (Winter 1981/82): 393-413.

Eayrs, James George
In Defence of Canada. 5 vols. Toronto: University of Toronto Press, 1965-1983.

Fayerweather, John
Foreign Investment in Canada: Prospects for National Policy. Toronto: Oxford University Press, 1974.

Field, Frederick William
Capital Investments in Canada: Some Facts and Figures Respecting One of the Most Attractive Investment Fields in the World. Montreal: Monetary Times of Canada, 1911.

French, Richard D., and Van Loon, Richard
How Ottawa Decides. Rev. ed. Toronto: James Lorimer in association with the Canadian Institute for Economic Policy, 1984.

Gilpin, Robert
"Integration and Disintegration on the North American Continent." *International Organization* 28 (Autumn 1974): 851-74.

Godfrey, Dave, ed.
Gordon to Watkins to You, A Documentary: The Battle for Control of Our Economy. Toronto: New Press, 1970.

Gordon, Myron J., and Fowler, David J.
The Drug Industry: A Case Study in Foreign Control. Toronto: James Lorimer in association with the Canadian Institute for Economic Policy, 1981.

Gordon, Walter Lockhart
A Political Memoir. Toronto: McClelland and Stewart, 1977.

Grant, George
Lament for a Nation: The Defeat of Canadian Nationalism. Toronto: McClelland and Stewart, 1967.

Hero, Alfred O. Jr., and Daneau, Marcel, eds.
Problems and Opportunities in U.S.-Quebec Relations. Boulder, Colo.: Westview Press, 1984.

Hutcheson, John
Dominance and Dependency: Liberalism and National Policies in the North Atlantic Triangle. Toronto: McClelland and Stewart, 1978.

Hymer, Stephen
"Direct Foreign Investment and the National Economic Interest." *The Multinational Corporation, A Radical Approach: Papers by Stephen Herbert Hymer*, pp. 173-82. Edited by Robert B. Cohen et al. Cambridge, Eng.: Cambridge University Press, 1979.

Innis, Harold A.
Essays in Canadian Economic History. Edited by Mary Q. Innis. Toronto: University of Toronto Press, 1956.

Jamieson, S.M.
Industrial Conflict in Canada, 1966-75. Economic Council of Canada Discussion Paper, no. 142. Ottawa: Economic Council of Canada, 1979.

Johnson, Harry G.
The Canadian Quandary. Toronto: McClelland and Stewart, 1977. (First published 1963.)

Kierans, Eric
Globalism and the National-State. C.B.C. Massey Lecture Series. C.B.C. Enterprises, 1984.

Laxer, James
Canada's Economic Strategy. Toronto: McClelland and Stewart, 1981.

Laxer, Robert, ed.
Canada's Unions. Toronto: James Lorimer, 1976.

(Canada) Ltd.: The Political Economy of Dependency. Toronto: McClelland and Stewart, 1973.

Layton, Jack
"Nationalism and the Canadian Bourgeoisie: Contradictions of Dependence." *Class State Ideology and Change*, pp. 220-34. Edited by J. Paul Grayson. Toronto: Holt, Rinehart & Winston, 1980.

Levitt, Kari
Silent Surrender: The Multinational Corporation in Canada. Toronto: Macmillan, 1970.

Litvak, I.A., and Maule, C.J.
The Canadian Multinationals. Toronto: Butterworth, 1981.

"Interest Group Tactics and Foreign Investment: The Time-Reader's Digest Case Study." *Canadian Journal of Political Science* 7 (December 1974): 616-29.

Litvak, I.A.; Maule, C.J.; and Robinson, R.D.
Dual Loyalty: Canadian-U.S. Business Arrangements. Toronto: McGraw-Hill, 1971.

Lumsden, Ian, ed.
Close the 49th Parallel Etc.: The Americanization of Canada. Toronto: University of Toronto Press, 1970.

Marchak, M. Patricia
In Whose Interests: An Essay on Multinational Corporations in a Canadian Context. Toronto: McClelland and Stewart, 1979.

Marshall, Herbert; Southard, Frank; and Taylor, Kenneth W.
Canadian-American Industry: A Study in International Investment. The Carle-

ton Library, no. 93. Toronto: McClelland and Stewart, 1976. (First published 1936.)

Moffett, Samuel E.
The Americanization of Canada. Toronto: University of Toronto Press, 1972. (First appeared in 1907 as a Columbia University Ph.D. thesis.)

Molot, Maureen Appel, and Williams, Glen
"A Political Economy of Continentalism." *Canadian Politics in the 1980s,* pp. 68-83. Edited by Michael S. Whittington and Glen Williams. Toronto: Methuen, 1981.

Naylor, R.T.
"Dominion of Capital: Canada and International Investment." *Domination,* pp. 33-56. Edited by A. Kontos. Toronto: University of Toronto Press, 1975.
The History of Canadian Business, 1867-1914. Vol. 2: *Industrial Development.* Toronto: James Lorimer, 1975.

Neufeld, E.P.
A Global Corporation: A History of the International Development of Massey-Ferguson Limited. Toronto: University of Toronto Press, 1969.

Niosi, Jorge
"The Canadian Bourgeoisie: Towards a Synthetical Approach." *Canadian Journal of Political and Social Theory* (Special issue: "Beyond Dependency") 7 (Fall 1983): 128-49.
Canadian Capitalism: A Study of Power in the Canadian Business Establishment. Toronto: James Lorimer, 1981.

Ontario. Task Force on Foreign Investment
Report of the Interdepartmental Task Force on Foreign Investment. Toronto: Queen's Printer, 1971.

Paquet, Gilles, ed.
The Multinational Firm and the Nation-State. Don Mills, Ont.: Collier-Macmillan, 1972.

Park, Frank, and Park, Libbie
Anatomy of Big Business. Toronto: James Lorimer, 1973. (First published 1962.)

Paterson, D.G.
British Direct Investment in Canada, 1890-1914. Toronto: University of Toronto Press, 1976.

Perry, Robert L.
Galt, U.S.A.: The "American Presence" in a Canadian City. A Financial Post Book. Toronto: Maclean-Hunter, 1971.

Preston, Richard A., ed.
The Influence of the United States on Canadian Development: Eleven Case Studies. Commonwealth Studies Centre. Publication no. 40. Durham, N.C.: Duke University Press, 1972.

Regehr, Ernie, and Rosenblum, Simon, eds.
Canada and the Nuclear Arms Race. Toronto: James Lorimer, 1983.

Resnick, Philip
"The Maturing of Canadian Capitalism." *Our Generation* 15 (Fall 1982): 11-25.

Resnick, Philip (con'd)
The Land of Cain: Class and Nationalism in English Canada 1945-1975. Vancouver: New Star Books, 1977.

Roby, Yves
Les Québécois et les investissements américains, 1918-1929. Québec: Presses de l'Université Laval, 1976.

Rosenbluth, G.
"The Relation Between Foreign Control and Concentration in Canadian Industry." *Canadian Journal of Economics* 3 (February 1970): 14-38.

Rotstein, Abraham
Rebuilding From Within: Remedies for Canada's Ailing Economy. Toronto: James Lorimer in association with the Canadian Institute for Economic Policy, 1984.

"Canada: The New Nationalism." *Foreign Affairs* 55 (October 1976): 97-118.

The Precarious Homestead: Essays on Economics, Technology and Nationalism. Toronto: New Press, 1973.

Rotstein, Abraham, and Lax, Gary, eds.
Independence: The Canadian Challenge. Toronto: Committee for an Independent Canada, 1972.

Russell, Peter H., ed.
Nationalism in Canada. Toronto: McGraw-Hill, 1966.

Safarian, A.E.
Foreign Ownership of Canadian Industry. Toronto: McGraw-Hill, 1966.

Saul, John, and Heron, Craig, eds.
Imperialism, Nationalism and Canada. Toronto: New Hogtown Press, 1977.

Scheinberg, Stephen
"Invitation to Empire: Tariffs and American Economic Expansion in Canada." *Enterprise and National Development: Essays in Canadian Business and Economic History*, pp. 80-100. Edited by Glenn Porter and Robert D. Cuff. Toronto: Hakkert, 1973.

Science Council of Canada. Working Group on Industrial Policies
Multinationals and Industrial Strategy: The Role of World Product Mandates: A Statement. Ottawa: Science Council of Canada, 1980.

Scott, Jack
Canadian Workers, American Unions. Vancouver: New Star Books, 1978.

Shaffer, Edward H.
Canada's Oil and the American Empire. Edited by José Druker. Edmonton: Hurtig, 1983.

Sharp, Mitchell
"Canada-U.S. Relations: Options for the Future." *International Perspectives.* (Special issue) (Autumn 1972): 1-24.

Stevenson, Garth
"Foreign Direct Investment and the Provinces: A Study of Elite Attitudes." *Canadian Journal of Political Science* 7 (December 1974): 630-47.

Swift, Jamie
The Big Nickel: Inco at Home and Abroad. Kitchener, Ont.: Between the Lines, 1977.

Taylor, C.
Snow Job: Canada, the United States and Vietnam, 1954-73. Toronto: Anansi, 1974.

Teeple, Gary, ed.
Capitalism and the National Question in Canada. Toronto: University of Toronto Press, 1972.

Thompson, Mark, and Blum, Albert A.
"International Unionism in Canada: The Move to Local Control." *Industrial Relations* 22 (Winter 1983): 71-86.

Warnock, Jack
Partner to Behemoth: The Military Policy of a Satellite Canada. Toronto: New Press, 1970.

Wilkins, Mira
The Maturing of Multinational Enterprise: American Business Abroad From 1914 to 1970. Cambridge, Mass.: Harvard University Press, 1974.

The Emergence of Multinational Enterprise: American Business Abroad From the Colonial Era to 1914. Cambridge, Mass.: Harvard University Press, 1970.

Williams, Glen
Not For Export: Toward a Political Economy of Canada's Arrested Industrialization. Toronto: McClelland and Stewart, 1983.

Zerker, Sally F.
The Rise and Fall of the Toronto Typographical Union 1832-1972: A Case Study of Foreign Domination. Toronto: University of Toronto Press, 1981.

11
Industrialization

TOM TRAVES

It is a weakness of the political economy tradition in Canada that the process of industrialization has rarely been considered as a major topic of much investigation in its own right. Industrial development has tended to be virtually ignored (as in some staples-based accounts), viewed as a global externality (as, for example, in some of Innis's writings about the wheat boom), or taken as a given, with real attention being reserved for different, albeit clearly related, issues such a foreign ownership and control. Consequently, much of what there is to know about Canada's industrialization must be gleaned from sources that would fit comfortably in other chapters of this guide. They range in subject matter from sectoral analyses through business biography to working-class history, and in method, from Marxist political economy through institutionalism to econometrics.

It was once common to identify Canada's "industrial revolution" with the wheat boom of the late 1890s and early twentieth century. This approach began with O.D. Skelton's celebration of the realization of National Policy industrialism during the Laurier period; it was taken up by the staples theorists for what it seemed to suggest about staples-led industrialization, and was reiterated in the 1950s and 1960s by the "take-off" theorists. More recently, however, this inter-pretation has been challenged on two fronts. As better statistical series describing the history of the economy were compiled, received notions about industrial stagnation in the pre-Laurier period were seriously shaken. In the mid-1970s, a great surge of interest in the history of work and workers produced much new information about manufacturing and related industries in the mid-nineteenth century. It now appears that if Canada had an "industrial revolution" — and the burden of that term is debatable — it was in the decade of the 1850s that it took shape and gathered momentum. While there is no consensus, the wheat boom is probably best seen as the period in which Canadian industrial capital was reorganized and consolidated and the basis of the political economy trans-formed from industrial to monopoly capitalism.

One of the central theoretical challenges for current Canadian political econ-omy is determining whether the staples approach, however modified, is adequate for a general understanding of economic development since the middle of the nineteenth century. While there is undoubtedly a strong case still to be made for the importance of staples-led industrialization, it is evident that the links between the staple and the industrial economy were both more complex and less direct than is usually acknowledged. Rigid demarcations between the manufacturing and the resource sectors are decreasingly useful. The continuing significance of resource exports and the reproduction of petty commodity production in Canadian agriculture throughout the period of industrial development and consolidation demand that industrialization be understood in the context of the total political economy. Similarly the political economy as a whole must be understood in a way that acknowledges industrial Canada. These theoretical issues will remain unresolved, however, until we have a firmer empirical grasp of the details of capital formation, manufactured-commodity markets, business organization and a number of other factors across a range of industrial sectors in the nineteenth and twentieth centuries.

Acheson, T.W.
"Changing Social Origins of the Canadian Industrial Elite, 1880-1910." *Business History Review* 47 (Summer 1973): 189-217.

"The Social Origins of the Canadian Industrial Elite, 1880-1885." *Canadian Business History, Selected Studies, 1497-1971*, pp. 144-74. Edited by D.S. Macmillan. Toronto: McClelland and Stewart, 1972.

"The Social Origins of Canadian Industrialism: A Study in the Structure of Entrepreneurship." Ph.D. dissertation, University of Toronto, 1971.

Aitken, H.G.J.
The Welland Canal Company: A Study in Canadian Enterprise. Cambridge, Mass.: Harvard University Press, 1954.

Alexander, David
Atlantic Canada and Confederation: Essays in Canadian Political Economy. Compiled by Eric W. Sager, Lewis R. Fischer and Stuart D. Pierson. Toronto: University of Toronto Press in association with Memorial University of Newfoundland, 1983.

The Decay of Trade: An Economic History of the Newfoundland Saltfish Trade, 1935-65. St. John's: Institute of Social and Economic Research, Memorial University of Newfoundland, 1977.

Alexander, David, and Ommer, Rosemary, eds.
Volumes Not Values: Canadian Sailing Ships and World Trades: Proceedings of the Third Conference of the Atlantic Canada Shipping Project, April 19-April 21, 1979. St. John's: Maritime History Group, Memorial University of Newfoundland, 1979.

Armstrong, Christopher.
"Making a Market: Selling Securities in Atlantic Canada Before World War I." *Canadian Journal of Economics* 13 (August 1980): 438-58.

Armstrong, Robert
"L'Industrie de l'amiante au Québec 1878-1929." *Revue d'histoire de l'Amérique française* 33 (septembre 1979): 187-95.

Ashley, C.A.
The First Twenty-Five Years: A Study of Trans-Canada Air Lines. Toronto: Macmillan, 1963.

Backler, Gary G., and Heaver, Trevor D.
"The Timing of a Major Investment in Railway Capacity: CPR's 1913 Connaught Tunnel Decision." *Business History* 24 (November 1982): 300-14.

Baskerville, Peter
"On the Rails: Trends in Canadian Railway Historiography." *American Review of Canadian Studies* 9 (Spring 1979): 63-72.

Bertram, G.W.
"Historical Statistics on Growth and Structure of Manufacturing in Canada, 1870-1957." *Canadian Political Science Association Conference on Statistics: 1962 and 1963 papers*, pp. 13-151. Edited by J. Henripin and A.A. Asimakopulos. Toronto: University of Toronto Press, 1964.

"Economic Growth in Canadian Industry, 1870-1915: The Staple Model and the Take-Off Hypothesis." *Canadian Journal of Economics and Political Science* 29 (May 1963): 159-84.

Bliss, Michael
A Canadian Millionaire: The Life and Business Times of Sir Joseph Flavelle, bart., 1858-1939. Toronto: Macmillan, 1978.

A Living Profit: Studies in the Social History of Canadian Business, 1883-1911. Toronto: McClelland and Stewart, 1974.

Blyth, J.A.
"The Development of the Paper Industry in Old Ontario, 1824-1867." *Ontario History* 62 (June 1970): 119-33.

Bothwell, Robert, and Kilbourn, William
C.D. Howe: A Biography. Toronto: McClelland and Stewart, 1979.

Bourgault, Pierre
Innovation and the Structure of Canadian Industry. Science Council of Canada, Special Study no. 23. Ottawa: Information Canada, 1972.

Brewis, T.N., ed.
Growth and the Canadian Economy. The Carleton Library, no. 39. Toronto: McClelland and Stewart, 1968.

Britton, John N.H., and Gilmour, James M.
The Weakest Link: A Technological Perspective on Canadian Industrial Underdevelopment. Background Study no.43. Ottawa: Science Council of Canada, 1978.

Cameron, James Malcolm
The Pictonian Colliers. Halifax: Nova Scotia Museum, Province of Nova Scotia, 1974.

Chambers, E.J., and Bertram, G.
"Urbanization and Manufacturing in Central Canada, 1870-90." *Conference on Statistics Papers* (1966). Canadian Political Science Association. Toronto: University of Toronto Press, 1966.

Chodos, Robert
The CPR: A Century of Corporate Welfare. Toronto: James Lorimer, 1973.

Clark, S.D.
The Canadian Manufacturers' Association: A Study in Collective Bargaining and Political Pressure. Toronto: University of Toronto Press, 1939.

Cook, Peter
Massey at the Brink: The Story of Canada's Greatest Multinational and Its Struggle to Survive. Toronto: Collins, 1981.

Craven, Paul
An Impartial Umpire: Industrial Relations and the Canadian State, 1900-1911. Toronto: University of Toronto Press, 1980.

Craven, Paul, and Traves, Tom
"Canadian Railways as Manufacturers, 1850-1880." Canadian Historical Association. *Historical Papers: A Selection from the Papers Presented at the Annual Meeting Held at Vancouver* (1983), pp. 254-81.

"Class Politics of the National Policy 1872-1933." *Journal of Canadian Studies* 14 (Fall 1979): 14-38.

Currie, Archibald William
The Grand Trunk Railway of Canada. Toronto: University of Toronto Press, 1957.

Dales, John Harkness
The Protective Tariff in Canada's Development: Eight Essays on Trade and Tariffs When Factors Move with Special Reference to Canadian Protectionism 1870-1955. Toronto: University of Toronto Press, 1966.

Hydroelectricity and Industrial Development: Quebec, 1898-1940. Cambridge, Mass.: Harvard University Press, 1957.

Dechêne, Louise
"Les Enterprises de William Price, 1810-1850." *Histoire sociale/Social History* 1 (avril 1968): 16-52.

Denison, Merrill
The Barley and the Stream: The Molson Story. Toronto: McClelland and Stewart, 1955.

Harvest Triumphant: The Story of Massey-Harris: A Footnote to Canadian History. Toronto: McClelland and Stewart, 1948.

Deverell, John
Falconbridge: A Portrait of a Canadian Mining Multinational. Toronto: James Lorimer, 1975.

Donald, W.J.A.
The Canadian Iron and Steel Industry: A Study in the Economic History of a Protected Industry. Boston: Houghton Mifflin, 1915.

Dreisziger, N.F., ed.
Mobilization for Total War: The Canadian, American and British Experience 1914-1918, 1939-1945. Waterloo, Ont.: Wilfrid Laurier University Press, 1981.

Durocher, René, et Linteau, Paul-André, éds.
Le 'Retard' du Québec et l'infériorité économique des Canadiens français. Collection d'études d'histoire du Québec, no. 1. Trois Rivières, Qué.: Boréal Express, 1971.

English, H.E.
"The Canadian Industrial Structure: An Essay on Its Nature and Efficiency." *Contemporary Canada*, pp. 81-103. Edited by Richard H. Leach. Toronto: University of Toronto Press, 1968.

Faucher, Albert
Québec en Amérique au XIXe siècle: essai sur les caractères économiques de la laurentie. Montréal: Fides, 1973.

Finkel, Alvin
Business and Social Reform in the Thirties. Toronto: James Lorimer, 1979.

Firestone, O.J.
Canada's Economic Development, 1867-1953: With Special Reference to Changes in the Country's National Product and National Wealth. London: Bowes and Bowes, 1958.

Fischer, Lewis R., and Sager, Eric W., eds.
The Enterprising Canadians: Entrepreneurs and Economic Development in Eastern Canada, 1820-1914: Proceedings of the Second Conference of the Atlantic Canada Shipping Project, March 30-April 1, 1978. St. John's: Maritime History Group, Memorial University of Newfoundland, 1979.

Forster, Ben
"The Coming of the National Policy: Business, Government and the Tariff, 1876-1879." *Journal of Canadian Studies* 14 (Fall 1979): 39-49.

Frank, David
"The Cape Breton Coal Industry and the Rise and Fall of the British Empire Steel Corporation." *Acadiensis* 7 (Autumn 1977): 3-34.

Gilbert, Heather
Awakening Continent: The Life of Lord Mount Stephen. Aberdeen: Aberdeen University Press, 1965- .

Gilmour, James M.
Spatial Evolution of Manufacturing: Southern Ontario, 1851-1891. Toronto: University of Toronto Press, 1972.

Glazebrook, G.P. deT.
A History of Transportation in Canada. 2nd ed. 2 vols. The Carleton Library, no. 11-12. Toronto: McClelland and Stewart, 1964.

Green, Alan G.
"Regional Aspects of Canada's Economic Growth, 1890-1929." *Canadian Journal of Economics and Political Science* 33 (May 1967): 232-45.

Greenberg, Dolores
"A Study of Capital Alliances: The St. Paul and Pacific." *Canadian Historical Review* 57 (March 1976): 25-39.

Hamelin, Jean, et Roby, Yves
Histoire économique du Québec, 1851-1896. Montréal: Fides, 1971.

Hann, Russell
Farmers Confront Industrialism: Some Historical Perspectives on Ontario Agrarian Movements. 3rd rev. ed. Toronto: New Hogtown Press, 1975.

Hartland, Penelope
"Factors in Economic Growth in Canada." *Journal of Economic History* 15:1 (1955): 13-22.

Hill, O. Mary
Canada's Salesman to the World: The Department of Trade and Commerce 1892-1939. Montreal: McGill-Queen's University Press, 1977.

Innis, H.A.
A History of the Canadian Pacific Railway. Toronto: McClelland and Stewart, 1923.

Jones, Robert Leslie
History of Agriculture in Ontario, 1613-1880. Toronto: University of Toronto Press, 1946.

Kilbourn, William
The Elements Combined: A History of the Steel Company of Canada. Toronto: Clarke, Irwin, 1960.

Lamb, William Kaye
History of the Canadian Pacific Railway. New York: Macmillan, 1977.

Linteau, Paul André
The Promoters' City: Building the Industrial Town of Maisonneuve, 1883-1918. Toronto: James Lorimer, 1985.

"Quelques réflexions autour de la bourgeoisie québécoise, 1850-1914." *Revue d'histoire de l'Amérique française* 30 (juin 1976): 55-66.

Lower, A.R.M.
Great Britain's Woodyard: British America and the Timber Trade, 1763-1867. Montreal: McGill-Queen's University Press, 1973.

Lukasiewicz, J.
The Railway Game. Toronto: McClelland and Stewart, 1976.

Macgillivray, Don
"Henry Melville Whitney Comes to Cape Breton: The Saga of a Gilded Age Entrepreneur." *Acadiensis* 9 (Autumn 1979): 44-70.

Macmillan, David S., ed.
Canadian Business History: Selected Studies, 1497-1971. Toronto: McClelland and Stewart, 1972.

Marshall, Herbert; Southard, Frank; and Taylor, Kenneth W.
Canadian-American Industry: A Study in International Investment. The Carleton Library, no. 93. Toronto: McClelland and Stewart, 1976. (First published 1936.)

Masters, D.C.
The Rise of Toronto, 1850-1890. Toronto: University of Toronto Press, 1947.

Matthews, Keith, and Panting, Gerald, eds.
Ships and Shipbuilding in the North Atlantic Region: Proceedings of the Conference of the Atlantic Canada Shipping Project, March 31-April 2, 1977. St. John's: Maritime History Group, Memorial University of Newfoundland, 1978.

McCalla, Douglas
The Upper Canada Trade, 1834-1872: A Study of the Buchanans' Business. Toronto: University of Toronto Press, 1979.

"The Commercial Politics of the Toronto Board of Trade, 1850-60." *Canadian Historical Review* 50 (March 1969): 51-67.

McCallum, J.
Unequal Beginnings: Agriculture and Economic Development in Quebec and Ontario Until 1870. Toronto: University of Toronto Press, 1980.

McCann, L.D.
"The Mercantile-Industrial Transition in the Metal Towns of Pictou County, 1857-1931." *Acadiensis* 10 (Spring 1981): 29-64.

McDiarmid, Orville John
Commercial Policy in the Canadian Economy. Cambridge, Mass.: Harvard University Press, 1946.
"Some Aspects of the Canadian Automobile Industry." *Canadian Journal of Economics and Political Science* 6 (May 1940): 258-74.

McDowall, Duncan
Steel at the Sault: Francis H. Clergue, Sir James Dunn and the Algoma Steel Corporation, 1901-1956. Toronto: University of Toronto Press, 1984.

Naylor, R.T.
The History of Canadian Business, 1867-1914. 2 vols. Toronto: James Lorimer, 1975.

Nelles, H.V.
"Public Ownership of Electrical Utilities in Manitoba and Ontario, 1906-30." *Canadian Historical Review* 57 (December 1976): 461-84.
The Politics of Development: Forest, Mines and Hydro-Electric Power in Ontario, 1840-1941. Toronto: Macmillan, 1974.

Neufeld, E.P.
A Global Corporation: A History of the International Development of Massey-Ferguson Limited. Toronto: University of Toronto Press, 1969.

Niosi, Jorge
Canadian Capitalism: A Study of Power in the Canadian Business Establishment. Toronto: James Lorimer, 1981.
"La Laurentide (1887-1928): pionnière du papier journal au Canada." *Revue d'histoire de l'Amérique française* 29 (décembre 1975): 375-415.

Otter, A.A. den
"Alexander Galt, the 1859 Tariff and Canadian Economic Nationalism." *Canadian Historical Review* 63 (June 1982): 151-78.
Civilizing the West: The Galts and the Development of Western Canada. Edmonton: University of Alberta Press, 1982.

Pentland, H. Clare
Labour and Capital in Canada, 1650-1860. Edited and with an introduction by Paul Phillips. Toronto: James Lorimer, 1981.

Phillips, W.G.
The Agricultural Implement Industry in Canada: A Study of Competition. Toronto: University of Toronto Press, 1956.

Plewman, William Rothwell
Adam Beck and the Ontario Hydro. Toronto: Ryerson, 1947.

Porritt, Edward
Sixty Years of Protection in Canada, 1846-1907: Where Industry Leans on the Politician. Toronto: Macmillan, 1908.

Porter, Glenn, and Cuff, Robert D., eds.
Enterprise and National Development: Essays in Canadian Business and Economic History. Toronto: Hakkert, 1973.

Regehr, T.D.
The Canadian Northern Railway: Pioneer Road of the Northern Prairies, 1895-1915. Toronto: Macmillan, 1976.

Reynolds, Lloyd G.
The Control of Competition in Canada. Cambridge, Mass.: Harvard University Press, 1940.

Rice, Richard
"The Wrights of Saint John: A Study in Shipbuilding and Shipowning in the Maritimes, 1839-1885." *Canadian Business History: Selected Studies, 1497-1971*, pp. 317-28. Edited by David S. Macmillan. Toronto: McClelland and Stewart, 1972.

Roby, Yves
Les Québécois et les investissements américains, 1918-1929. Québec: Presses de l'Université Laval, 1976.

Rosenbluth, G.
"Concentration and Monopoly in the Canadian Economy." *Social Purpose for Canada*, pp. 198-248. Edited by M. Oliver. Toronto: University of Toronto Press, 1961.

Ryerson, Stanley
Unequal Union: Confederation and the Roots of Conflict in the Canadas, 1815-1873. Toronto: Progress Books, 1968.

The Founding of Canada. 2nd ed. Toronto: Progress Books, 1975. (First published 1960.)

Safarian, E.A.
The Canadian Economy in the Great Depression. The Carleton Library, no. 54. Toronto: McClelland and Stewart, 1970. (First published 1959.)

Skelton, O.D.
"General Economic History, 1867-1912." *Canada and Its Provinces: A History of the Canadian People and Their Institutions By One Hundred Associates*, vol.9, pp. 95-274. Edited by Adam Shortt and Arthur G. Doughty. Toronto: printed by T. & A. Constable at the Edinburgh University Press for the Publishers' Association of Canada, 1913-1914. (Reprinted Toronto: Glasgow, Brook, 1914-1917.)

Spelt, Jacob
Urban Development in South-Central Ontario. The Carleton Library, no. 57. Toronto: McClelland and Stewart, 1972. (First published 1955.)

Starks, Richard
Industry in Decline: Why Canadian Industry Is So Weak, and What Can Be Done About It. Toronto: James Lorimer, 1978.

Stevens, George Roy
Canadian National Railways. 2 vols. Toronto: Clarke, Irwin, 1960.

Taylor, Graham D.
"Charles F. Sise, Bell Canada, and the Americans: A Study of Managerial Autonomy, 1880-1905." Canadian Historical Association. *Historical Papers: A Selection From the Papers Presented at the Annual Meeting Held at Ottawa* (1982), pp. 11-30.

Traves, Tom
The State and Enterprise: Canadian Manufacturers and the Federal Government, 1917-1931. Toronto: University of Toronto Press, 1979.

Traves, Tom, ed.
Essays in Canadian Business History. Toronto: McClelland and Stewart, 1984.

Tucker, Albert
Steam Into Wilderness: Ontario Northland Railway 1902-1962. Toronto: Fitzhenry & Whiteside, 1978.

Tulchinsky, Gerald
The River Barons: Montreal Businessmen and the Growth of Industry and Transportation, 1837-1853. Toronto: University of Toronto Press, 1977.

Tupper, Allan, and Doern, G. Bruce, eds.
Public Corporations and Public Policy in Canada. Montreal: Institute for Research on Public Policy, 1981.

Vaughn, W.
Sir William Van Horne. Toronto: Oxford University Press, 1926.

Weldon, J.C.
"Consolidations in Canadian Industry, 1900-19." *Restrictive Trade Practices in Canada: Selected Readings*, pp. 228-279. Edited by L.A. Skeoch. Toronto: McClelland and Stewart, 1966.

Wilkins, Mira
The Maturing of Multinational Enterprise: American Business Abroad From 1914 to 1970. Cambridge, Mass.: Harvard Universtiy Press, 1974.

The Emergence of Multinational Enterprise: American Business Abroad From the Colonial Era to 1914. Cambridge, Mass.: Harvard University Press, 1970.

Williams, Glen
Not For Export: Toward a Political Economy of Canada's Arrested Industrialization. Toronto: McClelland and Stewart, 1983.

Willoughby, William
The St. Lawrence Waterway: A Study in Politics and Diplomacy. Madison, Wisc.: University of Wisconsin Press, 1961.

Wynn, Graeme
Timber Colony: A Historical Geography of Early Nineteenth Century New Brunswick. Toronto: University of Toronto Press, 1981.

Young, Brian J.
George-Etienne Cartier: Montreal Bourgeois. Kingston, Ont.: McGill-Queen's University Press, 1981.

Promoters and Politicians: The North-Shore Railways in the History of Quebec, 1854-1885. Toronto: University of Toronto Press, 1978.

12

British Columbia

PATRICIA MARCHAK

British Columbia is a distinctive region of Canada for several reasons: the population is, and has always been, politically polarized; the economy is, and has always been, excessively dependent on the export of staples, particularly wood products; the region is becoming more of a periphery of the Pacific Rim; and it is a region that has not been adequately documented in national journals.

Included in this bibliography are books and articles that are either clearly within the political economy tradition or are particularly useful as resource materials. The subjects include native peoples, immigration and ethnic studies, labour and unions, community studies of general interest, class structure and politics, forestry, fishing, mining, investment, trade and commerce, exports, government policies and electoral politics of general interest. A few theses are also included. The journal, *B.C. Studies*, was systematically searched; other Canadian journals were less rigorously examined.

Interest in B.C. politics has generated a wealth of voting and general election studies, but few of these are likely to be of great interest beyond the particular election or the province. (Readers can find them in regular bibliographies in *BC Studies*.) The ''restraint politics'' of the Social Credit government since the 1983 election has generated an enormous output of protest articles in the popular press and in the form of essays distributed by the Pacific Group of the Canadian Centre for Policy Alternatives, Solidarity, Women Against the Budget and other organizations. These are not included in this bibliography, but readers can obtain them by writing to The Pacific Group, 22 East 8th Avenue, Vancouver, V5T 1R4.

The import of B.C.'s position within the Pacific Rim is only beginning to be recognized, and while there is not yet a literature on this subject, research is under way. The voluminous literature on forestry and fisheries tends to be technical and not likely to be of interest to political economists unless they are conducting very specialized studies. There is also a large literature on native peoples and a modest literature on the Chinese, Japanese and Sikh communities, but most of this is descriptive or well beyond the political economy framework.

The political economy literature takes liberal versions of B.C. society to task, but there is no continuing debate over, for example, staples and dependency approaches versus Marxist versions of development or similar theoretical discussions. Perhaps there is an inverse relationship between intellectual debate on the left and intensity of political activity.

Although the literature does not demonstrate it, there are debates in the political arenas of the left, some of the same variety as elsewhere between Marxists-Leninists and social democrats, others within the social democratic spectrum between centralists and decentralists. The debate on centralism appears to be considerably more intense than elsewhere in the country, and is concerned not only (and not even primarily) with federalism versus provincialism, but rather with the extent to which regional communities should control their resource industries. There are numerous small groups throughout the province producing newsletters, occasional studies and briefs advocating greater local control. So far, these have not generated much intellectual debate, but they have influenced NDP politics and relations between the social democratic left and the major unions. The debates ar not likely to emerge in the literature as long as all the participants are wholly engaged in struggles against common enemies on the right.

For further reference, the reader might consult the bibliographies listed at the end of this section.

Abella, Irving
"Communism and Anti-Communism in the B.C. Labour Movement: 1940-1948." *Western Perspectives 1: Papers of the Western Canadian Studies Conference, 1973*, pp. 88-98. Edited by David Jay Bercuson. Toronto: Holt, Rinehart & Winston, 1974.

Addie, John; Czepil, Allan; and Rumsey, Fred
"The Power Elite of British Columbia." *Essays in B.C. Political Economy*, pp. 25-32. Edited by Paul Knox and Philip Resnick. Vancouver: New Star Books, 1974.

Artibise, Alan F.J.
" 'A Worthy, If Unlikely Enterprise': The Labour Relations Board and the Evolution of Labour Policy and Practice in British Columbia, 1973-1980." *BC Studies*, no. 56 (Winter 1982-83), pp. 3-43.

Atherton, Jay
"The British Columbia Origins of the Federal Department of Labour." *BC Studies*, no. 32 (Winter 1976-77), pp. 93-105.

Barr, B.M., and Fairbairn, K.J.
"Growth Poles and Growth Centres: The Impact of the Kraft Pulp Industry on the Location of Growth in British Columbia." *Malaspina Papers: Studies in Human and Physical Geography*, pp. 67-77. Edited by Roger Leigh. B.C. Geographical Series, no. 17, Occasional Papers in Geography. Vancouver: Tantalus Research, 1973.

Bercuson, David J.
Fools and Wise Men: The Rise and Fall of the One Big Union. Toronto: McGraw-Hill Ryerson, 1978.

"Labour Radicalism and the Western Industrial Frontier, 1870-1919." *Canadian Historical Review* 58 (June 1977): 154-75.

Berger, Thomas R.
"Native History, Native Claims and Self-Determination." *BC Studies*, no. 57 (Spring 1983), pp. 10-23.

"The Banished Canadians: Mackenzie King and the Japanese Canadians." *Fragile Freedoms: Human Rights and Dissent in Canada*, pp. 93-126. Toronto: Clarke, Irwin, 1981.

"The Nishga Indians and Aboriginal Rights." *Fragile Freedoms: Human Rights and Dissent in Canada*, pp. 219-54. Toronto: Clarke, Irwin, 1981.

Bergren, Myrtle Woodward
Tough Timber: The Loggers of B.C. — Their Story. 2nd rev. ed. Toronto: Progress Books, 1967.

Bernard, Elaine
The Long Distance Feeling: A History of the Telecommunications Workers Union. Vancouver: New Star Books, 1982.

Black, E.R.
"British Columbia: The Politics of Exploitation." *Exploiting Our Economic Potential: Public Policy and the British Columbia Economy*, pp. 23-41. Edited by R.A. Shearer. Toronto: Holt, Rinehart & Winston, 1968.

Blake, Donald E.; Johnston, Richard; Elkins, David J.
"Sources of Change in the B.C. Party System." *BC Studies*, no. 50 (Summer 1981), pp. 3-28.

Bradbury, J.H.
"Class Structures and Class Conflicts in 'Instant' Resource Towns in British Columbia — 1965 to 1972." *BC Studies*, no. 37 (Spring 1978), pp. 3-18.

"Instant Towns in British Columbia: 1964-1972." Ph.D. dissertation, Simon Fraser University, 1977.

British Columbia. Royal Commission on Forest Resources.
Timber Rights and Forest Policy in British Columbia. Report of the Royal Commission on Forest Resources. 2 vols. Victoria: The Commission, 1976.

Byron, Ronald Neil
"Community Stability and Forest Policy in British Columbia." *Canadian Journal of Forest Research*, no. 8 (1978), pp. 61-66.

Campbell, Marie.
"Sexism in British Columbia Trade Unions, 1900-1920. *"In Her Own Right": Selected Essays on Women's History in B.C.*, pp. 167-86. Edited by Barbara Latham and Cathy Kess. Victoria: Camosun College, 1980.

Canada. Commission on Pacific Fisheries Policy
Turning the Tide: A New Policy for Canada's Pacific Fisheries: The Commission on Pacific Fisheries Policy Final Report. (The Pearse Report.) Vancouver: The Commission, 1982.

Careless, J.M.S.
"The Business Community in the Early Development of Victoria, British Columbia." *Canadian Business History: Selected Studies, 1497-1971*, pp. 104-23. Edited by David S. Macmillan. Toronto: McClelland and Stewart, 1972.

Clement, Wallace
"Canada's Coastal Fisheries: Formation of Unions, Cooperatives and Associations." *Journal of Canadian Studies* 19 (Spring 1984): 5-33.

Copithorne, Lawrence
"Natural Resources and Regional Disparities: A Skeptical View." *Canadian Public Policy* 5 (Spring 1979): 181-94.

Crommelin, Michael, and Thompson, Andrew R., eds.
Mineral Leasing as an Instrument of Public Policy. British Columbia Institute for Economic Policy Analysis Series, no. 5. Vancouver: University of British Columbia Press, 1977.

Cutler, Maurice
"How Foreign Owners Shape Our Cities." *Canadian Geographical Journal* 90 (June 1975): 34-48.

Deutsch, John J.; Jamieson, S.M.; Matuszewski, T.L.; Scott, A.D.; and Will, R.M.
Economics of Primary Production in British Columbia. Vancouver: n.p., 1959.

Evenden, L.J., ed.
Vancouver: Western Metropolis. Western Geographical Series, no. 16. Victoria: Dept. of Geography, University of Victoria, 1978.

Fisher, E.G.
"Strike Activity and Wildcat Strikes in British Columbia, 1945-1975." *Relations Industrielles/Industrial Relations* 37:2 (1982): 284-312.

"The Effects of Changes in Labour Legislation on Strike Activity in British Columbia: 1945-75." Ph.D. dissertation, University of British Columbia, 1979.

Friesen, J. and Ralston, H.K., eds.
Historical Essays on British Columbia. The Carleton Library, no. 96. Toronto: McClelland and Stewart, 1976.

Gibson, E.M.
"Lotus Eaters, Loggers and the Vancouver Landscape." *Cultural Discord in the Modern World: Geographical Themes*, pp. 57-74. Edited by L.J. Evenden and F.F. Cunningham. B.C. Geographical Series, no. 20. Vancouver: Tantalus Research, 1974.

Gough, Barry M.
"The Character of the British Columbia Frontier." *BC Studies*, no. 32 (Winter 1976-77), pp. 28-40.

Gunton, Thomas I.
Resources, Regional Development and Provincial Policy: A Case Study of British Columbia. Canadian Centre for Policy Alternatives, no. 7. Ottawa: Canadian Centre for Policy Alternatives, 1982.

Gutstein, Donald
Vancouver Ltd. Toronto: James Lorimer, 1975.

Hayter, Roger
"Research and Development in the Canadian Forest Product Sector — Another Weak Link?" *Canadian Geographer* 26 (Fall 1982): 256-63.

"Labour Supply and Resource-Based Manufacturing in Isolated Communities: The Experience of Pulp and Paper Mills in North-Central British Columbia." *Geoform* 10 (1979): 163-77.

"Corporate Strategies and Industrial Change in the Canadian Forest Product Industries." *Geographical Review* 66 (April 1976): 209-28.

Hayward, Brian
"The Co-op Strategy." *Journal of Canadian Studies* 19 (Spring 1984): 48-64.

"The B.C. Fishery: A Consideration of the Effects of Licensing." *BC Studies*, no. 50 (Summer 1981), pp. 39-51.

Helliwell, John F.
"National Fiscal and Monetary Policies: A Regional Interpretation." *BC Studies*, no. 13 (Spring 1972), pp. 54-59.

Helliwell, John F., and Broadbent, Jillian
"How Much Does Foreign Capital Matter?" *BC Studies*, no. 13 (Spring 1972), pp. 38-42.

Horsfall, R.B., et al.
Parameters of Healthful Community and Individual Functioning in Resource Frontier Towns. Burnaby, B.C.: Simon Fraser University, 1974.

Jamieson, Stuart M.
"The Nature and Character of Collective Bargaining in British Columbia — Its Challenges, Trials, Accomplishments and Failures — Introductory Statement." *Labour-Management Conference in Industrial Relations in British Columbia*, pp. 70-87. Edited by J.T. Montague and S.M. Jamieson. Vancouver: Institute of Industrial Relations, University of British Columbia, 1963.

"Regional Factors in Industrial Conflict: The Case of British Columbia." *Canadian Journal of Economics and Political Science* 28 (August 1962): 405-16.

Jamieson, Stuart M. and Gladstone, Percy
"Unionism in the Fishing Industry of British Columbia." *Canadian Journal of Economics and Political Science* 16 (February 1950): 1-11; (May 1950): 146-71.

Kardam, Nükhet
"Interest Group Power and Government Regulation: Period of New Democratic Party Government in British Columbia, 1972-1975." *BC Studies*, no. 60 (Winter 1983-84), pp. 48-74.

Knight, Rolf
Along the No. 20 Line: Reminiscences of the Vancouver Waterfront. Vancouver: New Star Books, 1980.

Indians At Work: An Informal History of Native Indian Labour in British Columbia, 1858-1930. Vancouver: New Star Books, 1978.

Knox, Paul
"The Passage of Bill 39: Reform and Repression in British Columbia's Labour Policy." M.A. dissertation, University of British Columbia, 1974.

Knox, Paul, and Resnick, Philip, eds.
Essays in B.C. Political Economy. Vancouver: New Star Books, 1974.

Koenig, Daniel, J., and Proverbs, Trevor B.
"Class, Regional and Institutional Sources of Party Support Within British Columbia." *BC Studies*, no. 29 (Spring 1976), pp. 19-28.

LaBonte, Ronald
"Racism and Labour: The Struggle of British Columbia's Farmworkers." *Canadian Forum* 62 (June/July 1982): 9-11.

Lewis, Hartley
"Statistics on the British Columbia Impact of National Fiscal and Monetary Policies." *BC Studies*, no. 13 (Spring 1972), pp. 43-53.

Marchak, M. Patricia
Green Gold: The Forestry Industry in British Columbia. Vancouver: University of British Columbia Press, 1983.

"Labour in a Staples Economy." *Studies in Political Economy*, no. 2 (Autumn 1979), pp. 7-35.

"Women, Work and Unions in Canada." *International Journal of Sociology* 5 (Winter 1975-76): 39-61.

"Class, Regional and Institutional Sources of Social Conflict in B.C." *BC Studies*, no. 27 (Autumn 1975), pp. 30-49.

McCandless, R.C.
"Vancouver's 'Red Menace' of 1935: The Waterfront Situation." *BC Studies*, no. 22 (Summer 1974), pp. 56-70.

McCormack, A. Ross
"The Emergence of the Socialist Movement in British Columbia." *BC Studies*, no. 21 (Spring 1974), pp. 3-27.

McDonald, Robert A.J.
"Business Leaders in Early Vancouver, 1886-1914." Ph.D. dissertation, University of British Columbia, 1977.

McLean, Bruce
"A Union Amongst Government Employees": A History of the B.C. Government Employees' Union, 1919-1979. Burnaby, B.C.: Government Employees' Union, 1979.

McMullan, John L.
"State, Capital and Debt in the British Columbia Fishing Fleet, 1970-1982." *Journal of Canadian Studies* 19 (Spring 1984): 65-88.

Morley, J. Terence, et al.
The Reins of Power: Governing British Columbia. Vancouver: Douglas & McIntyre, 1983.

Morton, James W.
In the Sea of Sterile Mountains: The Chinese in British Columbia. Vancouver: J.J. Douglas, 1973.

Muszynski, Alicja
"The Organization of Women and Ethnic Minorities in a Resource Industry: A Case Study of the Unionization of Shoreworkers in the B.C. Fishing Industry 1937-1949." *Journal of Canadian Studies* 19 (Spring 1984): 89-107.

Neher, Philip A.
"Capital Movement, Foreign Ownership and Dependence on 'Foreign Investment' in Canada and British Columbia." *BC Studies*, no. 13 (Spring 1972), pp. 31-37.

Norris, John
"The Vancouver Island Coal Miners, 1912-1914: A Study of an Organizational Strike." *BC Studies*, no. 45 (Spring 1980), pp. 56-72.

Ormsby, Margaret
British Columbia: A History. Toronto: Macmillan, 1958.

Paterson, D.G.
"European Financial Capital and British Columbia: An Essay on the Role of the Regional Entrepreneur." *BC Studies*, no. 21 (Spring 1974), pp. 33-47.

Paterson, D.G.; Blain, L; and Rae, J.D.
"The Regional Impact of Economic Fluctuations During the Inter-War Period: The Case of British Columbia." *Canadian Journal of Economics* 7 (August 1974): 381-401.

Payne, Raymond W.
"Corporate Power, Interest Groups and the Development of Mining Policy in British Columbia, 1972-77." *BC Studies*, no. 54 (Summer 1982), pp. 3-37.

Pentland, H. Clare
"The Western Canadian Labour Movement, 1847-1919." *Canadian Journal of Political and Social Theory* 3 (Spring-Summer 1979): 53-78.

Persky, Stan
Son of Socred: Has Bill Bennett's Government Gotten B.C. Moving Again? Vancouver: New Star Books, 1979.

Peters, J.E., and Shearer, R.A.
"The Structure of British Columbia's External Trade, 1939 and 1963." *BC Studies*, no. 8 (Winter 1970-71), pp. 34-46.

Phillips, Paul A.
No Power Greater: A Century of Labour in British Columbia. Vancouver: B.C. Federation of Labour, 1967.

Ralston, Keith
"Patterns of Trade and Investment on the Pacific Coast, 1867-1892: The Case of the British Columbia Salmon Canning Industry." *BC Studies*, no. 1 (Winter 1968-69), pp. 37-45.

Resnick, Philip
"Social Democracy in Power: The Case of British Columbia." *BC Studies*, no. 34 (Summer 1977), pp. 3-20.

Robin, Martin
Pillars of Profit: The Company Province, 1934-1972. Toronto: McClelland and Stewart, 1973.

The Rush for Spoils: The Company Province, 1871-1933. Toronto: McClelland and Stewart, 1972.

"The Social Basis of Party Politics in British Columbia." *Queen's Quarterly* 72 (Winter 1966): 675-90. (Rejoinder "Class Still Counts" *BC Studies*, no. 12 [Winter 1971-72], pp. 49-50.)

Schwindt, Richard
The Existence and Exercise of Corporate Power: A Case Study of MacMillan Bloedel Ltd. Canada. Royal Commission on Corporate Concentration. Study no. 15. Ottawa: Royal Commission on Corporate Concentration, 1977.

Schwindt, Richard, and Wanstall, Adrienne
"The Pearse Commission and the Industrial Organization of the British Columbia Forest Industry." *BC Studies*, no. 41 (Spring 1979), pp. 3-35.

Scott, Anthony, ed.
Natural Resource Revenues: A Test of Federalism. Vancouver: University of

Scott, Anthony (con'd)
British Columbia Press for the British Columbia Institute for Economic Policy Analysis, 1976.

Shearer, Ronald A.
"The Continuing International Monetary Crisis: A British Columbia Perspective." *BC Studies*, no. 13 (Spring 1972), pp. 16-30.

Shearer, Ronald A.; Young, John H.; and Munro, Gordon R.
"Trade Liberalization and a Regional Economy: Studies of the Impact of Free Trade on British Columbia." *Regional and Adjustment Aspects of Trade Liberalization*, pp. 1-204. Toronto: University of Toronto Press for the Private Planning Association of Canada, 1973.

Shearer, Ronald A., ed.
Exploiting Our Economic Potential: Public Policy and the British Columbia Economy. Toronto: Holt, Rinehart & Winston, 1968.

Sheils, Jean Evans, and Swankey, Ben
"Work and Wages!": Semi-Documentary Account of the Life and Times of Arthur H. (Slim) Evans. Vancouver: Trade Union Research Bureau, 1977.

Stanbury, William T.
"Indians in British Columbia: Level of Income, Welfare Dependency and Poverty Rate." *BC Studies*, no. 20 (Winter 1973-74), pp. 66-78.

Stanbury, William T., and McLeod, M.R.
"The Concentration of Timber Holdings in the British Columbia Forestry Industry, 1972." *BC Studies*, no. 17 (Spring 1973), pp. 57-68.

Swidinsky, Robert
"Poverty and the Welfare State I." *BC Studies*, no. 13 (Spring 1972), pp. 68-79.

Swift, Jamie
Cut and Run: The Assault on Canada's Forests. Toronto: Between the Lines, 1983.

Tennant, Paul
"Native Indian Political Activity in British Columbia, 1969-1983." *BC Studies*, no. 57 (Spring 1983), pp. 112-36.

"Native Indian Political Organization in British Columbia, 1900-1969: A Response to Internal Colonialism." *BC Studies*, no. 55 (Autumn 1982), pp. 3-49.

Wales, Terence J.
"Poverty and the Welfare State II." *BC Studies*, no. 13 (Spring 1972), pp. 80-86.

Warburton, Rennie
"Race and Class in British Columbia: A Comment." *BC Studies*, no. 49 (Spring 1981), pp. 79-85.

Warburton, Rennie, and Coburn, David
"The Rise of Non-Manual Work in British Columbia." *BC Studies*, no. 59 (Autumn 1983), pp. 5-27.

Ward, W. Peter
"Class and Race in the Social Structure of British Columbia, 1870-1939." *BC Studies*, no. 45 (Spring 1980), pp. 17-35.

Ward, W. Peter, and McDonald, Robert A.J., eds. and comps.
British Columbia: Historical Readings. Vancouver: Douglas & McIntyre, 1981.

Warriner, G. Keith, and Guppy, L. Neil
"From Urban Centre to Isolated Village: Regional Effects of Limited Entry in the British Columbia Fishery." *Journal of Canadian Studies* 19 (Spring 1984): 138-56.

Wilson, James Wood
People in the Way; The Human Aspects of the Columbia River Project. Toronto: University of Toronto Press, 1973.

BIBLIOGRAPHIES

Artibise, Alan F.J.
Western Canada Since 1870: A Select Bibliography and Guide. Vancouver: University of British Columbia Press, 1978.

Diamond, Sara
Women's Labour History in British Columbia: A Bibliography, 1930-1948. Vancouver: Press Gang Publishers, 1982.

Woodward, Frances M.
Cumulative Alphabetical Index to BC Studies, Numbers 1-50 (Winter 1968/ 69 to Summer 1981). Vancouver: University of British Columbia Press, 1981. Regular bibliographies in each issue of *BC Studies.*

13
The Prairies

J.F. CONWAY

There has been a phenomenal outpouring of research and writing on the Prairie West in the last decade. While some of this work has been from a clear-cut political economy perspective, most has been from the perspectives of the more orthodox social science disciplines, but with clear implications for a Prairie political economy.

The debates currently dominating this topic have two basic thrusts. On the one hand, there is a continuing revisionist re-examination of the interpretation and explanation of the history of the region; on the other, are debates about the nature of the current structural location of the region in the larger Canadian political economy, as well as, inevitably, the region's options and future trajectory.

Certain themes dominate the debates. The issues of class formation, class conflict and transformations affecting the agrarian petite bourgeoisie and the Western Canadian working class continue to be major focuses. The question of the nature of the regional fraction of the bourgeoisie — its early solid links with the national bourgeoisie during the heyday of the National Policy and its increasing separation from them on crucial issues — is central to understanding the politics of the region. The use of the provincial level of the state apparatus by emerging classes and class coalitions struggling for a regionally defined and centred political and economic strategy in Confederation also continues to be a vital focus of debate. These two inseparable themes — class and region — are at the heart of any discussions on the Prairie West in Confederation, both in historical studies and in contemporary analyses.

Finally, the most important issue — and one to which all analyses contribute — is the nature of the economic structural transformation of the Canadian economy, and the region's place in that changing economy. The transformation and modernization of agriculture and the resultant decline and fragmentation of the agrarian petite bourgeoisie continue to have crucial implications for the region's future. The growing diversification of the region's resource-based economy, and the impact of that on both federal-provincial relations and on regional politics, is also central to current debates, as are the decline of the national economy's focus on a tariff-protected road to industrialization, the lack of any commitment on the part of the national bourgeoisie to an integrated industrial strategy, and the implications for the Prairies of the national economy's continuing reliance on resource extraction.

These debates are far from resolved. Many are just beginning. But the agenda has been set, and students of the region can expect to see a growing literature that will strive to confront and resolve these controversies.

Due to the enormous amount of published material available on the region a number of decisions were made in order to whittle the list to an acceptable length. It was decided only published books, monographs and pamphlets would be included. The decisions were subjective, based partly on the works' relevance and easy accessibility, and partly on the need to strike a balance between analyses of the past and those of more recent times. Edited collections of works are entered only once, although many of them contain a number of relevant articles.

For undergraduates seeking a good general grasp of the region, past and present, I consider the following to be the ten most useful works: Conway, *The West*; Fowke, *The National Policy and the Wheat Economy*; Howard, *Strange Empire*; Lipset, *Agrarian Socialism*; Mackintosh, *The Economic Background of Dominion-Provincial Relations*; Macpherson, *Democracy in Alberta*; Mitchell, *The Politics of Food*; Morton, *The Progressive Party in Canada*; Richards and Pratt, *Prairie Capitalism*; and Stanley, *The Birth of Western Canada*.

Archer, John H.
Saskatchewan: A History. Saskatoon: Western Producer Prairie Books, 1980.

Avery, Donald
"Dangerous Foreigners": *European Immigrant Workers and Labour Radicalism in Canada, 1896-1932*. Toronto: McClelland and Stewart, 1979.

Barr, John
The Dynasty: The Rise and Fall of Social Credit in Alberta. Toronto: McClelland and Stewart, 1974.

Barr, John, and Anderson, Owen, eds.
The Unfinished Revolt: Some Views on Western Independence. Toronto: McClelland and Stewart, 1971.

Bechhofer, Frank, and Elliott, Brian, eds.
The Petite Bourgeoisie: Comparative Studies of the Uneasy Stratum. London: Macmillan, 1981.

Bercuson, David Jay
Opening the Canadian West. Toronto: Grolier, 1980.

Canada and the Burden of Unity. Toronto: Macmillan, 1977.

Bercuson, David J., and Palmer, Howard
Settling the Canadian West. Toronto: Grolier, 1984.

Breen, David H.
The Canadian Prairie West and the Ranching Frontier 1874-1924. Toronto: University of Toronto Press, 1983.

Britnell, G.E.
The Wheat Economy. Scholarly Reprint Series. Toronto: University of Toronto Press, 1974. (First published 1939.)

Britnell, G.E., and Fowke, V.C.
Canadian Agriculture in War and Peace, 1935-50. Stanford, Calif.: Stanford University Press, 1962.

Bruce, Jean
The Last Best West. Toronto: Fitzhenry & Whiteside, 1976.

Burnet, Jean
  Next-Year Country: A Study of Rural Social Organization in Alberta. Toronto:
  University of Toronto Press, 1951.

Canada. Royal Commission on Dominion-Provincial Relations
  Report. Ottawa: J.O. Patenaude, King's Printer, 1940.

Caragata, Warren
  Alberta Labour: A Heritage Untold. Toronto: James Lorimer, 1979.

Chodos, Robert
  The C.P.R.: A Century of Corporate Welfare. Toronto: James Lorimer, 1973.

Clark, S.D.
  Church and Sect in Canada. Toronto: University of Toronto Press, 1948.

Conway, J.F.
  The West: The History of a Region in Confederation. Toronto: James Lorimer,
  1983.

  *The Place of the Prairie West in the Canadian Confederation: An Inaugural
  Address in the University of Edinburgh.* Series of Inaugural Lectures (University of Edinburgh. Centre of Canadian Studies), no. 6. Edinburgh: University
  of Edinburgh, 1982.

Darling, Howard
  The Politics of Freight Rates: The Railway Freight Rate Issue in Canada.
  Toronto: McClelland and Stewart, 1980.

Dawson, C.A., and Younge, Eva R.
  Pioneering in the Prairie Provinces: The Social Side of the Settlement Process.
  Toronto: Macmillan, 1940.

Donnelly, Murray S.
  The Government of Manitoba. Toronto: University of Toronto Press, 1963.

Easterbrook, William T.
  Farm Credit in Canada. Toronto: University of Toronto Press, 1938.

Elias, P.D.
  Metropolis and Hinterland in Northern Manitoba. Winnipeg: Manitoba
  Museum of Man and Nature, 1975.

Fowke, Vernon
  The National Policy and the Wheat Economy. Toronto: University of Toronto
  Press, 1957.

  Canadian Agricultural Policy: The Historical Pattern. Toronto: University
  of Toronto Press, 1946.

Francis, R.D., and Palmer, H., eds.
  The Prairie West: Historical Readings. Edmondon: University of Alberta,
  forthcoming.

Fry, John A., ed.
  Contradictions in Canadian Society: Readings in Introductory Sociology.
  Toronto: John Wiley, 1983.

Gallagher, John
  To Kill the Crow. Moose Jaw, Alta.: Challenge Publishers, 1983.

Gibbins, Roger
  Prairie Politics and Society: Regionalism in Decline. Toronto: Butterworth,
  1980.

Glueck, Alvin C., Jr.
Minnesota and the Manifest Destiny of the Canadian Northwest. Toronto: University of Toronto Press, 1965.

Gray, James H.
Boomtime: Peopling the Canadian Prairies. Saskatoon: Western Producer Prairie Books, 1979.

Winter Years: The Depression on the Prairies. Toronto: Macmillan, 1966.

Hanson, Eric
Dynamic Decade: The Evolution and Effects of the Oil Industry in Alberta. Toronto: McClelland and Stewart, 1958.

Hedges, James Blaine
Building the Canadian West: The Land and Colonization Policies of the Canadian Pacific Railway. New York: Macmillan, 1939.

Hill, Douglas
The Opening of the Canadian West. London: Heinemann, 1967.

Howard, Joseph Kinsey
Strange Empire: Louis Riel and the Metis People. Toronto: James Lorimer, 1974. (First published 1952.)

Innis, Harold Adams
A History of the Canadian Pacific Railway. Toronto: University of Toronto Press, 1971. (First published 1923.)

Irvine, William
The Farmers in Politics. Toronto: McClelland and Stewart, 1976. (First published 1920.)

Irving, John
The Social Credit Movement in Alberta. Toronto: University of Toronto Press, 1959.

Kerr, Donald C., ed.
Western Canadian Politics: The Radical Tradition. 1st ed. Edmonton: NeWest Institute for Western Canadian Studies, 1981.

Lingard, Charles Cecil
Territorial Government in Canada: The Autonomy Question in the Old Northwest Territories. Toronto: University of Toronto Press, 1946.

Lipset, S.M.
Agrarian Socialism: The Cooperative Commonwealth Federation in Saskatchewan: A Study in Political Sociology. Rev. ed. Berkeley: University of California Press, 1971. (First published 1950.)

Liversedge, Ronald
Recollections of the On-to-Ottawa Trek. The Carleton Library, no. 66. Toronto: McClelland and Stewart, 1973. (First published 1963.)

Macdonald, Norman
Canada: Immigration and Colonization, 1841-1903. Toronto: Macmillan, 1966.

MacGibbon, D.A.
The Canadian Grain Trade, 1931-1951. Toronto: University of Toronto Press, 1952. (First published 1932.)

MacGregor, James G.
A History of Alberta. Rev. ed. Edmonton: Hurtig, 1981.

Mackintosh, W.A.
The Economic Background of Dominion-Provincial Relations. Royal
Commission Report on Dominion-Provincial Relations, Appendix III. Ottawa:
King's Printer, 1938. Reprinted by McClelland and Stewart: The Carleton
Library, no. 13. Edited by J.H. Dales. Toronto: 1964.

Agricultural Co-operation in Western Canada. Kingston, Ont.: Queen's
University, 1924.

Mackintosh, W.A., et al.
Economic Problems of the Prairie Provinces. Toronto: Macmillan, 1935.

Macpherson, C.B.
Democracy in Alberta: Social Credit and the Party System. 2nd ed. Toronto:
University of Toronto Press, 1968. (First edition 1955.)

Mallory, J.R.
Social Credit and the Federal Power in Canada. Toronto: University of Toronto
Press, 1977. (First published 1954.)

Manitoba
Manitoba's Case. A Submission Presented to the Royal Commission on
Dominion-Provincial Relations by the Government of the Province of Mani-
toba. Winnipeg: J.L. Cowie, King's Printer for Manitoba, 1937.

Martin, Chester
"Dominion Lands" Policy. Edited by Lewis H. Thomas. The Carleton Library,
no. 69. Toronto: McClelland and Stewart, 1973. (First published in 1938.)

"The Natural Resources Question": The Historical Basis of Provincial Claims.
Winnipeg: Printed by P. Purcell, 1920.

Mathias, Philip
*Forced Growth: Five Studies of Government Involvement in the Development
of Canada.* Toronto: James Lorimer, 1971.

McCormack, A. Ross
*Reformers, Rebels and Revolutionaries: The Western Canadian Radical
Movement, 1899-1919.* Toronto: University of Toronto Press, 1977.

McCrorie, James Napier
In Union Is Strength. Saskatoon: Centre for Community Studies, University
of Saskatchewan Campus, 1964.

Melnyk, George
Radical Regionalism. Edmonton: NeWest Press, 1981.

Mitchell, Don
The Politics of Food. Toronto: James Lorimer, 1975.

Moorhouse, Herbert Joseph [Hopkins Moorhouse]
*Deep Furrows: Which Tells of Pioneer Trails along which the Farmers of
Western Canada Fought their Way to Great Achievements in Co-operation.*
Toronto: G.J. McLeod, 1918.

Morton, Arthur S.
A History of the Canadian West to 1870-71. Toronto: Thomas Nelson, 1956.

History of Prairie Settlement. In *Canadian Frontiers of Settlement,* vol. 2.

Edited by W.A. Mackintosh and W.L.G. Joerg. Toronto: Macmillan, 1938. (Reprinted Millwood, N.J.: Kraus Reprint, 1974.)

Morton, W.L.
Manitoba: A History. 2nd ed. Toronto: University of Toronto Press, 1973. (First edition 1939.)

The Progressive Party in Canada. [Repr. with corrections.] Toronto: University of Toronto Press, 1967. (First published 1950.)

One Prairie Province Conference, Lethbridge, Alberta, 1970
Proceedings of One Prairie Province? A Question for Canada, and Selected Papers. Edited by David K. Elton. Lethbridge, Alta.: University of Lethbridge, 1970.

Otter, A.A. den
Civilizing the West: The Galts and the Development of Western Canada. Edmonton: University of Alberta Press, 1982.

Owram, Douglas
Promise of Eden: The Canadian Expansionist Movement and the Idea of the West, 1856-1900. Toronto: University of Toronto Press, 1980.

Palmer, Howard, ed.
The Settlement of the West. Calgary: University of Calgary, 1977.

Phillips, Paul
Regional Disparities: Why Ontario Has So Much and the Others Can't Catch Up. 2nd ed. Toronto: James Lorimer, 1982.

Porritt, Edward
Sixty Years of Protection in Canada: 1846-1912: Where Industry Leans on the Politician. 2nd ed. Rev. and brought up to date by Annie G. Porritt. Winnipeg: Grain Growers' Guide, 1913. (First published 1908.)

The Revolt in Canada Against the New Feudalism: Tariff History from the Revision of 1907 to the Uprising in the West in 1910. London: Cassell, for the Cobden Club, 1911.

Pratt, Larry
The Tar Sands: Syncrude and the Politics of Oil. Edmonton: Hurtig, 1976.

Pratt, Larry, and Stevenson, Garth, eds.
Western Separatism: The Myths, Realities and Dangers. Edmonton: Hurtig, 1981.

Priestley, Norman F., and Swindlehurst, Edward B.
Furrows, Faith and Fellowship. Edmonton: Co-op Press, 1967.

Rasmussen, Linda, et al.
A Harvest Yet to Reap: A History of Prairie Women. Toronto: Women's Press, 1975.

Richards, John, and Pratt, Larry
Prairie Capitalism: Power and Influence in the New West. Toronto: McClelland and Stewart, 1979.

Saskatchewan
An Historical Analysis of the Crow's Nest Pass Agreement and Grain Rates: A Study in National Transportation Policy. A Submission of the Province of Saskatchewan to the Royal Commission on Transportation. Regina: L. Amon, Queen's Printer, 1961.

Saskatchewan. Royal Commission on Agriculture and Rural Life
Report[s] Submitted to the Government of Saskatchewan. Regina: n.p., 1955-.

Sharp, Paul F.
The Agrarian Revolt in Western Canada: A Survey Showing American Parallels. Minneapolis: University of Minnesota Press, 1948.

Shortt, Adam, and Doughty, Arthur G., eds.
Canada and Its Provinces: A History of the Canadian People and Their Institutions, By One Hundred Associates. Vol. 19: *The Prairie Provinces I*, and vol. 20: *The Prairie Provinces II.* Printed by T. & A. Constable at the Edinburgh University Press for the Publishers' Association of Canada, 1913-1914. (Reprinted Toronto: Glasgow, Brook, 1914-17).

Silverman, Elaine Leslau
The Last Best West: Women on the Alberta Frontier: 1818-1930. Montreal: Eden Press, 1984.

Smith, David E.
The Regional Decline of a National Party: Liberals on the Prairies. Toronto: University of Toronto Press, 1981.

Prairie Liberalism: The Liberal Party in Saskatchewan, 1905-71. Toronto: University of Toronto Press, 1975.

Stanley, George F.G.
Louis Riel: Patriot or Rebel? Canadian Historical Association. Historical Booklet no. 2. Ottawa: Canadian Historical Association, 1979.

The Birth of Western Canada: A History of the Riel Rebellions. Toronto: University of Toronto Press, 1961.

Swainson, Donald, ed.
Historical Essays on the Prairie Provinces. The Carleton Library, no. 53. Toronto: McClelland and Stewart, 1970.

Thomas, Lewis G., ed.
The Prairie West to 1905: A Canadian Sourcebook. Toronto: Oxford University Press, 1975.

Thomas, Lewis Herbert
The Struggle for Responsible Government in the North-West Territories, 1870-97. 2nd ed. Toronto: University of Toronto Press, 1978.

The North-West Territories, 1870-1905. Canadian Historical Association. Historical Booklet no. 26. Ottawa: Canadian Historical Association, 1970.

Thompson, John Herd
The Harvests of War: The Prairie West, 1914-1918. Toronto: McClelland and Stewart, 1978.

Veeman, Terry, and Veeman, Michele
The Future of Grain. Toronto: James Lorimer in association with the Canadian Institute for Economic Policy, 1984.

Ward, Norman
Politics in Saskatchewan. Don Mills, Ont.: Longmans, 1968.

Warnock, John W.
Profit Hungry: The Food Industry in Canada. Vancouver: New Star Books, 1978.

Western Canadian Studies Conference, 12th, University of Calgary, 1980
The New Provinces: Alberta and Saskatchewan, 1905-1980. Edited by Howard Palmer and Donald Smith. B.C. Geographical Series, no. 30. Vancouver: Tantalus Research, 1980.

Western Canadian Studies Conference, 8th, University of Calgary, 1976
The Canadian West: Social Change and Economic Development. Edited by Henry C. Klassen. Calgary: University of Calgary; Comprint Pub., 1977.

Western Canadian Studies Conference, University of Calgary, 1972
The Twenties in Western Canada. Edited by S.M. Trofimenkoff. Mercury Series. History Division Paper no. 1. Ottawa: National Museum of Man, National Museums of Canada, 1972.

Wilson, Barry
Beyond the Harvest: Canadian Grain at the Crossroads. Saskatoon: Western Producer Prairie Books, 1981.

Wilson, Charles F.
A Century of Canadian Grain: Government Policy to 1951. Saskatoon: Western Producer Prairie Books, 1978.

Wiseman, Nelson
Social Democracy in Manitoba: A History of the CCF-NDP. Winnipeg: University of Manitoba Press, 1983.

Wood, Louis Aubrey
A History of Farmers' Movements in Canada: The Origins and Development of Agrarian Protest, 1872-1924. Toronto: University of Toronto Press, 1975. (First published 1924.)

Young, Walter D.
Democracy and Discontent: Progressivism, Socialism and Social Credit in the Canadian West. Toronto: Ryerson, 1969.

14

Ontario

ARTHUR DAVIS

In his thoughtful essay called "On Being an Ontarian," historian Peter Oliver shows how, after 1867, Ontario seemed to disappear in the minds of its people and in the works of its historians, social scientists and artists. In a very real sense, Ontario "became Canada" for a considerable time, so that A.R.M. Lower could pose the question: "Ontario. Does it exist?" While his answer was no, Oliver suggests it would be more appropriate to say that Ontario had been overlooked.

This bibliography shows that many historians, social scientists and artists are rediscovering the separate Ontario that has always been there, along with the Ontario that became Canada. Now Ontarians are being forced to acknowledge that they belong to a special region of Canada, that "the centre" is a region. The pressure is coming from the other regions of Canada, which, trying to develop their own economies, feel confined by the traditional centre-dominated Canada. Simultaneously, the pressure is being exerted from within the heartland itself by the deindustrialization of the branch-plant economy in the wake of fundamental changes in the American and world economies.

As I woke up to the need to focus on Ontario in the face of these pressures, I found, as many had found with Canada fifteen years ago, that although there are many gaps, a great deal of excellent work has been done. Much of Ontario's history, political economy and even literature lies "hidden" in the host of books written ostensibly about Canada from 1867 to the present. The best of these books must be reread to see how Ontario became the imperial centre of Canada and, as part of that becoming, masked its continuing existence as a separate region.

People from Ontario can no longer assume that being Ontarian and being Canadian can be so closely identified. Quebeckers, westerners, easterners and northerners have let it be known that a centrally dominated Canada is no longer acceptable to them. However, books like Hershel Hardin's *A Nation Unaware* can be given an "Ontario reading." Ontarians need to distinguish the Ontario component of their economic culture from the whole, and thereby clarify and strengthen the nation's awareness of itself. It is important, for example, to realize how much the public enterprise tradition is primarily an Ontario tradition, rather than a widespread Canadian one. Public enterprise initiatives suffer in both the East and West because what is natural in the centre is seen mainly as another form of central domination in the periphery.

National policies, such as the National Energy Policy and the National Industrial Policy (promised but never enacted), need to be redesigned with full acceptance of the fact that Canada is a country containing separate and radically different regional economies. A national policy that does not accept this fact cannot gather support and build a truly national movement. When the NEP was resisted or rejected by other regions, the national cause was not being defeated; rather the initiators were being taught a vital lesson. In matters of energy and industry, as in matters of art and the spirit, Ontarians need to be careful and articulate about what are primarily Ontario's concerns and what are genuine Canadian concerns. In an excellent recent study by the Science Council, *The Challenge of Diversity*, Michael Jenkin looks at problems of federal-provincial confrontation and cooperation in the context of a country with different regional economies. Such an approach indicates a sharp and welcome shift in policy development at "the centre."

Then there is the wealth of new work about Ontario, which indicates the rebirth, or rather the rediscovery, of the region as such. H.V. Nelles's book, *The Politics of Development*, is of giant stature and is indispensable for a sense of the structure of modern Ontario coming into being. He reveals the unfolding relationship between the people of Ontario, the large corporations and the Ontario government, along with the relationship of Ontario to the rest of Canada, to the federal government and to the U.S.A. He also shows Ontarians the formidable, deep-rooted framework they must engage if they choose to challenge the way the province functions as imperial centre of Canada and as gateway to American imperial control of Canada.

But the structure of Ontario, as Ontarians have known it, also appears to be breaking down. There are several matters pressing Ontarians from within to take on the task of rebuilding the region. First, the decline of the heartland's branch-plant economy is well under way and the manufacturing sector is in serious trouble. Second, at the same time, the great resource export industries in Ontario can no longer be counted on to yield as much wealth as the resource focus shifts west, north, east and to the Third World. Third, the great education, health and social service networks set up in Ontario with part of the wealth created in past primary and secondary production are now in great danger. Fourth, Ontarians remain energy-dependent and vulnerable, and they are still locked into Ontario Hydro's nuclear-electric strategy, which is a financial and ecological disaster. And finally, the microelectronics revolution is speeding up the transformation, elimination and exportation of jobs, and is steadily eroding the power of workers and citizens to influence the direction of policy.

One book I found vital for coming to grips with Ontario is Graeme Gibson's *Perpetual Motion*. The book is about the genesis of technological capitalism in Ontario, about the power and violence that drove those who brought it into being, about the terrible costs to Ontario's people and to their homeland, and about the strength of the forces that can impel Ontarians to rebuild the region.

Whether Ontarians will end up responding appropriately to the pressures to undertake this restructuring remains to be seen. The official responses by the federal and Ontario governments and the business community deny that the pressures are serious and continue to conduct themselves as before. Eventually we may see if a stronger response is brewing in other circles. One thing seems clear: an Ontario that does not address these challenges will not be able to gather the strength needed to heal the region and to help rebuild the nation.

Acton, Janice, et al., eds.
Women at Work: Ontario 1850-1930. Toronto: Canadian Women's Educational Press, 1974.

Aitken, H.G.J.
The Welland Canal Company: A Study in Canadian Enterprise. Cambridge, Mass.: Harvard University Press, 1954.

Armstrong, Christopher
The Politics of Federalism: Ontario's Relations with the Federal Government, 1867-1942. Toronto: University of Toronto Press, 1981.

Atwood, Margaret
Two-Headed Poems. Toronto: Oxford University Press, 1978.

Barber, John
"Crisis in the Heartland." *Financial Post Magazine* 75 (November 15, 1981): 15-19, 21-22.

Berger, Carl
The Writing of Canadian History. Toronto: Oxford University Press, 1976.

The Sense of Power: Studies in the Ideas of Canadian Imperialism, 1867-1914. Toronto: University of Toronto Press, 1970.

Birch Bark Alliance and the Ontario Public Interest Research Group
The Energy Booklet: A Critical Look at Nuclear Power in Ontario and a Guide to a Non-Nuclear Future Based on Conservation and Renewable Energy. Peterborough, Ont.: Birch Bark Alliance, and Ontario Public Interest Research Group, 1982.

Bliss, Michael
A Living Profit: Studies in the Social History of Canadian Business, 1883-1911. Toronto: McClelland and Stewart, 1974.

Calvert, J.
"The Ontario Development Corporation: The Politics of Stanley Randall." *Canadian Forum* 51 (June 1971): 23-28.

Canada. Federal Task Force on the Canadian Motor Vehicle and Automotive Parts Industries
An Automotive Strategy for Canada: Report of the Federal Task Force on the Canadian Motor Vehicle and Automotive Parts Industries to Edward C. Lumley, Minister of Industry, Trade and Commerce and Regional Economic Expansion. (Co-Chairmen: Patrick J. Lavelle and Robert White.) Ottawa: The Task Force, 1983.

Caplan, Gerald L.
The Dilemma of Canadian Socialism: The CCF in Ontario. Toronto: McClelland and Stewart, 1973.

Careless, J.M.S.
" 'Limited Identities' in Canada." *Canadian Historical Review* 50 (March 1969): 1-10.

Brown of the Globe. 2 vols. Toronto: Macmillan, 1956-1963.

Clement, Wallace
Hardrock Mining: Industrial Relations and Technological Changes at INCO. Toronto: McClelland and Stewart, 1981.

Cohen, Matt
The Sweet Second Summer of Kitty Malone. Toronto: McClelland and Stewart, 1979.

The Disinherited. Toronto: McClelland and Stewart, 1974.

Craig, Gerald, ed.
Discontent in Upper Canada. Vancouver: Copp Clark, 1974.

Creighton, Donald
''The Economic Background of the Rebellions of 1837.'' *Towards the Discovery of Canada*, pp. 103-21. Toronto: Macmillan, 1972.

John A. Macdonald. 2 vols. Toronto: Macmillan, 1952-55.

Denison, Merrill
The People's Power: The History of Ontario Hydro. Toronto: McClelland and Stewart, 1960.

Dewdney, Selwyn H.
Wind Without Rain. New Canadian Library, no. 103. Toronto: McClelland and Stewart, 1974. (First published 1946.)

Drury, Ernest Charles
Farmer Premier: Memoirs of the Honourable E.C. Drury. Toronto: McClelland and Stewart, 1966.

Dungan, Peter; Crocker, Douglas; and Garesché, Gay M.
The Ontario Economy 1982-1995. 2 vols. Toronto: Ontario Economic Council, 1983.

Dunham, Aileen
Political Unrest in Upper Canada, 1815-1836. The Carleton Library, no. 10. Toronto: McClelland and Stewart, 1963.

Foot, David K., et al.
The Ontario Economy 1977-1987. Toronto: Ontario Economic Council, 1977.

Gibson, Graeme
Perpetual Motion. Toronto: McClelland and Stewart, 1982.

Gibson, Thomas W.
Mining in Ontario. Toronto: T.E. Bowman, King's Printer, 1937.

The Mining Laws of Ontario and the Department of Mines. Toronto: Ontario. Dept. of Mines, 1933.

Gilmour, James M.
Spatial Evolution of Manufacturing: Southern Ontario, 1851-1891. Dept. of Geography. Research Publication no. 10. Toronto: University of Toronto Press, 1972.

Glazebrook, G.P. deT.
Life in Ontario: A Social History. Toronto: University of Toronto Press, 1968.

Gordon, Charles William [Ralph Connor]
Glengarry School Days: A Story of Early Days in Glengarry. Edited by Malcolm Ross. New Canadian Library, no. 118. Toronto: McClelland and Stewart, 1975. (First published 1902.)

Hann, Russell
Farmers Confront Industrialism: Some Historical Perspectives on Ontario Agrarian Movements. 3rd rev. ed. Toronto: New Hogtown Press, 1975.

Hodgins, Bruce W.
John Sandfield Macdonald, 1812-1872. Toronto: University of Toronto Press, 1971.

Houston, C.
The Orange Order in Nineteenth-Century Ontario: A Study in Institutional-Cultural Transfer. Discussion Paper no. 22. Toronto: Dept. of Geography. University of Toronto, 1977.

Hutchison, George
Grassy Narrows. Photographs by Dick Wallace. Toronto: Van Nostrand Reinhold, 1977.

Hynes, Ross
Provincial Mineral Policies: Ontario 1945-1975. Working Paper no. 5. Kingston, Ont.: Centre for Resource Studies, Queen's University, 1978.

Innis, Harold A.
"An Introduction to the Economic History of Ontario from Outpost to Empire." *Essays in Canadian Economic History*, pp. 108-22. Edited by Mary Q. Innis. Toronto: University of Toronto Press, 1956.

Jenkin, Michael
The Challenge of Diversity: Industrial Policy in the Canadian Federation. Background Study no. 50. Ottawa: Science Council of Canada, 1983.

Johnson, Leo A.
History of the County of Ontario, 1615-1875. Whitby, Ont.: Corporation of the County of Ontario, 1973.

"Land Policy, Population Growth and Social Structure in the Home District, 1793-1851." *Ontario History* 63 (March 1971): 41-60.

Jones, Robert Leslie
History of Agriculture in Ontario, 1613-1880. Toronto: University of Toronto Press, 1946.

Kealey, Gregory S.
Toronto Workers Respond to Industrial Capitalism, 1867-1892. Toronto: University of Toronto Press, 1980.

Kilbourn, William
The Firebrand: William Lyon Mackenzie and the Rebellion in Upper Canada. Toronto: Clarke, Irwin, 1956.

Kuyek, Joan Newman
The Phone Book: Working at the Bell. Kitchener, Ont.: Between the Lines, 1979.

Lambert, Richard Stanton, and Pross, Paul
Renewing Nature's Wealth: A Centennial History of the Public Management of Lands, Forests & Wildlife in Ontario, 1763-1967. Toronto: Ontario. Dept. of Lands and Forests, 1967.

Lamphier, Gary
"The Decline of Ontario: To Have and Have Not." *Today Magazine*, September 19, 1981, pp. 8-10, 12.

Lee, Dennis
Civil Elegies and Other Poems. Rev. ed. Toronto: Anansi, 1972.

Lower, A.R.M.
"Ontario — Does It Exist?" *Ontario History* 60 (June 1968): 65-69.

MacDonald, Donald C., ed.
Government and Politics of Ontario. Toronto: Macmillan, 1975.

Magee, William H.
"Ontario in Recent Canadian Literature." *Ontario History* 50 (1963): 107-16.

Main, O.D.
The Canadian Nickel Industry: A Study in Market Control and Public Policy. Toronto: University of Toronto Press, 1955.

Manthorpe, Jonathan
The Power and the Tories: Ontario Politics, 1943 to Present. Toronto: Macmillan, 1974.

Martin, Joe
The Role and Place of Ontario in the Canadian Confederation. The Evolution of Policy in Contemporary Ontario, no. 4. Toronto: Ontario Economic Council, 1974.

Masters, D.C.
The Rise of Toronto, 1850-1890. Toronto: University of Toronto Press, 1947.

"Toronto Versus Montreal: The Struggle for Financial Hegemony, 1860-1875. *Canadian Historical Review* 22 (June 1941): 133-46.

McKay, Paul
Electric Empire: The Inside Story of Ontario Hydro. Toronto: Between the Lines, 1983.

McKenty, Neil
Mitch Hepburn. Toronto: McClelland and Stewart, 1967.

Moodie, Susanna (Strickland)
Roughing It in the Bush: Or Forest Life in Canada. New Canadian Library, no. 31. Toronto: McClelland and Stewart, 1962. (Originally published 1913.)

Munro, Alice
Lives of Girls and Women: A Novel. New York: McGraw Hill, 1971.

Dance of the Happy Shades. Toronto: Ryerson, 1968.

Nasby, David
Permanence and Change: A Rural Ontario Document. Toronto: Anansi, 1973.

Nelles, H. Viv
"The Politics of Anaesthesia: How to Account for the Continuing Rule of the Conservatives in a Province that Was Once the Richest and Is Now Declining?" *Saturday Night* 96 (September 1981): 9-14.

The Politics of Development: Forests, Mines and Hydro-Electric Power in Ontario, 1840-1941. Toronto: Macmillan, 1974.

Oliver, Peter N.
G. Howard Ferguson: Ontario Tory. Toronto: University of Toronto Press, 1977.

"On Being an Ontarian." *Public and Private Persons: The Ontario Political Culture, 1914-1934*. Toronto: Clark, Irwin, 1975.

Oliver Mowat Colloquium, Kingston, Ont., 1970
Oliver Mowat's Ontario. Papers edited by Donald Swainson. Toronto: Macmillan, 1972.

Ontario. Advisory Committee on Energy
Energy in Ontario: The Outlook and Policy Implications. 2 vols. Toronto: Queen's Printer, 1972.

Ontario. Dept. of Economics
A Century of Industrial Development in Ontario. Toronto: Queen's Printer, 1965.

Ontario. Ministry of Energy
Ontario Energy Review. 3rd ed. Toronto: Ontario. Ministry of Energy, 1983.

Ontario. Ontario Economic Council
Issues and Alternatives. Toronto: The Council, 1977.

Ontario. Royal Commission on the Mineral Resources of Ontario.
Report. Toronto: Queen's Printer, 1890.

Ontario. Task Force on Foreign Investment
Report of the Interdepartmental Task Force on Foreign Investment. Toronto: Queen's Printer, 1971.

Ontario Historical Society
Profiles of a Province: Studies in the History of Ontario: A Collection of Essays Commissioned by the Ontario Historical Society to Commemorate the Centennial of Ontario. Toronto: Ontario Historical Society, 1967.

Palmer, Bryan D.
A Culture in Conflict: Skilled Workers and Industrial Capitalism in Hamilton, Ontario 1860-1914. Montreal: McGill-Queen's University Press, 1979.

Perry, Ross
The Future of Canada's Auto Industry: The Big Three and the Japanese Challenge. Toronto: James Lorimer in association with the Canadian Institute for Economic Policy, 1982.

Plewman, William Rothwell
Adam Beck and the Ontario Hydro. Toronto: Ryerson, 1947.

Prentice, Alison
The School Promoters: Education and Social Class in Mid-Nineteenth Century Upper Canada. Toronto: McClelland and Stewart, 1977.

Salutin, Rick, and Theatre Passe Muraille
1837: William Lyon Mackenzie and the Canadian Revolution. Toronto: James Lorimer, 1976.

Schindeler, Frederick Fernand
Responsible Government in Ontario. Toronto: University of Toronto Press, 1973.

Schull, Joseph
Ontario Since 1867. Toronto: McClelland and Stewart, 1978.

Souster, Raymond
A Local Pride: Poems. Toronto: Contact Press, 1962.

Spelt, Jacob
Urban Development in South-Central Ontario. The Carleton Library, no. 57. Toronto: McClelland and Stewart, 1972. (First published 1955.)

Splane, Richard B.
Social Welfare in Ontario, 1791-1893: A Study of Public Welfare Administration. Toronto: University of Toronto Press, 1965.

Stelter, G.A.
"Community Development in Toronto's Commercial Empire: The Industrial Towns of the Nickel Belt, 1883-1931." *Laurentian University Review* 6 (June 1974): 3-53.

Swift, Jamie
Cut and Run: The Assault on Canada's Forests. Toronto: Between the Lines, 1983.

The Big Nickel: INCO at Home and Abroad. Kitchener, Ont.: Between the Lines, 1977.

Thompson, Austin Seton
Spadina: A Story of Old Toronto. Toronto: Pagurian, 1975.

Underhill, Frank
"Some Aspects of Upper Canadian Radical Opinion in the Decade Before Confederation." *In Search of Canadian Liberalism*, pp. 43-67. Toronto: Macmillan, 1960. (A selection of articles written between ca.1930 and 1960.)

Walker, David F., and Baker, James H.
Industrial Development in Southern Ontario: Selected Essays. Dept. of Geography, Publication Series, no. 3. Waterloo, Ont.: University of Waterloo, 1974.

Warkentin, Germaine, ed.
Stories From Ontario. Toronto: Macmillan, 1974.

Warkentin, John
"Southern Ontario: A View From the West." *Canadian Geographer* 10:3 (1966): 157-71.

Wise, S.F.
"Upper Canada and the Conservative Tradition." *Profiles of a Province: Studies in the History of Ontario*, pp. 20-33. Toronto: Ontario Historical Society, 1967.

Zaslow, Morris
"Does Northern Ontario Possess a Regional Identity?" *Laurentian University Review* 5 (September 1973): 9-20.

Zaslow, Morris, ed.
The Defended Border: Upper Canada and the War of 1812. Toronto: Macmillan, 1964.

15

Atlantic Canada

R. JAMES SACOUMAN

Arguably, no other area in Canada has moved forward so far in the last five years as Atlantic Canada. No other region has more concerted debate at regional academic conferences. No other set of academics has been pushed so rigorously by such a relatively large number of underemployed and unemployed "intelligentsia." No other region has contributed to more debate in Canadian political economy. No other region has been so unevenly developed by capitalism and its expanding state.

In order to investigate the validity of the preceding claims, the reader should critically examine the more recent materials cited in this section. Those wishing to keep up to date with changing struggles on the East Coast can subscribe to the monthly newspaper *New Maritimes* (Enfield, Hants County, Nova Scotia B0N 1N0).

Labour, gender and social history in the region have advanced in closer critical contact with more openly theoretical political economy than in other regions. It is even becoming popular to overstate the cohesion or "the new Maritime political economy/labour history." Certainly, debate within the region is sustained, substantively grounded and often constructive. There are no final words; our analyses are emergent. Nevertheless, out of a multiplicity of concrete political economic analyses have come a number of important theoretical, substantive and, therefore, political insights that have challenged not only earlier analyses of the region, but also many of the accepted notions of Canada-wide political economy.

Central to this challenge has been the shared theoretical-substantive-political focus of much of the work in Atlantic Canada on the almost incredible, but necessary (if entirely inhumane), unevenness of capitalist development in Canada. The Atlantic Canada literature has demonstrated the changing *complexity* of the Canadian class structure in order to explain a wide variety of struggles in the region. It is argued that this complexity in class structure flows necessarily from the historical expansion of Canada as a "middle power" capitalist state through processes of *both* expanded accumulation *and* simple primary/"primitive" accumulation. In other words, the Canadian class structure cannot be reduced analytically to a two-class structure but is better seen heuristically as a two-bloc or two-alliance structure of the capitalist class, state and allies, on the one hand, and the full-time working class, semi-proletarianized working class, "independent" producer class and allies, on the other hand.

Attention to uneven development and class structural complexity within a two-block heuristic model has allowed the recapturing and rethinking of a wider variety of class-rooted struggles than other regional and national approaches. Regionalist, nationalist, non-political and populist struggles, as well as the labour movement per se, in Atlantic Canada have been reanalyzed as block responses (and blocked responses) to uneven capitalist development, instead of being discarded from analysis for being somehow impure.

Equally as instructive, analyses of these struggles have made evident the fundamentally coercive nature of the capitalist state in the region and in Canada — a healthy purgative for those elsewhere who have a tendency to emphasize legitimation without coercion. Anti-democratic state coercion is, probably, daily more apparent in Atlantic Canada than elsewhere because of the higher degree of super-exploitation through primary accumulation.

Two of the most exciting areas of Canadian political economy — "women's work" and state-led capitalist initiatives — are also currently being researched in Atlantic Canada. Because they further build on versions of the above uneven development problematic, they will, no doubt, lead to more heated debate across Canada. Analyses of concrete state-coercive initiatives in the Atlantic fisheries and analyses of the complexity and diversity of the work women actually do in the region will add immensely to our still too narrow Canadian treatments.

In Atlantic Canada, then, creative Marxism is the many-pronged leading edge of analysis. Here, as elsewhere, there are many problems with the gaps between Marxist intellectuals and others — gaps that limit the insights and advances of political economy. A truly "organic" political economy of Atlantic Canada remains distant. Our failures of analysis are nothing new; the new is still be be accomplished.

Acheson, T.W.
   "The Maritimes and 'Empire Canada'." *Canada and the Burden of Unity*, pp. 87-114. Edited by D.J. Bercuson. Toronto: Macmillan, 1977.

   "The Social Origins of Canadian Industrialization: A Study in the Structure of Entrepreneurship." Ph.D. dissertation, University of Toronto, 1972.

Alexander, David
   Atlantic Canada and Confederation: Essays in Canadian Political Economy. Compiled by Eric W. Sager, Lewis R. Fischer and Stuart O. Pierson. Toronto: University of Toronto Press in association with Memorial University of Newfoundland, 1983.

   The Decay of Trade: An Economic History of the Newfoundland Saltfish Trade, 1935-1965. St. John's: Institute of Social and Economic Research, Memorial University of Newfoundland, 1977.

Alexander, David, and Ommer, Rosemary, eds.
   Volumes Not Values: Canadian Sailing Ships and World Trade: Proceedings of the Third Conference of the Atlantic Canada Shipping Project, April 19-April 21, 1979. St. John's: Maritime History Group, Memorial University of Newfoundland, 1979.

Allain, Greg
   "L'Affaire Kouchibougouac: bilan du rapport de la Commission spéciale d'enquête sur le parc national de Kouchibougouac." *Egalité*, no. 7 (automne 1982), pp. 51-94.

Archibald, Bruce
   "Atlantic Regional Underdevelopment and Socialism." *Essays on the Left: Essays in Honour of T.C. Douglas*, pp. 103-20. Edited by Laurier Lapierre et al. Toronto: McClelland and Stewart, 1971.

Babcock, Robert H.
   "The Saint John Street Railwaymen's Strike and Riot, 1914." *Acadiensis* 11 (Spring 1982): 3-27.

Bailey, Alfred Goldsworthy
   Culture and Nationality: Essays. The Carleton Library, no. 58. Toronto: McClelland and Stewart, 1972.

Baker, Melvin; Cuff, Robert; and Gillespie, Bill
   Workingmen's St. John's: Aspects of Social History in the Early 1900s. St. John's, Nfld.: Cuff Publications, 1982.

Barrett, L. Gene
   Floundering in Troubled Waters: The Political Economy of the Atlantic Fishery and the Task Force on Atlantic Fisheries. Halifax: Gorsebrook Research Institute, St. Mary's University, 1983.

   "Perspectives on Dependency and Underdevelopment in the Atlantic Region." *Canadian Review of Sociology and Anthropology* 17 (August 1980): 273-86.

Beck, J. Murray, ed.
   Joseph Howe: Voice of Nova Scotia: A Selection. The Carleton Library, no. 20. Toronto: McClelland and Stewart, 1964.

Bercuson, David J., and Buckner, Phillip A., eds.
   Eastern and Western Perspectives: Papers from the Joint Atlantic Canada/Western Canadian Studies Conference. Toronto: University of Toronto Press, 1981.

Bickerton, James
   "Underdevelopment and Social Movements in Atlantic Canada: A Critique." *Studies in Political Economy*, no. 9 (Fall 1982), pp. 191-202.

Boyd, Mary
   The Irish Moss 'Strikes' in Prince Edward Island. Wolfville, N.S.: Regional Centre for the Study of Contemporary Social Issues, Acadia University, 1983.

Brebner, John Bartlet
   New England's Outpost: Acadia Before the Conquest of Canada. New York: Columbia University Press, 1927.

Brookes, Alan
   "Out-Migration From the Maritime Provinces, 1860-1900: Some Preliminary Considerations." *Acadiensis* 5 (Spring 1976): 26-55.

Brown, Cassie
   Death on the Ice: The Great Newfoundland Sealing Disaster of 1914. Toronto: Doubleday, 1974.

Brox, Ottar
   Maintenance of Economic Dualism in Newfoundland. St. John's: Institute of Social and Economic Research, Memorial University of Newfoundland, 1969.

Brun, Régis
   De Grand-Pré à Kouchibouagouac: l'histoire d'un peuple exploité: essai. Moncton: Editions d'Acadie, 1982.

Brunton, R.; Overton, J.; and Sacouman, J.
"Uneven Underdevelopment and Song: Expressions of Popular Class Culture in Atlantic Canada." *Communication Studies in Canada*, pp. 105-32. Edited by Liora Salter. Toronto: Butterworth, 1981.

Brym, Robert J., and Sacouman, R. James, eds.
Underdevelopment and Social Movements in Atlantic Canada. Toronto: New Hogtown Press, 1979.

Calhoun, Sue
The Lockeport Lockout: An Untold Story in Nova Scotia's Labour History. Halifax: n.p., 1983. (Printed by Kentville Publishing, Kentville, N.S.)

Cameron, James Malcolm
The Pictonian Colliers. Halifax: Nova Scotia Museum, 1974.

Industrial History of the New Glasgow District. New Glasgow, N.S.: Hector Publishing, 1960.

Cameron, Silver Donald
The Education of Everett Richardson: The Nova Scotia Fishermen's Strike, 1970-71. Toronto: McClelland and Stewart, 1977.

Canada. Bureau of Statistics
The Maritime Provinces in Their Relation to the National Economy of Canada: A Statistical Study of Their Social and Economic Condition. Ottawa: King's Printer, 1948.

Canada. Bureau of Statistics
The Maritime Provinces Since Confederation. A Statistical Study of Their Social and Economic Condition During the Past Sixty Years. Ottawa: F.A. Acland, King's Printer, 1927.

Canada. Royal Commission on Coal
Report of the Royal Commission on Coal, 1946. Ottawa: E. Cloutier, King's Printer, 1947.

Canada. Task Force on Atlantic Fisheries
Navigating Troubled Waters: A New Policy for the Atlantic Fisheries: Highlights and Recommendations: Report of the Task Force on Atlantic Fisheries. (The Kirby Report.) Ottawa: The Task Force, 1982.

Chanteloup, Robert, ed.
Labour in Atlantic Canada. St. John, N.B.: University of New Brunswick at St. John, 1981.

Clow, Michael
Politics and Uneven Capitalist Development: The Maritime Challenge to the Study of Canadian Political Economy. Halifax: Gorsebrook Research Institute, St. Mary's University, 1983.

Connelly, M. Patricia, and MacDonald, Martha
"Women's Work: Domestic and Wage labour in a Nova Scotia Community." *Studies in Political Economy*, no. 10 (Winter 1983), pp. 45-72.

Côté, Serge
"Les Obstacles structurels au développement en Acadie." *Revue de l'Université de Moncton* 13 (janvier/mai 1980): 61-73.

Daigle, Jean, ed.
Acadians of the Maritimes: Thematic Studies. Moncton, N.B.: Centre d'études acadiennes, 1982.

Fay, C.R.
Life and Labour in Newfoundland. Toronto: University of Toronto Press, 1956.

Fay, C.R., and Innis, H.A.
"The Economic Development of Canada, 1867-1921: The Maritime Provinces." *The Cambridge History of the British Empire*, vol. 6, pp. 657-71. Edited by J. Holland Rose et al. Cambridge, Eng.: Cambridge University Press, 1930.

Ferguson, C.B.
The Labour Movement in Nova Scotia Before Confederation. Halifax: Public Archives of Nova Scotia, 1964.

Fingard, Judith
Jack in Port: Sailortowns of Eastern Canada. Toronto: University of Toronto Press, 1982.

"The Winter's Tale: The Seasonal Contours of Pre-industrial Poverty in British America, 1815-1860." Canadian Historical Association. *Historical Papers* (1974): 65-94.

Fischer, Lewis R., and Sager, Eric W., eds.
Merchant Shipping and Economic Development in Atlantic Canada: Proceedings of the Fifth Conference of the Atlantic Canada Shipping Project, June 25-27, 1981. St. John's: Maritime History Group, Memorial University of Newfoundland, 1982.

The Enterprising Canadians: Entrepreneurs and Economic Development in Eastern Canada, 1820-1914: Proceedings of the Second Conference of the Atlantic Canada Shipping Project, March 30-April 1, 1978. St. John's: Maritime History Group, Memorial University of Newfoundland, 1979.

Forbes, Ernest R.
Aspects of Maritime Regionalism, 1867-1927. Historical Booklet no. 36. Ottawa: Canadian Historical Association, 1983.

The Maritime Rights Movement, 1919-1927: A Study in Canadian Regionalism. Montreal: McGill-Queen's University Press, 1979.

"Misguided Symmetry: The Destruction of Regional Transportation Policy for the Maritimes." *Canada and the Burden of Unity*, pp. 60-86. Edited by D.J. Bercuson. Toronto: Macmillan, 1977.

Forsey, Eugene
"Some Notes on the Early History of Unions in P.E.I." *Canadian Historical Review* 46 (December 1965): 346-51.

National Problems of Canada: Economic and Social Aspects of the Nova Scotia Coal Industry. McGill University Economic Studies, no. 5. Toronto: Macmillan, 1926.

Frank, David
"The Cape Breton Coal Industry and the Rise and Fall of the British Empire Steel Corporation." *Acadiensis* 7 (Autumn 1977): 3-34.

"Class Conflict in the Coal Industry: Cape Breton 1922." *Essays in Canadian Working Class History*, pp. 161-84. Edited by Gregory S. Kealey and Peter Warrian. Toronto: McClelland and Stewart, 1976.

Fraser, Dawn
Echoes From Labour's War: Industrial Cape Breton in the 1920's. Toronto: New Hogtown Press, 1976.

Frost, James D.
"The 'Nationalization' of the Bank of Nova Scotia, 1880-1910." *Acadiensis* 12 (Autumn 1982): 3-38.

George, Roy E.
A Leader and a Laggard: Manufacturing Industry in Nova Scotia, Quebec, and Ontario. Toronto: University of Toronto Press, 1970.

Grant, Ruth Fulton
The Canadian Atlantic Fishery. Toronto: Ryerson, 1934.

Great Britain. Newfoundland Royal Commission, 1933
Newfoundland Royal Commission, 1933: Report. (The Amulree Report.) London: H.M.S.O., 1933.

Gwyn, Richard J.
Smallwood: The Unlikely Revolutionary. Rev. ed. Toronto: McClelland and Stewart, 1972.

Henry, Frances
The Forgotten Canadians: The Blacks of Nova Scotia. Don Mills, Ont.: Longmans, 1973.

Hiller, James
"The Origins of the Pulp and Paper Industry in Newfoundland." *Acadiensis* 11 (Spring 1982): 42-68.

Hunt, Russell, and Campbell, Robert
K.C. Irving: The Art of the Industrialist. Toronto: McClelland and Stewart, 1973.

Innis, Harold Adams
The Cod Fisheries: The History of an International Economy. Rev. ed. Toronto: University of Toronto Press, 1954. (First edition 1940.)

Kealey, Gregory; McKay, Ian; and Reilly, Nolan
"Canada's 'Eastern Question': A Reader's Guide to Regional Underdevelopment." *Canadian Dimension* 13:2 (1978): 37, 40.

Kierstead, B.D.
The Economic Effects of the War on the Maritime Provinces of Canada. Halifax: Institute of Public Affairs, Dalhousie University, 1944.

Laidlaw, Alexander F., ed.
The Man From Margaree: Writings and Speeches of M.M. Coady. Toronto: McClelland and Stewart, 1971.

Leyton, Elliott
Dying Hard: The Ravages of Industrial Carnage. Toronto: McClelland and Stewart, 1975.

MacEwan, Paul
Miners and Steelworkers: Labour Unions in Cape Breton. Toronto: Hakkert, 1975.

Macgillivray, Don
"Military Aid to the Civil Power: The Cape Breton Experience in the 1920's." *Acadiensis* 3 (Spring 1974): 45-65.

Macgillivray, Don (con'd)
"Cape Breton in the 1920's: A Community Besieged." *Essays in Cape Breton History*, pp. 49-67. Edited by B. Tennyson. Windsor, N.S.: Lancelot Press, 1973.

Macgillivray, Don, and Tennyson, Brian, eds.
Cape Breton Historical Essay. Sydney, N.S.: College of Cape Breton Press, 1979.

MacPherson, Ian
"Patterns in the Maritime Co-operative Movement 1900-1945." *Acadiensis* 5 (Autumn 1975): 67-83.

Mathias, Philip
Forced Growth: Five Studies of Government Involvement in the Development of Canada. Toronto: James Lorimer, 1971.

Matthews, Keith, and Panting, Gerald, eds.
Ships and Shipbuilding in the North Atlantic Region: Proceedings of the Conference of the Atlantic Canada Shipping Project, March 31-April 2, 1977. St. John's: Maritime History Group, Memorial University of Newfoundland, 1978.

Matthews, Ralph
The Creation of Regional Dependency. Toronto: University of Toronto Press, 1983.

"There's No Better Place Than Here": Social Change in Three Newfoundland Communities. Toronto: Peter Martin Associates, 1976.

McFarland, Joan
"Underdevelopment and Economic Theory in Atlantic Canada." *Acadiensis* 11 (Spring 1982): 135-40.

"Changing Modes of Social Control in a New Brunswick Fish Packing Town." *Studies in Political Economy*, no. 4 (Autumn 1980), pp. 99-113.

McKay, Ian
"Strikes in the Maritimes, 1901-1914." *Acadiensis* 13 (Autumn 1983): 3-46.

Muise, D.A.
"Parties and Constituencies: Federal Elections in Nova Scotia, 1867-1896." Canadian Historical Association. *Historical Papers* (1971): 183-202.

Neary, Peter
"Canadian Immigration Policy and the Newfoundlanders, 1912-1939." *Acadiensis* 11 (Spring 1982): 69-83.

Neary, Peter, ed.
The Political Economy of Newfoundland 1929-1972. Toronto: Copp Clark, 1973.

Noel, S.J.R.
Politics in Newfoundland. Toronto: University of Toronto Press, 1971.

Ommer, Rosemary, and Panting, Gerald, eds.
Working Men Who Got Wet: Proceedings of the Fourth Conference of the Atlantic Canada Shipping Project, July 24-July 26, 1980. St. John's: Maritime History Group, Memorial University of Newfoundland, 1980.

O'Neill, Brian
Safety in the Offshore. Wolfville, N.S.: Regional Centre for the Study of

Contemporary Social Issues, Acadia University, 1984.

Overton, James
"Promoting 'The Real Newfoundland': Culture as Tourist Commodity." *Studies in Political Economy*, no. 4 (Autumn 1980), pp. 115-37.

"Uneven Regional Development in Canada: The Case of Newfoundland." *Review of Radical Political Economics* 10 (Fall 1978): 106-16.

Panting, G.E.
"The Fishermen's Protective Union of Newfoundland and the Farmers' Organizations in Western Canada." *Canadian Historical Association Report* (1963): 141-51.

Prowse, D.W.
A History of Newfoundland, from the English, Colonial, and Foreign Records. 3rd ed. St. John's, Nfld.: Dicks, 1971. (First published 1895.)

Pryke, Ken
"Labour and Politics: Nova Scotia at Confederation." *Social History* 6 (November 1970): 33-55.

Rawlyk, G.A., ed.
The Atlantic Provinces and the Problems of Confederation. St. John's, Nfld.: Breakwater Books, 1979.

Historical Essays on the Atlantic Provinces. The Carleton Library, no. 35. Toronto: McClelland and Stewart, 1967.

Reilly, Nolan
"The General Strike in Amherst, Nova Scotia, 1919." *Acadiensis* 9 (Spring 1980): 56-77.

Ridler, Neil B., ed.
Issues in Regional/Urban Development of Atlantic Canada. St. John, N.B.: Division of Social Science, University of New Brunswick at St. John, 1977.

Sacouman, R. James
"Broken-Up Canada and Breaking-Up Britain: Some Comparative Lessons in Uneven Development, Nationalism and Regionalism." *Political Action and Social Identity: Class, Locality and Culture.* Edited by G. Rees. London: Macmillan, forthcoming.

"Regional Uneven Development, Regionalism and Struggle." *Introduction to Sociology: An Alternative Approach*, pp. 149-69. Edited by J. Paul Grayson. Toronto: Gage, 1983.

"The 'Peripheral' Maritimes and Canada-Wide Marxist Political Economy." *Studies in Political Economy*, no. 6 (Autumn 1981), pp. 135-50.

"Semi-Proletarianization and Rural Underdevelopment in the Maritimes." *Canadian Review of Sociology and Anthropology* 17 (August 1980): 232-45.

Saunders, S.A.
The Economic History of the Maritime Provinces. A Study Prepared for the Royal Commission on Dominion-Provincial Relations. Ottawa: King's Printer, 1939.

Studies in the Economy of the Maritime Provinces. Studies of the Institute of Public Affairs at Dalhousie University. Toronto: Macmillan, 1939.

The Economic Welfare of the Maritime Provinces. Wolfville, N.S.: Acadia University, 1932.

Seager, Allen
"Minto, New Brunswick: A Study in Canadian Class Relations Between the Wars." *Labour/Le Travailleur*, no. 5 (Spring 1980), pp. 81-132.

Sharpe, Errol
A People's History of Prince Edward Island. Toronto: Steel Rail Press, 1976.

Smallwood, Joseph Robert
The Book of Newfoundland. 6 vols. St. John's: Newfoundland Book Publishers, 1976. (First published 1937.)

I Chose Canada: The Memoires of the Hon. Joseph R. ("Joey") Smallwood. Toronto: Macmillan, 1973.

Coaker of Newfoundland: The Man Who Led the Deep-Sea Fishermen to Political Power. London: Labour Publishing, 1927.

Smith, Philip
Brinco: The Story of Churchill Falls. Toronto: McClelland and Stewart, 1976.

Smitheram, Vernon; Milne, David; and Dasgupta, Satadal, eds.
The Garden Transformed: Prince Edward Island, 1945-1980. Charlottetown: Ragweed Press, 1982.

Social Action Commission, Diocese of Charlottetown
The Work Book: Witness to Injustice. Charlottetown: Social Action Commission, 1982.

Sterns, Maurice A., ed.
Newfoundland and Labrador: Social Science Research: A Select Annotated Bibliography. St. John's: Department of Sociology, Memorial University of Newfoundland, 1975.

Tennyson, Brian, ed.
Cape Breton: A Bibliography. Halifax: Dept. of Education, 1978.

Thomson, Anthony
"The Nova Scotia Civil Service Association, 1956-1967." *Acadiensis* 12 (Spring 1983): 81-105.

Trépanier, Pierre
"Clio en Acadie." *Acadiensis* 11 (Spring 1982): 95-103.

Wadel, Cato
Now Whose Fault Is That? The Struggle for Self Esteem in the Face of Chronic Unemployment. St. John's: Institute of Social and Economic Research, Memorial University of Newfoundland, 1973.

Wynn, Graeme
Timber Colony: A Historical Geography of Early Nineteenth Century New Brunswick. Toronto: University of Toronto Press, 1981.

16

The North

JENNIFER MAURO

Since the first edition of this guide was published in 1978, northern issues have changed little in context. The competing interests between homeland and hinterland, between self-determination and assimilation, and between traditional and wage economy, are still the basis of the conflict over control and management of development in the North. This is manifested through the consistent drive for non-renewable resource development, the restraints imposed upon the renewable resource economy, aboriginal claims and constitutional negotiations. What *has* changed is the polysymmetrical/multidimensional nature of the issues' complexity and content.

This change has occurred because of the emergence of a strong bureaucratic and political infrastructure, not only within the traditional colonial framework of the territorial/federal systems, but also as aboriginal organizations and control have developed. This infrastructure has altered the relationships between the aboriginal peoples and the state. Some of the more important organizational developments have been the Committee for Original Peoples Entitlement settlement, the Council for Yukon Indians signing of an Agreement-in-Principle, and the establishment of various local, regional and territorial economic development corporations.

In terms of the study of the North, there has been an explosion of interest, witnessed by the myriad published research and papers, although few independent books have been written. Key books that have been published since 1977 and should not be overlooked, include:

- Bregha (1979), who takes a close look at the political economy of the North from a project-specific basis;
- Dacks (1981), who gives a thorough outline of the primary issues — constitutional development, aboriginal rights and economic development — their policy relationships and inherent conflicts;
- Brody (1981), who, by using land as the focus, offers a definitive study of the relationships between different modes of production and the resulting conflict that did exist and continues to exist today; and
- Asch (1984)), whose excellent work considers aboriginal rights and constitutional development in Canada and the North.

Most of the other references are either articles, papers or reports prepared for one of the entrenched institutions — that is, either government (federal or territorial), industry (multinational oil or mining), or aboriginal — as can be seen in the incomplete 1983 bibliography compiled by the Arctic Institute of North

America. One should also not forget the work done on Labrador (Brice-Bennett, 1977), northern Quebec and James Bay regions (LaRusic et al., 1979; Müller-Willie, 1983), and the northern sections of the provinces (Justus et al., 1983). There is an obvious commonality in the political and economic struggles of these areas, based on the power relationships and the clash between various modes of production, ideologies, institutions and their interrelationships.

The best of the literature addresses the implications of research as a political tool (ACUNS, 1984). Brody, Cruikshank, Gibson and Usher are four authors who deal with this inherent socio-political conflict — the concept of values and knowledge, the power relations of a particular model of knowledge in our society and the way that power is used by institutions. Harvey Feit has also done excellent work on this issue and its effect on resource management institutions. Much of his work has been done within the Anthropology Department at McMaster University and the Centre for Northern Studies at McGill University. Peter Cummings has written several perceptive analyses on the political economy of energy and its links to jurisprudence and aboriginal rights in the North. These can be found in the *Alberta Law Review* and the *Canadian Resources Law Centre Journal* (based at the University of Calgary). Chamberlain's (1983) paper explains the conflict in considering aboriginal claims in the context of development as opposed to development in the context of aboriginal claims.

The other references are equally important and thorough in their treatment of the issues. However, a great bulk of material deserving reference is that produced through the hearing and public review process. Since 1977, the action by the state has virtually institutionalized conflict through the use of the public review process. Since the 1977 Berger Inquiry, each region of the North has been subjected to several hearings, reviews, commissions, task forces, committees, etc. Some examples include:

- Environmental Assessment and Reviews (EARPs) have been done for the Alaska Highway Gas Pipeline (1979, 1981, 1982), Lancaster Sound (1979), Davis Strait (1978), Arctic Pilot Project (1980), Normal Wells Field Expansion and Pipeline (1981), Beaufort Hydrocarbon Development (1984).
- National Energy Board has held hearings on the Norman Wells/Interprovincial Pipeline Application (1981) and the Arctic Pilot Project (1982)).
- Government committees on Indian self-government (1984), Senate Committee on Transportation of Hydrocarbons (1983), Task Force on Beaufort Development (1981) and Constitutional Development (1981).
- Water Board hearings into Norman Wells (1981) and Placer Mining claims and use in the Yukon (1981, 1982 and 1983).

The materials, papers and reports prepared for the above, and the evidence presented at the hearings are excellent sources of information. Special attention and credit must be given to the work done by the aboriginal organizations including the Déné Nation, the Council for Yukon Indians, the Committee for Original Peoples' Entitlement, the Métis Association of the N.W.T., and the Inuit Tapirisat of Canada and, more recently, their bands and/or regional associations. A good reference is the evidence and submissions given by both the Mackenzie Delta Déné Regional Council and the Déné Nation to the Beaufort Environmental

Assessment and Review Panel in November 1983. For sources that are not available in libraries, refer directly to the individual aboriginal organizations. Many universities and large city libraries hold the reports or transcripts of public hearings and reviews.

Another ongoing source of political economic analysis and development is the process of constitutional development — concerned in the Northwest Territories with partition and with the First Ministers' Meetings on National Aboriginal Rights. The work done by the aboriginal organizations is again extremely valuable. For a list of the work done for the Western and/or Nunavut Constitutional Forums, details are available through their respective coordinating offices in Yellowknife, N.W.T., or through the Department of Indian Affairs and Northern Development in Ottawa. For work done on aboriginal rights and the Canadian Constitution, a good university library specializing in northern aboriginal and constitutional law should have the papers, as should Ottawa and/or the respective organization.

A further issue that seems to be regaining importance is that of the militarization of the North.

Clearly, the Canadian state's activities in resource and constitutional development have great impact on the North and its political economic development. Whether pertaining to the search for oil, or sovereignty, or international pressures, the policies and developments in the North can and should be questioned, not only in terms of the political and economic benefits, as defined by "southern-centralist" values, but in terms of the political and economic value base of the people indigenous to the region.

Abele, Frances, and Dosman, E.J.
"Intergovernmental Coordination and Northern Development." *Canadian Public Administration* 24 (Fall 1981): 428-51.

Asch, Michael
Aboriginal Rights in the Canadian State. Toronto: Methuen, 1984.
"Déné Self-Determination and the Study of Hunter-Gatherers in the Modern World." *Politics and History in Band Societies*, pp. 347-72. Edited by Eleanor Leacock and Richard Lee. Cambridge, Eng.: Cambridge University Press, 1982.

Association of Canadian Universities for Northern Studies
Social Science in the North: Communicating Northern Values. Occasional Publication no. 9. Ottawa: Association of Canadian Universities for Northern Studies, 1984.

Bankes, Nigel
Resource-Leasing Options and the Settlement of Aboriginal Claims. Ottawa: Canadian Arctic Resources Committee, 1983.

Banting, Keith, and Simeon, Richard, eds.
And No One Cheered: Federalism, Democracy, and the Constitution Act. Toronto: Methuen, 1983.

Berger, Thomas
Northern Frontier, Northern Homeland: The Report of the Mackenzie Valley Pipeline Inquiry. Ottawa: Supply and Services Canada, 1977.

Bourgault, Ron G.
"The Indians, the Métis and the Fur Trade: Class, Sexism and Racism in the Transition from 'Communism' to Capitalism." *Studies in Political Economy*, no. 12 (Fall 1983), pp. 45-80.

Bregha, François
Bob Blair's Pipeline: The Business and Politics of Northern Energy Development Projects. New ed. Toronto: James Lorimer, 1979.

Brice-Bennett, Carol, ed.
Our Footprints Are Everywhere: Inuit Land Use and Occupancy in Labrador. Nain, Nfld.: Labrador Inuit Association, 1977.

Brody, Hugh
Maps and Dreams: Indians and the British Columbia Frontier. Vancouver: Douglas & McIntyre, 1981.

The People's Land: Eskimos and Whites in the Eastern Arctic. Harmondsworth: Penguin, 1975.

Canada. Special Representative for Constitutional Development in the Northwest Territories
Constitutional Development in the Northwest Territories: Report of the Special Representative. Ottawa: Special Representative for Constitutional Development in the Northwest Territories, 1980.

Canadian Arctic Resources Committee
Canadian Arctic Marine Energy Projects. Presentation to the Special Committee of the Senate on the Northern Pipeline. Ottawa: The Committee, 1982.

Chamberlin, J.E.
Native Land Claims and Northern Hydrocarbon Development in the Beaufort Sea-Mackenzie Delta Region: A Report. Ottawa: Beaufort Sea Alliance, 1983.

The Harrowing of Eden: White Attitudes Toward North American Natives. Toronto: Fitzhenry & Whiteside, 1975.

Cruikshank, Julie
"Oral Tradition and Scientific Research: Approaches to Knowledge in the North." *Social Science in the North: Communicating Northern Values*. Occasional Publication no. 9. Ottawa: Association of Canadian Universities for Northern Studies, 1984.

"Legend and Landscape: Convergence of Oral and Scientific Traditions in the Yukon Territory." *Arctic Anthropology* 18:2 (1981): 67-93.

Cummings, Peter
"Native Rights and Law in an Age of Protest." *Alberta Law Review* 11 (1973):238.

Dacks, Gurston
A Choice of Futures: Politics in the Canadian North. Toronto: Methuen, 1981.

Davis, H.C., and Hainsworth, G.B.
"A Critical Appraisal of the Economic Aspects of the Proposed Beaufort Sea Development." Vancouver: School of Community and Regional Planning, 1983.

Dimitrov, P.
So That the Future Will Be Ours. A Report Prepared for the Ross River Indian Band. Ross River, Yukon: n.p., 1984.

Dosman, Edgar J.
"The Mackenzie Valley Pipeline Inquiry: The Politics of Catharsis." *Canadian Ethnic Studies* 10:1 (1978): 135-41.

The National Interest: The Politics of Northern Development 1968-75. Toronto: McClelland and Stewart, 1975.

Feit, Harvey A.
"The Future of Hunters Within Nation-States: Anthropology and the James Bay Cree." *Politics and History in Band Societies*, pp. 373-411. Edited by Eleanor Leacock and Richard Lee. Cambridge, Eng.: Cambridge University Press, 1982.

Fumoleau, René
As Long as This Land Shall Last: A History of Treaty 8 and Treaty 11, 1870-1939. Toronto: McClelland and Stewart, 1973.

Gamble, Don
"Destruction by Insignificant Increments." *Northern Perspectives* 7:6 (1979): 1-10.

Gibson, Robert B.
Values, Interests and Preferences: Non-Factual Considerations in the Work of the Beaufort Sea Environmental Assessment Panel. Ottawa: Beaufort Sea Research Coalition, 1982.

The Strathcona Sound Mining Project: A Case Study of Decision Making. Background Study no.42. Ottawa: Science Council of Canada, 1978.

International Symposium on Renewable Resources and the Economy of the North
Proceedings: First International Symposium on Renewable Resources and the Economy of the North, Banff, Alberta, May 1981. Edited by Milton M.R. Freeman. Ottawa: Association of Canadian Universities for Northern Studies, 1981.

Inuit Tapirisat of Canada
Political Development in Nunavut: A Report Prepared for the Board Directors of Inuit Tapirisat of Canada, and Discussed at the Annual General Meeting, September 3-7, 1979, Igloolik. Ottawa: Information Services, Inuit Tapirisat of Canada, 1980.

Jackson, Ted
"Resisting Pipeline Imperialism: The Struggle for Self-Determination in the Canadian North." *Alternatives* 7 (Autumn 1978): 40-51.

James Bay and Northern Quebec Native Harvesting Research Committee
The Wealth of Our Land. Quebec: n.p., 1982.

Jull, Peter, and Bankes, Nigel
"Inuit Interests in the Arctic Offshore." *Northern Perspectives* 11 (December 1983).

Justus, R., and Simonetta, J.
From Where We Stand. Fort McKay Tribal Administration. Fort McMurray, Alta.: n.p., 1983.

La Rusic, I., et al.
Negotiating a Way of Life: Initial Cree Experience with the Administrative Structure Arising from the James Bay Agreement. Report Prepared for the Research Division, Policy Research and Evaluation Group of the Dept. of

La Rusic, I., et al. (con'd)
Indian and Northern Affairs. Montreal: Dept. of Indian Affairs and Northern Development, 1979.

Laxer, James
Oil and Gas: Ottawa, the Provinces and the Petroleum Industry. Toronto: James Lorimer, 1983.

Leacock, Eleanor, and Lee, Richard, eds.
Politics and History in Band Societies. Cambridge, Eng.: Cambridge University Press, 1982.

McCullum, Hugh, and McCullum, Karmel
This Land is Not for Sale. Toronto: Anglican Book Centre, 1975.

McCullum, Hugh; McCullum, Karmel; and Olthuis, John
Moratorium: Justice, Energy, North and the Native People. Toronto: Anglican Book Centre, 1977.

McInnis, Simon
"The Inuit and the Constitutional Process: 1978-1981." *Journal of Canadian Studies* 16 (Summer 1981): 53-68.

Milton Freeman Research Limited
Inuit Land Use and Occupancy Project: Report. 3 vols. Ottawa: Minister of Indian and Northern Affairs, 1976.

Müller-Wille, Ludger, ed.
Conflict in Development in Nouveau-Québec. McGill Subarctic Research Paper no. 37. Montreal: Centre for Northern Studies and Research, McGill University, 1983.

National Northern Development Conference
Ninth National Northern Development Conference, 1982: Proceedings, Oct. 27, 28, 29, 1982, Edmonton, Alberta: Theme: Partners in Progress. Edmonton: National Northern Development, 1982.

National Workshop on People, Resources and the Environment North of 60°
Ocean Policy and Management in the Arctic Ocean Management Working Group, Third National Workshop on People, Resources and the Environment North of 60°, 1-3 June 1983. Ottawa: Canadian Arctic Resources Committee, 1984.

Nicholls, W.G.
Aishihik: The Politics of Hydro Planning in the Yukon. Yukon Series. Research Monograph no. 5. Ottawa: Canadian Arctic Resources Committee, 1981.

O'Malley, Martin
The Past and Future Land: An Account of the Berger Inquiry into the Mackenzie Valley Pipeline. Toronto: Peter Martin Associates, 1976.

Path Economics Ltd.
An Analysis of the Minimum Economic Scale of Developing Beaufort Sea Oil Reserves. A Report Prepared for Beaufort Sea Alliance. Calgary: Path Economics, 1983.

Pearse, Peter H., ed.
The Mackenzie Pipeline: Arctic Gas and Canadian Energy Policy. Toronto: McClelland and Stewart, 1974.

Peterson, E.B., and Wright, J.B., eds.
Northern Transitions. Vol. 1: *Northern Resources and Land Use Policy Study*.
Ottawa: Canadian Arctic Resources Committee, 1978.

Pimlott, D.H.
Oil Under the Ice. Ottawa: Canadian Arctic Resources Committee, 1976.

Pimlott, D.H., et al.
Arctic Alternatives. Ottawa: Canadian Arctic Resources Committee, 1973.

Ponting, J. Rick, and Gibbins, Roger
Out of Irrelevance: A Socio-Political Introduction to Indian Affairs in Canada.
Toronto: Butterworth, 1980.

Rea, K.J.
The Political Economy of Northern Development. Background Study no. 36.
Ottawa: Science Council of Canada, 1976.

Stabler, Jack C., and Alfert, M. Rose
"Gaslight Follies: The Political Economy of the Western Arctic." *Canadian Public Policy* 6 (Spring 1980): 374-88.

Symposia on Folk Law and Legal Pluralism
Papers of the Symposia on Folk Law and Legal Pluralism: XI International Congress of Anthropological and Ethnological Sciences, Vancouver, Canada, August 19-23, 1983. 2 vols. Compiled by Harold W. Finkler. Ottawa: Indian and Northern Affairs Canada, 1983.

Usher, Peter J.
Assessing the Impact of Industry in the Beaufort Sea Region: A Report Prepared for the Beaufort Sea Alliance. Ottawa: Beaufort Sea Alliance, 1982.

"Staple Production and Ideology in Northern Canada." *Culture, Communication, and Dependency: The Tradition of H.A. Innis*, pp. 177-86. Edited by William H. Melody, Liora Salter and Paul Heyer. Norwood, N.J.: Ablex Publishing, 1981.

The Bankslanders: Economy and Ecology of a Frontier and Trapping Community. 3 vols. Ottawa: Information Canada, 1970.

Watkins, Mel, ed.
Dene Nation — The Colony Within. Toronto: University of Toronto Press, 1977.

Wetzel, Jerry, et al.
Freedom to Live Our Own Way in Our Own Land. Edited by Peter J. Usher. Conne River, Nfld.: Ktaqamkuk Ilnui Saqimawoutie and the Conne River Indian Band Council, 1980.

White, Pam
Essential Elements in Social Impact Assessment. Ottawa: Beaufort Sea Alliance, 1982.

World Council of Indigenous People
"Fort McKay, Alberta, Canada." *World Council of Indigenous People Newsletter*, no. 3 (August 1983), pp. 5-25.

17
Native Peoples

MICHAEL ASCH

The study of native peoples in Canada in the political economy tradition is the study of the effect on the indigenous population of the development of its territory into a majority European-settler state under liberal-democratic government and capitalism. It is also a study that runs the gamut of all topics found within the political economy tradition, albeit from the specific perspective of their relationship to aboriginal peoples and societies.

The focus of such a study cannot be limited solely to the actions of capitalism and the state. Such an approach fails to account for the ability of aboriginal peoples to respond creatively to the challenges to their ways of life and their determination to struggle to maintain autonomy against pressures to assimilate them into a national norm. Nor would it be proper to overgeneralize the nature of how such settler states interact with aboriginal entities, although speaking generally the theme has always been to attempt to encapsulate and destroy their autonomy. Recent events indicate that Canada may be among the first to reverse this general process. This possibility is symbolized by the incorporation of a clause protecting "existing aboriginal rights" in the new Canadian Constitution. This implies state recognition of aboriginal peoples as ethnonational entitities with special rights based on their presence in the territory prior to the arrival of settlers. It is the only such acknowledgement among such settler states and, as a result, enables Canada to lead the others in finding a means to accommodate the aspirations of aboriginal nations within their polity.

This bibliography is intended to introduce students to the range and complexity of issues that belong to the study of native peoples within a political economy tradition. It includes, however, many references that are not themselves in that tradition and, among these, some that refer to issues, such as language and culture, that may not always be perceived as falling into the scope of concerns signaled by that tradition. They are included because I believe they indicate the range of responses aboriginal peoples have made to the pressures that have accompanied the expansion of settler society into their lives, and so are important to that tradition. There is a bias, as well, towards anthropological literature, primarily because most research on the topic of native societies has come from that discipline. However, as the political economy orientation is only now growing beyond basic roots within anthropology, again, of necessity, the literature that reflects it will not be large, especially when one selects on the basis of quality as well as orientation.

Two topics have dominated a political economy tradition in research over the past decade and a half, and these are most prominently represented in the bibliography. The first pertains to the economic and policy aspects of contact between aboriginal nations and the expanding settler population. Central to such research has been the recent work on the fur trade, and as it is the case with other foci included in the bibliography, this work incorporates studies both of the dynamics of expansion and of response. The second area concerns the contemporary period. Here, in addition to a wide selection of readings that range from the severe economic, social, educational and health problems faced by aboriginal peoples to the literature that demonstrates the continuities that persist even in the face of the exploitation of these peoples, I have included a number of references that point particulary to the experiences of aboriginal peoples in the Northwest Territories, northern Quebec and Labrador. This research has brought to light what I consider to be the most significant new fact of the past fifteen years in this area: hunting-trapping economies still persist and help to shape both subsistence and social life among major segments of aboriginal peoples. It is a finding that is clearly within the political economy tradition of research. As well, I have made reference to an area that is now developing a literature in the political economy tradition: the political aspirations of aboriginal nations for self-government within Canada. In this, as in all other matters, I have tried to provide citations that are widely diverse geographically and representative of the three groupings of aboriginal peoples defined in our Constitution: the Indians, the Inuit and the Métis.

While the reading list includes only English-language titles, this is not because French-speaking social scientists neither discuss native peoples nor use a political economy context to do so. In fact, the opposite is the case. The French-language literature, specifically concerning the relationship of aboriginal nations to Quebec, surpasses in scope and equals in theoretical strength the research represented here. Indeed, it is the very scope of this literature that renders the task of including it within such a brief bibliography impossible. Instead, I have provided reference to an essay available in English (by Gold and Tremblay) that describes the recent history of this literature in Quebec. It is hoped that from the extensive set of references listed in that essay, it will be possible to pursue the topic more fully than would be the case were I merely to indicate a few sources here.

Adams, Howard
Prison of Grass: Canada from the Native Point of View. Toronto: New Press, 1975.

Asch, Michael I.
Home and Native Land: Aboriginal Rights and the Canadian Constitution. Toronto: Methuen, 1984.

''Dene Self-Determination and the Study of Hunter-Gatherers in the Modern World.'' *Politics and History in Band Societies*, pp. 347-72. Edited by Eleanor Leacock and Richard Lee. Cambridge, Eng.: Cambridge University Press, 1982.

''The Economics of Dene Self-Determination.'' *Challenging Anthropology*, pp. 339-52. Edited by David H. Turner and Gavin A. Smith. Toronto: McGraw-Hill Ryerson, 1979.

''The Dene Economy.'' *Dene Nation — The Colony Within*, pp. 47-61. Edited by Mel Watkins. Toronto: University of Toronto Press, 1977.

Bailey, Alfred Goldsworthy
The Conflict of European and Eastern Algonkian Cultures, 1504-1700: A Study in Canadian Civilization. Publications of the New Brunswick Museum, Saint John, N.B. Monograph Series, no. 2. Sackville, N.B.: The Tribune Press, 1937. (Reprinted Toronto: University of Toronto Press, 1969, 1976.)

Barsh, Russell Lawrence, and Henderson, James Youngblood
"Aboriginal Rights, Treaty Rights, and Human Rights: Indian Tribes and 'Constitutional Renewal'." *Journal of Canadian Studies* 17 (Summer 1982): 55-81.

Bennett, Gordon
Aboriginal Rights in International Law. Occasional Paper of the Royal Anthropological Institute of Great Britain and Ireland, no. 37. London: Royal Anthropological Institute of Great Britain and Ireland in association with Survival International, 1978.

Berger, Thomas
Northern Frontier, Northern Homeland: The Report of the Mackenzie Valley Pipeline Inquiry. 2 vols. Ottawa: Supply and Services Canada, 1977.

Bishop, Charles A.
The Northern Ojibwa and the Fur Trade: An Historical and Ecological Study. Toronto: Holt, Rinehart & Winston, 1974.

Braroe, Niels W.
Indian and White: Self-Image and Interaction in a Canadian Plains Community. Stanford, Calif.: Stanford University Press, 1975.

Briggs, Jean L.
Never in Anger: Portrait of an Eskimo Family. Cambridge, Mass.: Harvard University Press, 1970.

Brody, Hugh
Maps and Dreams: Indians and the British Columbia Frontier. Vancouver: Douglas & McIntyre, 1981.

The People's Land: Eskimos and Whites in the Eastern Arctic. Harmondsworth: Penguin Books, 1975.

Indians on Skid Row. Ottawa: Information Canada, 1971.

Brown, Dougald
"Indian Hunting Rights and Provincial Law: Some Recent Developments." *University of Toronto Faculty of Law Review* 39 (1981): 121-32.

Brown, Jennifer S.H.
Strangers in Blood: Fur Trade Company Families in Indian Country. Vancouver: University of British Columbia Press, 1980.

Canada. Indian and Northern Affairs
In All Fairness: A Native Claims Policy: Comprehensive Claims. Ottawa: Supply and Services Canada, 1981.

Indian Conditions: A Survey. Ottawa: Supply and Services Canada, 1980.

Canada. Indian Land Claims Commission
Statements and Submissions: A Report. Ottawa: Supply and Services Canada, 1977.

Canada. Parliament. House of Commons. Special Committee on Indian Self-Government

Indian Self-Government in Canada: Report of the Special Committee. Minutes of Proceedings of the Special Committee on Indian Self-Government, 1st session, 32nd Parliament, issue no. 40, Oct.12-20, 1983. Ottawa: Queen's Printer for Canada, 1983.

Cardinal, Harold

The Unjust Society: The Tragedy of Canada's Indians. Edmonton: Hurtig, 1969.

Chamberlin, J.E.

The Harrowing of Eden: White Attitudes Toward North American Natives. Toronto: Fitzhenry & Whiteside, 1975.

Clark, A. McFadyen, ed.

Proceedings: Northern Athapaskan Conference, 1971. 2 vols. Mercury Series. Canadian Ethnology Service Paper no. 27. Ottawa: National Museum of Man, National Museums of Canada, 1975.

Conference on Aboriginal Rights

Aboriginal Rights: Toward an Understanding: Proceedings. Conference on Aboriginal Rights, sponsored by the Alberta Law Foundation and the Dept. of Native American Studies, the University of Lethbridge, January 18-21, 1983. Edited by J. Anthony Long, Menno Boldt, and Leroy Little Bear. Lethbridge, Alta.: University of Lethbridge, 1983.

Cumming, Peter A., and Mickenberg, Neil H., eds.

Native Rights in Canada. 2nd ed. Toronto: Indian-Eskimo Association of Canada in association with General Publishing, 1972. (Reprinted Toronto: Canadian Association in Support of the Native Peoples, 1980.)

Dacks, Gurston

A Choice of Futures: Politics in the Canadian North. Toronto: Methuen, 1981.

Dene Nation and the Metis Association of the N.W.T.

Public Government for the People of the North. Yellowknife, N.W.T.: Dene Nation and the Metis Association of the N.W.T., 1981.

Dickason, Olive Patricia

The Myth of the Savage and the Beginnings of French Colonialism in the Americas. Edmonton: University of Alberta Press, 1983.

Dobbin, Murray

The One-and-a-Half Men: The Story of Jim Brady and Malcolm Norris, Metis Patriots of the Twentieth Century. Vancouver: New Star Books, 1981.

Duff, Wilson

The Indian History of British Columbia. Vol. 1: *The Impact of the White Man.* Anthropology in British Columbia Memoirs, no. 5. Victoria: Provincial Museum of Natural History and Anthropology, 1965.

Dunning, Robert William

Social and Economic Change Among Northern Ojibwa. Toronto: University of Toronto Press, 1959.

Dyck, Noel, ed.

Indigenous Peoples and the Nation-State: Fourth World Politics in Canada, Australia and Norway. St. John's: Institute of Social and Economic Research, Memorial University of Newfoundland, 1983.

Elias, D.
"Indian Politics in the Canadian Political System." *The Patterns of "Amerindian" Identity*, pp. 35-64. Edited by Marc-Adelard Tremblay. Québec: Presses de l'Université Laval, 1976.

Feit, Harvey A.
"The Future of Hunters Within Nation-States: Anthropology and the James Bay Cree." *Politics and History in Band Societies*, pp. 373-411. Edited by Eleanor Leacock and Richard Lee. Cambridge, Eng.: Cambridge University Press, 1982.

Flanagan, Thomas
"The Case Against Métis Aboriginal Rights." *Canadian Public Policy* 9 (September 1983): 314-25.

"Louis Riel and Aboriginal Rights." *As Long as the Sun Shines and the Water Flows: A Reader in Canadian Native Studies*, pp. 247-62. Edited by Ian A.L. Getty and Antoine S. Lussier. Vancouver: University of British Columbia Press, 1983.

Riel and the Rebellion: 1885 Reconsidered. Saskatoon: Western Producer Prairie Books, 1983.

Frideres, James S.
Native People in Canada: Contemporary Conflicts. 2nd ed. Scarborough, Ont.: Prentice-Hall, 1983.

Fumoleau, René
As Long as This Land Shall Last: A History of Treaty 8 and Treaty 11, 1870-1939. Toronto: McClelland and Stewart, 1975.

Getty, Ian A.L., and Lussier, Antoine S., eds.
As Long as the Sun Shines and Water Flows: A Reader in Canadian Native Studies. Vancouver: University of British Columbia Press, 1983.

Gold, G.L., and Tremblay, M.A.
"Steps Towards an Anthropology of Quebec, 1960-1980." *Consciousness and Inquiry: Ethnology and Canadian Realities*. Edited by Frank Manning. Mercury Series. Canadian Ethnology Service Paper no. 89E. Ottawa: National Museum of Man, National Museums of Canada, 1983.

Green, L.C.
"Aboriginal Peoples, International Law and the Canadian Charter of Rights and Freedoms." *Canadian Bar Review* 61 (March 1983): 339-53.

Guédon, Marie-Françoise
People of the Tetlin, Why Are You Singing? Mercury Series. Ethnology Division Paper no. 9. Ottawa: National Museum of Man, National Museums of Canada, 1974.

Hara, Hiroko Sue
The Hare Indians and Their World. Mercury Series. Canadian Ethnology Service Paper no. 63. Ottawa: National Museum of Man, National Museums of Canada, 1980.

Helm, June, et al.
"The Contact History of the Subarctic Athapaskans: An Overview." *Proceedings: Northern Athapaskan Conference*, vol. 1, pp. 302-36. Mercury Series. Canadian Ethnology Service Paper no. 27. Edited by A. McFadyen Clark. Ottawa: National Museum of Man, National Museums of Canada, 1975.

Helm, June, ed.
Handbook of North American Indians. Vol. 6: *Subarctic*. William C. Sturtevant, general editor. Washington: Smithsonian Institution, 1981.

Hickerson, Harold
"The Southwestern Chippewa: An Ethnohistorical Study." *American Anthropological Association Memoirs*. Memoir no. 92, vol. 16, no. 2, pt. 2 (June 1962).

Hunt, George T.
The Wars of the Iroquois: A Study in Intertribal Trade Relations. Madison, Wisc.: University of Wisconsin Press, 1940.

Indian Brotherhood of the N.W.T. and the Metis Association of the N.W.T., 2nd Joint General Assembly, 19 July 1975 at Fort Simpson
"Dene Declaration." *Dene Nation — The Colony Within*, pp. 3-4. Edited by Mel Watkins. Toronto: University of Toronto Press, 1977.

Innis, Harold A.
The Fur Trade in Canada: An Introduction to Canadian Economic History. Rev. ed. Toronto: University of Toronto Press, 1956. (First edition 1930.)

International Symposium on Renewable Resources and the Economy of the North
Proceedings of the First International Symposium on Renewable Resources and the Economy of the North, Banff, Alberta, May 1981. Edited by Milton M.R. Freeman. Ottawa: Association of Canadian Universities for Northern Studies, 1981.

Knight, Rolf
"A Reexamination of Hunting, Trapping, and Territoriality Among the Northeastern Algonkian Indians." *Man, Culture and Animals: The Role of Animals in Human Ecological Adjustments*, pp. 27-42. Publication no. 78. Edited by Anthony Leeds and Andrew P. Vayda. Washington, D.C.: American Association for the Advancement of Science, 1965.

La Rusic, Ignatius E., ed.
Negotiating a Way of Life: Initial Cree Experience with the Administrative Structure Arising from the James Bay Agreement. Ottawa: Research Division, Policy, Research and Evaluation Group of the Dept. of Indian and Northern Affairs, 1979.

Leacock, Eleanor
"The Montagnais 'Hunting Territory' and the Fur Trade." *American Anthropological Association Memoirs*. Memoir no. 78, Vol. 56, no. 5, pt. 2 (1954).

Leacock, Eleanor, and Lee, Richard, eds.
Politics and History in Band Societies. Cambridge, Eng.: Cambridge University Press, 1982.

Leacock, Eleanor, and Lurie, Nancy Oestreich, eds.
North American Indians in Historical Perspective. New York: Random House, 1971.

Little Bear, Leroy; Boldt, Menno; and Long, J. Anthony, eds.
Pathways to Self-Determination: Canadian Indians and the Canadian State. Toronto: University of Toronto Press, 1983.

Lysyk, Kenneth M.
"The Rights and Freedoms of the Aboriginal Peoples of Canada." The Canadian Charter of Rights and Freedoms: Commentary, pp. 467-88. Edited by

Lysyk, Kenneth M. (con'd)
Walter S. Tarnopolsky and Gérard-A. Beaudoin. Toronto: Carswell, 1982.

"The Indian Title Question in Canada: An Appraisal in the Light of Calder." *Canadian Bar Review* 51 (September 1973): 450-80.

"Indian Hunting Rights: Constitutional Considerations and the Role of Indian Treaties in British Columbia." *University of British Columbia Law Review* 2:3 (1966): 401-21.

Mackenzie, Alexander
Voyages from Montreal on the River St. Lawrence, through the Continent of North America to the Frozen and Pacific Oceans in the Years 1789 and 1793, with a Preliminary Account of the Rise, Progress, and Present State of the Fur Trade of that Country. New. ed. Rutland, Vt.: Tuttle, 1971. (First published 1801.)

Manuel, George, and Posluns, M.
The Fourth World: An Indian Reality. Don Mill, Ont.: Collier-Macmillan, 1974.

Manyfingers, Wallace
"Commentary: Aboriginal Peoples and the Constitution." *Alberta Law Review* 19:3 (1981): 428-32.

Maybury-Lewis, David, ed.
The Prospects for Plural Societies: 1982 Proceedings of the American Ethnological Society. Washington: American Ethnological Society, 1984.

McCaskill, D.
"The Urbanization of Indians in Winnipeg, Toronto, Edmonton, and Vancouver: A Comparative Analysis." *Culture* 1 (1981): 82-89.

Metis and Non-Status Indian Constitutional Review Commission
Native People and the Constitution of Canada: The Report of the Metis and Non-Status Indian Constitutional Review Commissions. Harry W. Daniels, Commissioner. Ottawa: The Commission, 1981.

Metis National Council
Opening Address to the First Ministers' Conference on the Rights of the Aboriginal Peoples. [Briefs Presented to the First Ministers' Conference on Aboriginal Constitutional Matters, no. 5. Ottawa: Minister of Supply and Services], 1983.

Morris, Alexander
The Treaties of Canada with the Indians of Manitoba and the North-West Territories: Including the Negotiations on Which They Were Based and Other Information Relating Thereto. Toronto: Belfords, Clarke, 1880. (Facsimile repr. Toronto: Coles: 1971.)

Morrison, R. Bruce, and Wilson, C.R.
Native Peoples: The Canadian Experience. Toronto: McClelland and Stewart, forthcoming.

Murphy, Robert F., and Steward, Julien H.
"Tappers and Trappers: Parallel Processes in Acculturation." *Economic Development and Cultural Change* 4 (1955-56): 335-55.

Niedermeyer, Lynn
"Aboriginal Rights: Definition or Denial?" *Queens Law Journal* 6 (1980-81): 568-86.

Paine, Robert, ed.

The White Arctic: Anthropological Essays on Tutelage and Ethnicity. St. John's: Institute of Social and Economic Research, Memorial University of Newfoundland, 1977.

Patrons and Brokers in the East Arctic. St. John's: Institute of Social and Economic Research, Memorial University of Newfoundland, 1971.

Ponting, J. Rick, and Gibbins, Roger

Out of Irrelevance: A Socio-Political Introduction to Indian Affairs in Canada. Toronto: Butterworth, 1980.

Ray, Arthur J.

Indians in the Fur Trade: Their Role as Trappers, Hunters and Middlemen in the Lands Southwest of Hudson Bay, 1660-1860. Toronto: University of Toronto Press, 1974.

Ray, Arthur J., and Freeman, Donald

"Give Us Good Measure": An Economic Analysis of Relations Between the Indians and the Hudson's Bay Company Before 1763. Toronto: University of Toronto Press, 1978.

Rea, K.J.

The Political Economy of the Canadian North: An Interpretation of the Course of Development in the Northern Territories of Canada to the Early 1960s. Toronto: University of Toronto Press, 1968.

Richardson, Boyce

Strangers Devour the Land. Toronto: Macmillan, 1976.

James Bay: The Plot to Drown the North Woods. Toronto: Clarke, Irwin, 1973.

Rogers, Edward S.

The Quest for Food and Furs: The Mistassini Cree, 1953-1954. Mercury Series. Ethnology Division Paper no. 5. Ottawa: National Museum of Man, National Museums of Canada, 1973.

Sanders, Douglas E.

"The Re-Emergence of Indigenous Questions in International Law." *Aboriginal Rights: Toward an Understanding: Proceedings.* Conference on Aboriginal Rights sponsored by the Alberta Law Foundation and the Dept. of Native American Studies, January 18-21, 1983, University of Lethbridge, Lethbridge, Alta. Edited by J. Anthony Long, Menno Boldt, and Leroy Little Bear. Lethbridge, Alta.: University of Lethbridge, 1983.

"The Rights of the Aboriginal Peoples of Canada." *Canadian Bar Review* 61 (March 1983): 314-38.

"Aboriginal Peoples and the Constitution." *Alberta Law Review* 19 (1981): 410-27.

Savishinsky, Joel S.

The Trail of the Hare: Life and Stress in an Arctic Community. Library of Anthropology, vol. 2. New York: Gordon and Breach, 1974.

Sawchuk, Joe, and the Metis Association of Alberta

Metis Land Rights in Alberta: A Political History. Edmonton: Metis Association of Alberta, 1981.

Simpson, George

Fur Trade and Empire: George Simpson's Journal Entitled Remarks Connected

Simpson, George (con'd)
with the Fur Trade in the Course of a Voyage from York Factory to Fort George and Back to York Factory 1824-25, with Related Documents. Rev. ed. Edited by Frederick Merk. Cambridge, Mass.: Belknap Press of Harvard University Press, 1968. (Earlier edition 1931.)

Slattery, Brian
"The Constitutional Guarantee of Aboriginal and Treaty Rights." *Queen's Law Journal* 8 (1982-83): 232-72.

Slobodin, Richard
Métis of the Mackenzie District. Ottawa: Canadian Research Centre for Anthropology, Saint-Paul University, 1966.

Smith, Derek G.
Natives and Outsiders: Pluralism in the Mackenzie River Delta, Northwest Territories. Social Science Note no. 5. Ottawa: Dept. of Indian and Northern Affairs, 1974.

Smith, Derek G., ed.
Canadian Indians and the Law: Selected Documents, 1663-1972. The Carleton Library, no. 87. Toronto: McClelland and Stewart, 1975.

Stanbury, W.T.
Success and Failure: Indians in Urban Society. Vancouver: University of British Columbia Press, 1975.

Stymeist, David H.
Ethnics and Indians: Social Relations in a Northwestern Ontario Town. Toronto: Peter Martin Associates, 1975.

Sutton, C. Gerald
"Aboriginal Rights." *Dene Nation — The Colony Within*, pp. 149-62. Edited by Mel Watkins. Toronto: University of Toronto Press, 1977.

Tanner, Adrian
Bringing Home Animals: Religious Ideology and Mode of Production of the Mistassini Cree Hunters. London: C. Hurst, 1979.

Tanner, Adrian, ed.
The Politics of Indianness: Case Studies of Native Ethnopolitics in Canada. St. John's: Institute of Social and Economic Research, Memorial University of Newfoundland, 1983.

Tobias, John L.
"Protection, Civilization, Assimilation: An Outline History of Canada's Indian Policy." *As Long as the Sun Shines and Water Flows: A Reader in Canadian Native Studies*, pp. 39-55. Edited by Ian A.L. Getty and Antoine S. Lussier. Vancouver: University of British Columbia Press, 1983.

Trigger, Bruce G.
The Children of Aataentsic: A History of the Huron People to 1660. 2 vols. Montreal: McGill-Queen's University Press, 1976.

Turner, David H., and Wortman, Paul
Shamattawa: The Structure of Social Relations in a Northern Algonkian Band. Mercury Series. Canadian Ethnology Service Paper no. 36. Ottawa: National Museum of Man, National Museums of Canada, 1977.

Upton, L.F.S.
"The Origins of Canadian Indian Policy." *Journal of Canadian Studies* 8 (November 1973): 51-61.

Usher, Peter
"Evaluating Country Food in the Northern Native Economy." *Arctic* 29 (June 1976): 105-20.

The Bankslanders: Economy and Ecology of a Frontier and Trapping Community. 3 vols. Ottawa: Information Canada, 1970.

Watkins, Melville, ed.
Dene Nation — The Colony Within. Toronto: University of Toronto Press, 1977.

Weaver, Sally M.
Making Canadian Indian Policy: The Hidden Agenda, 1968-70. Toronto: University of Toronto Press, 1981.

Wolforth, John
The Evolution and Economy of the Delta Community. Mackenzie Delta Research Project Report no. 11. Ottawa: Northern Science Research Group, Dept. of Indian Affairs and Northern Development, 1971.

Woodcock, George
Gabriel Dumont: The Métis Chief and His Lost World. Edmonton: Hurtig, 1975.

18

English-Canadian Nationalism

DANIEL DRACHE

English Canadian nationalism has changed greatly in the last decade. In the 1960s and 1970s, it was a counter-ideology, propogated by various groups and organizations (including the Waffle, the Canadian Artists' Representation, etc.) that offered an alternative to liberalism, to Canada's relations with the U.S. and to the country's reliance on foreign investment. In the 1980s, however, nationalism has been appropriated by the state and used extensively for state ends. The nationalist turn by the Trudeau Liberal government extended right across the board, from the National Energy Program to the patriation of the Constitution, from the creation of the Macdonald Commission Canada's future to Trudeau's so-called peace initiative.

Nationalism's large, ''official'' role in Canadian affairs might be expected to have generated a comprehensive re-examination of its importance. Not so. The writing on English Canadian nationalism remains cast in the mould shaped by Grant's *Lament for a Nation*, Ramsay Cook's *The Maple Leaf Forever* and Abe Rotstein's various articles cited throughout this bibliography. While journal articles abound, recent full-length studies of English Canadian nationalism are few and far between. An important exception is Stephen Clarkson's *Canada and the Reagan Challenge: Crisis in the Canadian-American Relationship*, which offers a contemporary account of the American response to Trudeau's nationalism of convenience. It is essential reading (an updated edition carrying this story up to early 1985 is now in print).

With the exception of Clarkson's book, the fact remains that there is no English Canadian equivalent to the perspective developed by Nicole Laurin-Frenette, Leon Dion, Gilles Bourque or even Pierre Trudeau in his early writing on the cultural and political role nationalism played in the formation of Quebec. The study of English Canadian nationalism continues to be narrow and issue-oriented, examining single aspects of foreign domination or cultural identity rather than combining them in a single analysis. One recent book that reverses this trend is Susan Crean and Marcel Rioux's *Two Nations: An Essay on the Culture and Politics of Canada and Quebec in a World of American Pre-eminence* which attempts to develop a political economy approach to the study of culture and nationalism.

The absence of a more dynamic approach to the study of Canadian nationalism is due, in part, to the fact that English Canadian liberal scholarship has been interested primarily in attacking nationalism on ideological grounds. Not surprisingly, there is no shortage of anti-nationalism critiques, mostly in the form of individual studies by economists and historians, as well as government studies by the Economic Council of Canada and studies by such business organizations as the C.D. Howe Institute and the Business Council on National Issues. English Canadian Marxists have also been critical of nationalism and often indifferent to the various aspects of Canada's national question. And while they have grappled somewhat successfully with the origins of Canadian dependency and foreign domination, they have failed to come to terms with Quebec's quest for sovereignty association or, failing that, its quest for a new relationship with Canada. All these factors have contributed to a certain under-theorization on the subject of nationalism that is reflected in the available literature on the subject.

However, because state nationalism is a force to be reckoned with, writers of various political persuasions are beginning to seriously address the questions "nationalism" poses. Nationalism, like gender, is seen to have a specificity of its own and cannot be explained simply by a narrow focus on class. Hopefully, this realization will result in some provocative studies on the relationship between nationalism and class, region and the state, and, particularly, on how the issue of nationalism is regarded in the various political arenas across the country.

The books and articles that follow concentrate on specific aspects of nationalism and on the broader nationalist question. The reader should also consult other sections of this bibliography, including "State Policy and Politics," "Federalism," "Quebec" and "Class Formation," which deal with such specific issues as the National Energy Program, federal-provincial relations, Quebec nationalism and working-class politics.

Abella, Irving, and Troper, Harold
None Is Too Many: Canada and the Jews of Europe, 1933-1948. Toronto: Lester & Orpen Dennys, 1982.

Acorn, Milton
More Poems for People. Toronto: NC Press, 1972.

I've Tasted My Blood: Poems 1956-1968. Toronto: Ryerson, 1969.

Ajzenstat, Janet
"Liberalism and Nationality." *Canadian Journal of Political Science* 14 (September 1981): 587-609.

Alexander, David
"New Notions of Happiness: Nationalism, Regionalism and Atlantic Canada." *Journal of Canadian Studies* 15 (Summer 1980): 29-42.

Armatage, Kay
"Canadian Women's Cinema." *Canadian Forum* 62 (February 1982): 24-25.

Atwood, Margaret
Surfacing. Toronto: McClelland and Stewart, 1972.

Survival: A Thematic Guide to Canadian Literature. Toronto: Anansi, 1972.

Audley, Paul
"Proposals for Canada's Cultural Industries." *Canadian Forum* 62 (March 1983): 6-10.

Bailey, Alfred Goldsworthy
  Culture and Nationality: Essays by A.G. Bailey. The Carleton Library, no. 58. Toronto: McClelland and Stewart, 1972.

Bell, David
  "The Loyalist Tradition in Canada." *Journal of Canadian Studies* 5 (May 1970): 22-33.

Berger, Carl
  The Writing of Canadian History. Toronto: Oxford University Press, 1976.

  The Sense of Power: Studies in the Ideas of Canadian Imperialism, 1867-1914. Toronto: University of Toronto Press, 1970.

Bothwell, Robert, and Kirton, John
  "A Sweet Little Country: American Attitudes Towards Canada, 1925 to 1963." *Queen's Quarterly* 90 (Winter 1983): 1078-1102.

Bourque, Gilles, et Dostaler, Gilles
  Socialisme et indépendance. Montréal: Boréal Express, 1980.

Braybrooke, David
  "In Search of Canadian Philosophy." *Queen's Quarterly* 90 (Autumn 1983): 688-92.

Bullen, John
  "The Ontario Waffle and the Struggle for an Independent Socialist Canada: Conflict Within the NDP." *Canadian Historical Review* 64 (June 1983): 188-215.

Cairns, Alan C.
  "Political Science in Canada and the Americanization Issue." *Canadian Journal of Political Science* 8 (June 1975): 191-234.

Cameron, David
  Nationalism, Self-Determination and the Quebec Question. Toronto: Macmillan, 1974.

Canada. Royal Commission on National Development in the Arts, Letters and Sciences
  The Massey Report. Ottawa: King's Printer, 1951.

Canada. Royal Commission on Publications
  The O'Leary Report. Ottawa: Queen's Printer, 1961.

Canada. Senate Report
  "The Uncertain Mirror." *Report of the Special Senate Committee on Mass Media.* Ottawa: Information Canada, 1970.

  Words, Music, and Dollars: A Study of the Economics of Publishing and Broadcasting. Report of the Special Senate Committee on Mass Media. Ottawa: Information Canada, 1970.

Canadian Dimension
  "The NDP and the Waffle." (Special Supplement) 1 (April 1971).

Carr, Graham
  "Imperialism and Nationalism in Revisionalist Historiography: A Critique of Some Recent Trends." *Journal of Canadian Studies* 17 (Summer 1982): 91-99.

Clarkson, Stephen
Canada and the Reagan Challenge: Crisis and Adjustment, 1981-1985. 2nd ed. Toronto: James Lorimer, 1985.

Clements, Kevin, and Drache, Daniel, eds.
"Symposium on Creative Modes of Nationalism in New Zealand, Canada and Australia." *Australian and New Zealand Journal of Sociology* 14:3, pt. 2 (October 1978): 15-20.

Colman, S.J.
"Margaret Atwood, Lucien Goldmann's Pascal, and the Meaning of 'Canada'." *University of Toronto Quarterly* 48 (Spring 1979): 245-62.

Cook, Ramsay
"Has the Quiet Revolution Ended?" *Queen's Quarterly* 90 (Summer 1983): 330-42.

Canada and the French-Canadian Question. Toronto: Macmillan, 1966.

The Maple Leaf Forever: Essays on Nationalism and Politics in Canada. Toronto: Macmillan, 1971.

Cook, Ramsay, ed.
French-Canadian Nationalism: An Anthology. Toronto: Macmillan, 1969.

Crean, Susan
"The Thirty Per Cent Solution: Sexism as a Fine Art." *This Magazine* 17 (January 1984): 26-31, 38.

"Understanding Applebert." *Canadian Forum* 63 (April 1983): 14-17, 42.

Who's Afraid of Canadian Culture? Don Mills, Ont.: General Publishing, 1976.

Crean, Susan, and Rioux, Marcel
Two Nations: An Essay on the Culture and Politics of Canada and Quebec in a World of American Pre-eminence. Toronto: James Lorimer, 1983.

Dewar, Ken
"The CBC: A Note on the Past with an Eye to the Future." *Canadian Forum* 59 (October 1979): 6-9.

Drache, Daniel
"Whatever Happened to Canadian Nationalism?" *Canadian Dimension* 18 (October-November 1984): 15-20.

"Rediscovering Canadian Political Economy." *A Practical Guide to Canadian Political Economy*, pp. 1-53. Edited by Wallace Clement and Daniel Drache. Toronto: James Lorimer, 1978.

"Going Down the Nationalist Road...Slowly." *This Magazine* 7 (August 1973): 28-30.

"The Canadian Bourgeoisie and Its National Consciousness." *Close the 49th Parallel Etc.: The Americanization of Canada*, pp. 3-25. Edited by Ian Lumsden. Toronto: University of Toronto Press, 1970.

Drache, Daniel, and Kroker, Arthur, eds.
"The Labyrinth of Dependency." *Canadian Journal of Political and Social Theory* 7 (Fall 1983): 5-24.

Ferguson, Barry
"Political Economists and Queen's Quarterly, 1893-1939." *Queen's Quarterly* 90 (Autumn 1983): 623-43.

Frye, Northrop
The Bush Garden: Essays on the Canadian Imagination. Toronto: Anansi, 1971.

Gagne, Wallace, ed.
Nationalism, Technology and the Future of Canada. Toronto: Macmillan, 1976.

Gordon, Walter L.
Storm Signals: New Economic Policies for Canada. Toronto: McClelland and Stewart, 1975.

A Choice for Canada: Independent or Colonial Status. Toronto: McClelland and Stewart, 1966.

Troubled Canada: The Need for New Domestic Policies. Toronto: McClelland and Stewart, 1961.

Grant, George
Lament for a Nation: The Defeat of Canadian Nationalism. Toronto: McClelland and Stewart, 1967.

Hackett, Robert
"Pie in the Sky: A History of the Ontario Waffle." *Canadian Dimension* 15 (October-November 1980): 1-72. Replies by Dan Heap and Jim Harding: 15-16 (December 1981): 43-46.

Harcourt, Peter
"Feature Films in English Canada." *Canadian Forum* 61 (February 1982): 15-18. Addendum: "Isolated Incidents." 62 (June-July 1982): 48.

Hardin, Herschel
A Nation Unaware: The Canadian Economic Culture. Vancouver: J.J. Douglas, 1974.

Hodgetts, A.B.
What Culture? What Heritage? A Study of Civic Education in Canada. Toronto: Ontario Institute for Studies in Education, 1968.

Horowitz, Gad
"Conservatism, Liberalism, and Socialism in Canada: An Interpretation." *Canada: A Sociological Profile*, 2nd ed., pp. 8-23. Edited by W.E. Mann. Toronto: Copp Clark, 1971. (Original in *Canadian Journal of Economics and Political Science* 32 [May 1966]: 143-71.)

Johnson, Harry G.
"Problems of Canadian Nationalism." *The Canadian Quandary*, pp. 11-21. Toronto: McClelland and Stewart, 1977.

Kierans, Eric
"Canada and the New U.S. Empire." *Canadian Forum* 63 (January 1984): 5-6.

Kroker, Arthur
"The Cultural Imagination and the National Questions." *Canadian Journal of Political and Social Theory* 6 (Winter-Spring 1982): 5-11.

Laurin-Frenette, Nicole
"Quebec and the Theory of the Nation." *Our Generation* 4 (Spring 1980): 29-35.

Production de l'état et formes de la nation. Montréal: Nouvelle optique, 1978.

Laxer, James, and Laxer, Robert
The Liberal Idea of Canada. Toronto: James Lorimer, 1977.

Lee, Dennis
"Writing in Colonial Space." *Open Letter*, Second Series, 6 (Fall 1973).

Levitt, Kari
"Decolonizing Canada and Quebec." *Canadian Forum* 51 (March 1972).

Lumsden, Ian, ed.
Close the 49th Parallel, Etc.: The Americanization of Canada. Toronto: University of Toronto Press, 1970.

Macpherson, C.B.
"After Strange Gods: Canadian Political Science 1973." *Perspectives on the Social Sciences in Canada*, pp. 52-76. Edited by T.N. Guinsberg and Grant Reuber. Toronto: University of Toronto Press, 1974.

MacPherson, Ian
"Creighton's Empire." *Canadian Forum* 60 (September 1980): 7-8.

Marchak, M. Patricia
Ideological Perspectives on Canada. 2nd ed. Toronto: McGraw-Hill Ryerson, 1981.

Mathews, Robin
Canadian Literature. Toronto: Steel Rail Press, 1978.

"Canadian Culture and the Liberal Ideology." *Canada Ltd.: The Political Economy of Dependency*, pp. 213-31. Edited by Robert Laxer. Toronto: McClelland and Stewart, 1973.

Mathews, Robin, and Steele, James, eds.
The Struggle for Canadian Universities: A Dossier. Toronto: New Press, 1969.

Mathie, William
"Political Community and the Canadian Experience: Reflections on Nationalism, Federalism, and Unity." *Canadian Journal of Political Science* 12 (March 1979): 3-20.

McRoberts, Kenneth
"English Canada and the Quebec Nation." *Canadian Forum* 59 (February 1980): 11-14.

Moore, Steve, and Wells, Debbi
Imperialism and the National Question in Canada. Toronto: New Hogtown Press, 1975.

Morris, Peter
"After Grierson: The National Film Board 1945-1953." *Journal of Canadian Studies* 16 (Spring 1981): 3-12.

Morrow, Ray
"Deux pays pour vivre: Critical Sociology and Canadian Political Economy." *Canadian Journal of Political and Social Theory* 6 (Winter-Spring 1982): 61-105.

Neatby, Hilda
So Little For the Mind. 2nd ed. Toronto: Clark, Irwin, 1953.

Ontario. Royal Commission on Book Publishing
Canadian Publishers and Canadian Publishing. Ottawa: Queen's Printer, 1971.

Ornstein, Michael D. et al.
"Region, Class and Political Culture in Canada." *Canadian Journal of Political Science* 13 (June 1980): 227-71.

Ouellet, Fernand
"D.-G. Creighton et les racines de la nation." *Canadian Forum* 60 (September 1980): 11-12.

Peers, Frank
The Politics of Canadian Broadcasting, 1920-1951. Toronto: University of Toronto Press, 1969.

Reid, Malcolm
"An Open Letter to Sneezy Waters." *This Magazine* 13 (July-August 1979): 4-8.

Repo, Satu
"The American Comic Book: Proletarian Literature for Children." *This Magazine* 8 (March 1974): 8-11.

"From Pilgrim's Progress to Sesame Street: 125 Years of Colonial Readers." *This Magazine"* 7 (August 1973): 11-15.

Resnick, Philip
The Land of Cain: Class and Nationalism in English Canada 1945-1975. Vancouver: New Star Books, 1977.

Rioux, Marcel, and Crean, Susan
"Overcoming Dependency: A Plea for Two Nations." *Canadian Journal of Political and Social Theory* 7 (Fall 1983): 50-67.

Rosenblum, Simon
"Economic Nationalism and the English-Canadian Socialist Mind." *Our Generation* 11 (Fall 1975): 5-15.

Rotstein, Abraham
"Is There an English-Canadian Nationalism?" *Journal of Canadian Studies* 13 (Summer 1978): 109-18.

"The World Upside Down." *Canadian Journal of Political and Social Theory* 2 (Spring-Summer 1978): 5-30.

"Canada: The New Nationalism." *Foreign Affairs* 55 (October 1976): 97-118.

The Precarious Homestead: Essays on Economics, Technology and Nationalism. Toronto: New Press, 1973.

Rotstein, Abraham, and Lax, Gary, eds.
Getting It Back: A Program for Canadian Independence. Toronto: Clarke, Irwin, 1974.

Independence: The Canadian Challenge. Toronto: Committee For An Independent Canada, 1972.

Rush, G.B., et al.
"Lament for a Notion: The Development of Social Science in Canada." *Canadian Review of Sociology and Anthropology* 18 (November 1981): 519-44.

Russell, Peter, ed.
Nationalism in Canada. Toronto: McGraw-Hill, 1966.

Salutin, Rick
Marginal Notes: Challenges to the Mainstream. Toronto: Lester & Orpen

Dennys, 1984.

Saul, J., and Heron, Craig, eds.
Imperialism, Nationalism and Canada. Toronto: New Hogtown Press, 1977.

Schafer, R. Murray
"Canadian Culture: Colonial Culture." *Canadian Forum* 63 (March 1984): 14-19.

Sher, Julian
"Rephrasing the National Question." *Canadian Dimension* 16 (June 1982): 33-34. With reply by R.T. Naylor: 35-36.

Shore, Marlene
"'Overtures of an Era Being Born' F.R. Scott: Cultural Nationalism and Social Criticism 1925-1939." *Journal of Canadian Studies* 15 (Winter 1980-81): 31-42.

Smart, Patricia
"Culture, Revolution and Politics in Quebec." *Canadian Forum* 62 (May 1982): 7-10.

Smith, Denis
Gentle Patriot: A Political Biography of Walter Gordon. Edmonton: Hurtig, 1973.

Solecki, Sam
"Criticism and the Anxiety of Identity." *Queen's Quarterly* 90 (Winter 1983): 1026-33.

Sullivan, Rosemary
"Nationalism: Were We Wrong." *This Magazine* 18 (June 1984): 22-23, 38.

Sutherland, John
Essays, Controversies and Poems. New Canadian Library Original. Edited by Miriam Waddington. Toronto: McClelland and Stewart, 1972.

Symons, T.H.B.
To Know Ourselves: The Report of the Commission on Canadian Studies. 3 vols. Ottawa: AUCC, 1975-1984. Also *The Symons Report*. 1 vol. abridged. Toronto: McClelland and Stewart, 1977. (Title of vol. 3: *Some Questions of Balance*, by T.H.B. Symons and James E. Page.)

Teeple, Gary, ed.
Capitalism and the National Question in Canada. Toronto: University of Toronto Press, 1972.

Vano, Gerard S.
Neo-Feudalism: The Canadian Dilemma. Toronto: Anansi, 1981.

Vigod, B.L.
"Canadian Books in French: The Study of Postwar Ideologies." *Canadian Historical Review* 64 (June 1983): 257-67.

Watkins, Mel
"Laxer's Choice." *This Magazine* 18 (April 1984): 16-19, 36.

"Coming Apart Together: The Report of the Task Force on Canadian Unity." *This Magazine* 13 (May-June 1979): 4-9.

Wright, Judy, and Magidson, Debbie
"Making Films For Your Own People." *This Magazine* 8 (November-December 1974): 21-27.

19
Canadian Political Theory

ARTHUR KROKER

English Canada: Refusing Liberalism

Political theory in English Canada is typified by a compelling, highly original and thorough critique of liberalism, old and new. Perhaps because of Canada's domination by the United States — the society George Grant has described as the "dynamic" centre of liberalism today — the most critical Canadian thinkers of *all* political stripes have seriously reflected on the inadequacies of the liberal account of politics and, more generally, on the deep insufficiencies of liberalism as a theory of society. For example, C.B. Macpherson (Canada's leading socialist theorist), George Grant (Canada's most important conservative philosopher) and George Woodcock (Canada's anarchist writer par excellence) all unanimously reject the liberal account of politics and society. It is this refusal of liberalism that is the legacy of English Canadian political thought.

In an important series of essays, political scientist Howard Aster argues that "vilifying liberalism" is the primary characteristic of Canadian political thought and that it is, in fact, Canada's most important contribution to North American discourse. Canadian political theorists' writings have succeeded in developing historically specific critiques of liberalism within the Canadian context into more extensive examinations of the foundations of the liberal account of politics and society. And, interestingly enough, the writing is almost always marked by its emphasis on both sides of the issues: the Canadian side and the international side, which develops liberalism beyond a purely Canadian context into a more global vision.

C.B. Macpherson's *Democracy in Alberta: Social Credit and the Party System*, for example, is a classic study of the tragic failure of the "radical experiment" in popular democracy in Prairie politics to overcome the ideological, class and psychological barriers of a dependent, capitalist society. This work is the first to chronicle the emergence of a radical experiment in popular democracy and its swift eclipse by the ascendant petit-bourgois world of capitalism in its liberal phase. It is this tension of the early, tragic encounter between the economic (capitalist) logic of liberalism and the political (democratic) logic of the Prairie populists that has shaped all Macpherson's thinking.

So too with George Grant's critique of liberalism as the "animating vision" of technological society in North America. Grant's first major publication — *Lament for a Nation* — bitterly yet eloquently criticizes the old, liberal elite of Montreal and Toronto for short-circuiting Canadian independence from the American dynamo. The tragic sense in *Lament for a Nation* derives from Grant's insight that Canadian liberal political leadership has simply adopted the American "technocratic" world view. All Grant's subsequent works — including his account of the liberal theory of justice in *English-speaking Justice* and his meditation on technology and power in *Technology and Empire* — are fundamentally a reflection on the "intimations of deprival" in the society of technological liberalism. The seeds for Grant's austere and searing account of modern liberalism in *Time as History* follow from his realization, articulated in *Lament for a Nation*, that liberalism has always been the "language of willing" in a universe that doesn't recognize human purpose as the animator of North American politics and economy.

In addition to Macpherson and Grant, two other articulate critics of liberalism must be acknowledged. Gad Horowitz wrote a brilliant interpretation of socialism, liberalism and conservatism in the Canadian context (*Canadian Labour in Politics*) and followed that triumph with an equally brilliant account of the cultural foundations of modern domination (*Repression: Basic and Surplus Repression in Psychoanalytic theory*). And Charles Taylor, perhaps Canada's most distinguished political philosopher, has translated a dualistic theory of liberalism in the Canadian context (*The Pattern of Politics*) into a deeper account of the origins of this dualism in Western political philosophy. Taylor's most famous philosophical study, *Hegel*, examines the deep split between romanticism (private life) and instrumentalism (public life) and expands upon the basic thematic criticism of liberal ideology established in *The Pattern of Politics* . In his article "The Villany of Liberalism: The Case of Charles Taylor," Aster has this to say about Taylor's place in the rejectionist wing on the question of liberalism: "Taylor has shown us that while we may indulge in romantically inspired rebellions against the dominant spirit of our liberal age, we can still not escape from it. We cannot shed our Enlightenment skin."

Quebec: Pluralist Socialism

Michael Weinstein, in a book on Fernand Dumont, one of Quebec's leading thinkers of the twentieth century, states that Dumont is "in his politics, an adherent of that characteristic tendency in French thought, pluralistic socialism, the great nineteenth-century expositor of which was Proudhon and which in the twentieth century has been expressed with greatest lucidity by Georges Gurvitch." The basis for Weinstein's remarks stems from the fact that all Dumont's theoretical writing is an attempt to develop a socialist theory that links the emergence of popular culture with an understanding of an ever-changing Quebec society.

Weinstein's comments about Dumont might be applied more generally to contemporary Quebec critical thought, which combines a culturally informed theory of politics with a politically mature analysis of social transformation. Reflecting the depth and profound originality of their nation's sociological tradition, Quebec political theorists have produced a series of popular, utopian and emancipatory analyses of Quebec's place in the New World, thereby interspersing their *political interpretations with superb accounts of Quebec society*.

Marcel Rioux, for example, has examined the question of Quebec's fate in the broadest and most historical of terms in *Québec in Question* and *Two Nations*. According to Rioux, to be a "Québécois is to agree to live dangerously" to the extent that Quebec's survival holds open the possibility of an entirely new culture appearing in North America. English Canadian political theorists might examine liberalism from all sides, but Quebec political theorists are actively thinking about how liberal society might be replaced by a socialist alternative, and how, in fact, *le virage technologie* might be resisted in the name of preservation of Quebec popular culture. Thus, Rioux's thought swings between the utopian (*La Question du Québec*) and fatalistic ("Québec, Québec"), between genuine admiration for other critical traditions in North America and bitter satire (*Pour rendre publiquement congé de quelques salauds*), reflecting the fact that in Quebec, unlike English Canada, political thought is a *living* part of popular culture. Other examples of this fact include Denis Monière, whose political theories concerning the defence of "small cultures" is of immediate political relevance in the face of the modernization of Quebec, and Jean-Guy Vaillancourt, Quebec's foremost scholar in the analysis of contemporary social movements and a leading political participant in the ecological and peace movements.

What lends special dynamism to Quebec political theory are the sharp oppositions that exist between contending schools of thought. The strategy of *autogestion*, as elaborated by Rioux, Lise Gauvin and others of the Quebec "cultural left," is highly contested. And what better exemplifies the opposing schools than a comparison of Gilles Bourque's *L'Etat capitaliste et la question nationale* and Rioux's *Two Nations*, or the contrast between the political analysis of *Les Cahiers du Socialism* (production focused, capital-logic) and that of *Possibles* (the primacy of cultural politics). Even individual Quebec thinkers shift back and forth, adopting radically different intellectual positions in response to ruptures in Quebec politics and society. Thus, for example, Nicole Laurin-Frenette may have written a classic book (using the political economy model) on the Quebec state — *Production de l'état et formes de la nation* (1978) — but her more recent writings, particularly her tragic and unforgettable reflections on the Quebec referendum — "Divertimento pour deux états" (1983) — evince a mind that is deeply existentialist. And, finally, two recent manifestos, *Pour un Québec socialist* (Le Comité des cent) and the *Black Rock Manifesto* (for a "Quebec that doesn't kill its poets"), show the breadth and depth of the Quebec political spectrum at a time of ferment and change.

Emergent Tendencies: The Feminist Challenge

Finally, this survey of Canadian political theoretical writings would be incomplete without mentioning one of the most influential developments: the emergence of critical writings in feminist theory and practice. Feminist discourse has been most notable for its provocative rethinking of gender and politics, including pornography, power, and the politics of reproduction. Feminist writings show the deep sexism of social and political thought and the ideological consequences that follow from a patriarchal political science and a male-stream politics. The reader should also consult the section concerning "Women" in this bibliography.

A. ENGLISH CANADA: REFUSING LIBERALISM

Canadian Journal of Political and Social Theory
"Beyond Dependency." 7 (Fall 1983). (Special journal issue.)

Christian, William
"A Note on Rod Preece and Red Tories." *Canadian Journal of Political and Social Theory* 2 (Spring-Summer 1978): 128-34. (The Red Tory debate.)

Crépeau, Paul-André, and Macpherson, C.B., eds.
The Future of Canadian Federalism. Toronto: University of Toronto Press, 1965.

Grant, George
English-Speaking Justice. The Josiah Wood Lectures, 1974. Sackville, N.B.: Mount Allison University, 1974.

Technology and Empire: Perspectives on North America. Toronto: Anansi, 1969.

Time as History. Massey Lectures. Series 9. Toronto: Canadian Broadcasting Corporation, 1969.

Lament for a Nation: The Defeat of Canadian Nationalism. Toronto: McClelland and Stewart, 1967.

"An Ethic of Community." *Social Purpose for Canada*, pp. 3-26. Edited by Michael Oliver. Toronto: University of Toronto Press, 1961.

Philosophy in the Mass Age. Vancouver: Copp Clark, 1959.

Horowitz, Gad
Repression: Basic and Surplus Repression in Psychoanalytic Theory: Freud, Reich & Marcuse. Toronto: University of Toronto Press, 1977.

Canadian Labour in Politics. Toronto: University of Toronto Press, 1968.

Horowitz, Gad, et al.
Canadian Political Culture: Essays. Canadian Dimension Kit no. 4. Winnipeg: Canadian Dimension, 1970.

Innis, Harold A.
Empire and Communications. Rev. by Mary Q. Innis. Toronto: University of Toronto Press, 1972.

The Strategy of Culture. Toronto: University of Toronto Press, 1952.

Macpherson, C.B.
The Life and Times of Liberal Democracy. Oxford: Oxford University Press, 1977.

Democratic Theory: Essays in Retrieval. Oxford: Clarendon Press, 1973.

Democracy in Alberta: Social Credit and the Party System. 2nd ed. Toronto: University of Toronto Press, 1968. (First edition 1953.)

The Real World of Democracy. Massey Lectures. Series 4. Toronto: C.B.C. Publications, 1965.

The Political Theory of Possessive Individualism, Hobbes to Locke. Oxford: Clarendon Press, 1962.

Macpherson, C.B., ed.
Property: Mainstream and Critical Positions. Toronto: University of Toronto Press, 1978.

Marchak, M. Patricia
Ideological Perspectives on Canada. 2nd ed. Toronto: McGraw-Hill Ryerson, 1981.

Preece, Rod
"Tory Myth and Conservative Reality: Horowitz Revisited." *Canadian Journal of Political and Social Theory* 2 (Winter 1978): 175-8. (The Red Tory debate.)

"Liberal-Conservatism & Feudalism in Canadian Politics: A Response to Christian." *Canadian Journal of Political and Social Theory* 2 (Spring-Summer 1978): 135-41. (The Red Tory debate.)

"The Myth of the Red Tory." *Canadian Journal of Political and Social Theory* 1 (Spring-Summer 1977): 3-28. (The Red Tory debate.)

Resnick, Philip
The Land of Cain: Class and Nationalism in English Canada 1945-1975. Vancouver: New Star Books, 1977.

Scott, Frank R.
Essays on the Constitution: Aspects of Canadian Law and Politics. Toronto: University of Toronto Press, 1977.

The Canadian Constitution and Human Rights. Four Radio Talks as Heard on CBC University of the Air. Toronto: Canadian Broadcasting Corporation, 1959.

Civil Liberties and Canadian Federalism. Alan B. Placent Memorial Lectures, 1959. Toronto: University of Toronto Press in cooperation with Carleton University, 1959.

Studies in Political Economy
"Rethinking Canadian Political Economy.", no. 6 (Autumn 1981). (Special journal issue.)

Taylor, Charles
Hegel. Cambridge, Eng.: Cambridge University Press, 1975.

Hegel and Modern Society. Cambridge, Eng.: Cambridge University Press, 1974.

"Interpretation and the Sciences of Man." *Review of Metaphysics* 25 (September 1971): 3-51.

"The Agony of Economic Man, Excerpt from *Essays on the Left*." *Canadian Forum* 51 (April-May 1971): 43-49.

The Pattern of Politics. Toronto: McClelland and Stewart, 1970.

"Neutrality in Political Science." *Philosophy, Politics and Society*, pp. 25-57. Third Series. Edited by Peter Laslett and W.C. Runciman. Oxford: Basil Blackwell, 1967.

"Nationalism and the Political Intelligentsia: A Case Study." *Queen's Quarterly* 72 (Spring 1965): 150-68.

The Explanation of Behaviour. London: Routledge & Kegan Paul, 1964.

Teeple, Gary, ed.
Capitalism and the National Question in Canada. Toronto: University of Toronto Press, 1972.

Trudeau, Pierre Elliott
A Time for Action: Toward the Renewal of the Canadian Federation. Ottawa: Government of Canada, 1978.

Conversation with Canadians. Toronto: University of Toronto Press, 1972.

Les Cheminements de la politique. Montréal: Editions du Jour, 1970.

Federalism and the French Canadians. Toronto: Macmillan, 1968; reprinted 1977.

Trudeau, Pierre Elliott, ed.
The Asbestos Strike. Toronto: James Lorimer, 1974. (First published 1956.)

Underhill, Frank
The Image of Confederation. The Massey Lectures, 3rd Series. Toronto: C.B.C. Publications, 1964.

In Search of Canadian Liberalism. Toronto: Macmillan, 1960.

Whitaker, Reginald
"Reason, Passion and Interest: Pierre Trudeau's Eternal Liberal Triangle." *Canadian Journal of Political and Social Theory* 4 (Winter 1980): 5-31.

B. QUEBEC: PLURALISTIC SOCIALISM

Adams, Danny; Fennario, David; Salmela, John; et al.
"Black Rock Manifesto." *Canadian Journal of Political and Social Theory* 6 (Winter 1982): 139-42. (A Quebec manifesto.)

Arnaud, Nicole, and Dofny, Jacques
Nationalism and the National Question. Montreal: Black Rose Books, 1977.

Boismenu, Gérard, et al.
Espace régional et nation: pour un nouveau débat sur le Québec. Montréal: Boréal Express, 1983.

Bourque, Gilles
L'Etat capitaliste et la question nationale. Montréal: Presses de l'Université de Montréal, 1977.

Question nationale et classes sociales au Québec (1760-1840). Montréal: Parti Pris, 1970.

Bourque, Gilles, et Dostaler, Gilles
Socialisme et indépendance. Montréal: Boréal Express, 1980.

Comité des Cent
"For a Socialist Québec." *Canadian Journal of Political and Social Theory* 6 (Winter 1982): 109-38. (A Quebec manifesto.)

Dion, Leon
Nationalismes et politique au Québec. Montréal: Hurtubise HMH, 1975.

La Prochaine Révolution. Montréal: Leméac, 1973. (English edition: *Quebec: The Unfinished Revolution.* Montreal: McGill-Queen's University Press, 1976.)

Dumont, Fernand
The Vigil of Quebec. Toronto: University of Toronto Press, 1974.

Dumont, Fernand; Montminy, Jean-Paul; et Hamelin, Jean, éds.
Idéologies au Canada français. 4 vols. Québec: Presses de l'Université Laval, 1971-1981. (See especially vol. 4: *Idéologies au Canada français, 1900-1929.* [1973].)

Fournier, Marcel
"Autour de la spécificité." *Possibles* 8:1 (1983): 85-114.

Freeman, Bill
"The Ecology Movement and the Radical Project, Ecology vs. Marxism."
Our Generation 13 (Fall 1979): 16-17.

Laurin-Frenette, Nicole
Classes et pouvoir: les théories fonctionnalistes. Montréal: Presses de l'Université de Montréal, 1978.

Production de l'état et formes de la nation. Montréal: Nouvelle optique, 1978.

Laurin-Frenette, Nicole, et Léonard, Jean-François, éds.
L'Impasse: enjeux et perspectives de l'après-référendum. Montréal: Nouvelle optique, 1980.

Monière, Denis
Le Développement des idéologies au Québec: des origines à nos jours. Montréal: Editions Québec/Amérique, 1977.

Morrow, Ray
"Deux Pays pour vivre: Critical Sociology and Canadian Political Economy."
Canadian Journal of Political and Social Theory 6 (Winter 1982): 61-105.

Rioux, Marcel
"Une Porte de plus en plus étroite." *Possibles* 8:1 (1983): 19-22.

"Québec, Québec (désillusions et espoirs)." *Possibles* 7:2 (1983): 103-11.

Pour prendre publiquement congé de quelques salauds Montréal: L'Hexagone, 1980.

Quebec in Question. 2nd ed. Toronto: James Lorimer, 1978. (First published 1969.)

"Sur l'évolution des idéologies au Québec." *Revue de l'Institut de sociologie* (Bruxelles), no. 1 (1968), pp. 95-124.

Rioux, Marcel, et Crean, Susan
Deux Pays pour vivre: un plaidoyer. Laval, Qué.: Editions coopératives Albert Saint-Martin, 1980.

Rocher, Guy
Le Québec en mutation. Montréal: Hurtubise HMH, 1973.

Roussopolos, Dimitri
"Root and Branch: The Political Origins of the 1960's New Left and the Future." *Our Generation* 14 (Summer-Fall 1980): 5-11.

Ryerson, Stanley B.
Le Capitalisme et la conféderation: aux sources du conflit Canada-Québec, 1760-1873. Montréal: Parti Pris, 1972.

Séguin, Maurice
L'Idée d'indépendence au Québec: genèse et historique. 2e éd. Trois-Rivières: Boréal Express, 1977.

Vaillancourt, Jean Guy
"The Ecology Question: Some Strategies: The Ecology Manifesto and the Growth of the Movement in Quebec." *Our Generation* 13 (Fall 1979): 5-7.

Vandycke, Robert
"La Question nationale: où en est la pensée marxist?" *Recherches sociographiques* 21 (janvier-août 1980): 97-129.

C. EMERGENT TENDENCIES: THE FEMINIST CHALLENGE

Alexander, Judith
"Women and Unpaid Work: The Economic Consequences." *Atlantis* 4 (Spring 1979): 200-11.

Alternate Routes
"Feminism." 6 (1983). (Special theme issue.)

Armstrong, Pat, and Armstrong, Hugh
"Beyond Sexless Class & Classless Sex: Towards Feminist Marxism." *Studies in Political Economy*, no. 10 (Winter 1983), pp. 7-43.

Briskin, Linda
"Toward a Socialist Feminist Movement." *Our Generation* 10 (Fall 1974): 23-35.

Canadian Journal of Political and Social Theory
"Feminism Now: Contemporary Feminist Theory and Practice." 10 (Winter/ Spring 1985). (Special theme issue.)

Clark, Lorenne M.G., and Lange, Lynda, eds.
The Sexism of Social and Political Theory: Women and Reproduction From Plato to Nietzsche. Toronto: University of Toronto Press, 1979.

Finn, Geraldine
"Women and the Ideology of Science." *Our Generation* 15 (Winter 1982): 40-50.

"Reason and Violence: More than a False Antithesis — A Mechanism of Patriarchal Power." *Canadian Journal of Political and Social Theory* 6 (Fall 1982): 162-8.

Fireweed: A Feminist Quarterly
"Lesbian Issue." 13 (July 1982). (Special theme issue.)

FitzGerald, Maureen; Guberman, Connie; Wolfe, Margie, eds.
Still Ain't Satisfied! Canadian Feminism Today. Toronto: Women's Press, 1982.

Fox, Bonnie, ed.
Hidden in the Household: Women's Domestic Labour Under Capitalism. Toronto: Women's Press, 1980.

Lamoureux, Diane
"Nationalisme et feminisme: impasses et coïncidences." *Possibles* 8:1 (1983): 43-59.

Miles, Angela
"Economism and Feminism." *Studies in Political Economy*, no. 11 (Summer 1983), pp. 197-209.

"The Integrative Feminine Principle in North American Feminism: Value Basis of a New Feminism." *Women's Studies International Quarterly* 4:4 (1981): 481-95.

Miles, Angela, and Finn, Geraldine, eds.
Feminism in Canada: From Pressure to Politics. Montreal: Black Rose Books, 1982.

O'Brien, Mary
The Politics of Reproduction. Boston: Routledge & Kegan Paul, 1981.

Room of One's Own
"Tessera." 8:4 (1984). (Special theme issue.)

Smith, Dorothy E., and Davids, Sara J., eds.
Women Look at Psychiatry. Vancouver: Press Gang, 1975.

Trofimenkoff, Susan, and Prentice, Alison, eds.
The Neglected Majority: Essays in Canadian Women's History. Toronto: McClelland and Stewart, 1977.

D. THE CRITIQUE OF LIBERALISM

Angus, Ian H.
"On Macpherson's Developmental Liberalism." *Canadian Journal of Political Science* 15 (March 1982): 145-50.

Badertscher, John
"The Prophecy of George Grant." *Canadian Journal of Political and Social Theory* 4 (Winter 1980): 183-9.

Box, Ian
"Reply: Thinking Through Technology." *Canadian Journal of Political Science* 16 (June 1983): 355-9.

"George Grant and the Embrace of Technology." *Canadian Journal of Political Science* 15 (September 1982): 503-15.

Carmichael, D.J.C.
"Reply: Macpherson vs. the Text of *Leviathan*." *Canadian Journal of Political Science* 16 (December 1983): 807-9.

"C.B. Macpherson's 'Hobbes': A Critique." *Canadian Journal of Political Science* 16 (March 1983): 61-80.

Christian, William
"George Grant and Love: A Commentary on Ian Box's 'George Grant and the Embrace of Technology'." *Canadian Journal of Political Science* 16 (June 1983): 349-54.

Horowitz, Gad
"Conservatism, Liberalism and Socialism in Canada: An Interpretation." *Canada: A Sociological Profile*, 2nd ed., pp. 8-23. Edited by W.E. Mann. Toronto: Copp Clark, 1971. (Original in *Canadian Journal of Economics and Political Science* 32 [May 1966]: 143-71.)

"Tories, Socialists and the Demise of Canada." *Canadian Dimension* 23 (1965).

Innis, H.A.
Political Economy in the Modern State. Toronto: Ryerson, 1946.

Kroker, Arthur
"Technological Dependency: George Grant as the Nietzche of the New World." *Technology and the Canadian Mind: Innis/McLuhan/Grant*. Montreal: New World Perspectives, 1984.

Macpherson, C.B.
"Leviathan Restored: A Response to Carmichael." *Canadian Journal of Political Science* 16 (December 1983): 795-805.

"Humanist Democracy and Elusive Marxism: A Response to Minogue and Svacek." *Canadian Journal of Political Science* 9 (September 1976): 422-30.

Mandel, Eli
"George Grant: Language, Nation, the Silence of God." *Canadian Literature*, no. 83 (Winter 1979), pp. 163-75. (Special issue: "Intellectual History".)

Minogue, K.R.
"Humanist Democracy: The Political Thought of C.B. Macpherson." *Canadian Journal of Political Science* 9 (September 1976): 377-94.

Noel, S.J.R.
"Domination and Myth in the Works of George Grant and C.B. Macpherson." *Dalhousie Review* 59 (Autumn 1979): 534-51.

Radwanski, George
Trudeau. Toronto: Macmillan, 1978.

Stewart, Walter
Shrug: Trudeau in Power. Toronto: New Press, 1971.

Svacek, Victor
"The Elusive Marxism of C.B. Macpherson." *Canadian Journal of Political Science* 9 (September 1976): 395-422.

Trudeau, Pierre Elliott
Les Cheminements de la politique. Montréal: Editions du Jour, 1970.

Weinstein, Michael A.
"Lament and Utopia: Responses to American Empire in George Grant and Leopoldo Zea." *Canadian Journal of Political and Social Theory* 5 (Fall 1981): 44-55.

E. NEW DIRECTIONS: TECHNOLOGY AND COMMUNICATIONS

Kroker, Arthur
Technology and the Canadian Mind: Innis/McLuhan/Grant. Montreal: New World Perspectives, 1984.

Leiss, William
The Limits to Satisfaction: An Essay on the Problem of Needs and Commodities. Toronto: University of Toronto Press, 1976.

The Domination of Nature. New York: G. Braziller, 1972.

Leiss, William, ed., for the University League for Social Reform
Ecology Versus Politics in Canada. Toronto: University of Toronto Press, 1979.

20

Canadian Education: Economics and Society

GEORGE MARTELL

The readings listed below have been gathered together under a very broad rubric that encompasses the wide range of economic, social, political and cultural forces at work in Canadian education. Included are many works not traditionally associated with the ''political economy'' of education, particularly within its Marxist parameters. These works emphasize the relations between modes of production, the state and education. I believe this material to be essential, however, given the relative weakness of the political economy tradition in terms of education and the contribution these works make to an understanding of the Canadian school system as a whole. There are, however, wide gaps in the subject areas covered, primarily because of space limitations, and my original list of some 360 items was whittled down to 100. Consequently, subsections on the critical history of schooling, school finance, Canadian universities, and childhood and schooling in Canadian literature were dropped and the remainder substantially cut. Furthermore, even the original list omitted a number of significant subject areas, including the interrelated topics of working-class curriculum, psycho- and socio-linguistics, and adult and union education. Finally, what is offered is far too Ontario-centred, while some of the provinces are grievously neglected. I intend to compile a more complete set of readings, to which readers of the *Guide* are invited to contribute. Please send further entries to me, c/o The Department of Social Science, Atkinson College, York University, Downsview, Ontario, M3J 2R7. The expanded list will be mailed out on request.

To the general selection of works in subsection A, I have added subsections that focus on subject areas that are coming under increasing scholarly and journalistic scrutiny. Subsection B, on minorities and the working class, reflects a growing focus on racial and class conflict in our schools, with particular emphasis on understanding the dynamic of oppression and resistance within the educational system. This theme links in with works included in subsection C, on women and education, where the concentration on women's schooling does not deny the necessity of integrating questions of gender, race and class if one is to understand the entirety of the educational system — a system produced in capitalist and imperial hegemony and in struggle against that hegemony. Subsection D focuses on Canadian teachers and, especially, on the growth of their union militancy during the last five decades. While this list indicates that teachers unions have been the most powerful opposition to government policies during this time, it also makes clear that this opposition has been articulated primarily within the framework of economic demands made at the bargaining table. Canadian teachers have yet to develop their long-run interests in power sharing and curriculum development. Similar studies on the growth of union militancy among the large numbers of "non-teaching" staff in our educational institutions have yet to be produced.

For their help in developing the original list, I would like to thank Willard Brehaut, Howard Buchbinder, Jane Gaskell, Beth Light, David Livingstone, Alison Prentice and Eleanor Smollett.

A. CANADIAN EDUCATION — ECONOMICS AND SOCIETY, POLITICS AND CULTURE

Axelrod, Paul
   "Cops in the Classroom — No Answer to Hall-Dennis." *This Magazine* 11 (March-April 1977): 12-15.

Berland, Jody, and McGee, Diane
   "The Literary Crisis: Beyond Banality and 'Basics' and Down to Business." *This Magazine* 12 (March 1978): 12-14.

Brown, Alan F.
   Changing School Districts in Canada. Toronto: Ontario Institute for Studies in Education, 1968.

Cameron, David
   Schools For Ontario: Policy-Making, Administration, and Finance in the 1960s. Toronto: University of Toronto Press, 1972.

Canada
   Review of Educational Policies in Canada. Paris: Organization for Economic Cooperation and Development, 1976.

Carleton, Richard A., Colley, Louise A; and MacKinnon, Neil J., eds.
   Education, Change and Society: A Sociology of Canadian Education. Toronto: Gage, 1977.

Chaiton, Alf, and McDonald, Neil, eds.
   Canadian Schools and Canadian Identity. Toronto: Gage, 1977.

Cistone, Peter J., ed.
   School Boards and the Political Fact: A Report on the Conference, The Politics of Education: Some Main Themes and Issues. Toronto: Ontario Institute for Studies in Education, 1972.

Close, D., and Bartels, B.
   "The Socializing Effects of Regime Supportive Textbooks." *Socialist Studies* 1:1 (1979). (Published by the Society for Socialist Studies, Winnipeg.)

Dupré, J. Stefan, et al.
   Federalism and Policy Development: The Case of Adult Occupational Training in Ontario. Toronto: University of Toronto Press, 1973.

Goulson, Cary F.
   A Source Book of Royal Commissions and Other Major Governmental Inquiries in Canadian Education, 1787-1978. Toronto: University of Toronto Press, 1981.

Harp, John
"Social Inequalities and the Transmission of Knowledge: The Case Against the Schools." *Structured Inequality in Canada*, pp. 219-46. Edited by John Harp and John R. Hofley. Scarborough, Ont.: Prentice-Hall, 1980.

Hodgetts, A.B.
What Culture? What Heritage? A Study of Civic Education in Canada. Toronto: Ontario Institute for Studies in Education, 1968.

Hodgetts, A.B., and Gallagher, Paul
Teaching Canada for the '80s. Toronto: Ontario Institute for Studies in Education, 1978.

Hodgson, Ernest D.
Federal Intervention in Public Education. Toronto: Canadian Education Association, 1976.

Ivany, J.W. George, and Manley-Casimir, Michael E., eds.
Federal-Provincial Relations: Education Canada. Papers Presented at the symposium Education Canada: Federal-Provincial Relations in Education, held at Simon Fraser University, Vancouver, B.C., February 1981. Toronto: OISE Press, 1981.

Katz, Joseph
Society, Schools and Progress in Canada. Oxford: Pergamon, 1969.

Lind, Loren Jay
The Learning Machine: A Hard Look at Toronto Schools. Toronto: Anansi, 1974.

Livingstone, David W.
"Class, Educational Ideologies and Mass Opinion in Capitalist Crisis." *Sociology of Education*, forthcoming.

Class Ideologies and Educational Futures. New York: International Publications Service, Falmer Press, 1983.

Lloyd, Woodrow Stanley
The Role of Government in Canadian Education. Quance Lectures in Canadian Education, 1959. Toronto: Gage, 1959.

Lorimer, James
"Canadian Textbooks and the American 'Knowledge Industry'." *This Magazine Is About Schools* 5 (Summer 1971): 47-57.

Martell, George
"Bureaucrats Are Beautiful or Learning (Still) to Love Your Keeper." *Mudpie* 1 (April 1980): 7, 16.

"Bureaucrats Are Beautiful or Learning to Love Your Keepers." *This Magazine* 9 (November-December 1975): 13-14.

"Community Control of the Schools: In New York and Toronto." *This Magazine Is About Schools* 4 (Summer 1970): 6-53.

Martell, George, ed.
The Politics of the Canadian Public School. Toronto: James Lorimer, 1974.

Morris, Lorenzo
"The Politics of Education and Language in Quebec: A Comparative Perspective." *Canadian and International Education* 5 (December 1976): 1-36.

Myers, Doug, ed.
The Failure of Educational Reform in Canada. Toronto: McClelland and Stewart, 1973.

Nelson, Randle W., and Nock, David, eds.
Reading, Writing and Riches: Education and the Socio-Economic Order in North America. Toronto: Between the Lines, 1978.

Olsen, C. Paul
"Inequality Remade: The Theory of Correspondence and the Context of French Immersion in Northern Ontario." *Journal of Education* (Boston), no. 165 (Winter 1983), pp. 75-98.

Pammett, Jon H.
"The Development of Political Orientations in Canadian School Children." *Canadian Journal of Political Science* 4 (March 1971): 132-41.

Pitman, Walter G.
"The Limits to Diversity: The Separate School Issue in the Politics of Ontario." *Government and Politics of Ontario*. Edited by Donald C. MacDonald. Toronto: Macmillan, 1975.

Point [St. Charles] Improvement of Education Committee
"Organizing English Parents in Point St. Charles, Montreal." *This Magazine Is About Schools* 6 (Summer 1972): 6-30.

Repo, Satu, ed.
This Book Is About Schools. New York: Pantheon Books, 1970.

Schecter, Stephen
"Capitalism, Class and Educational Reform in Canada." *The Canadian State: Political Economy and Political Power*, pp. 373-416. Edited by Leo Panitch. Toronto: University of Toronto Press, 1977.

Stamp, Robert M.
"Government and Education in Post-War Canada. *Canadian Education: A History*, pp. 444-70. Edited by J. Donald Wilson. Scarborough, Ont.: Prentice-Hall, 1970.

Stevenson, Hugh A., and Wilson, J. Donald, comps. and eds.
Precepts, Policy and Process: Perspectives on Contemporary Canadian Education. London, Ont.: Alexander, Blake Associates, 1977.

Symons, T.H.B.
The Symons Report. 1 vol. abridged. Toronto: McClelland and Stewart, 1977. (An abridged version of the first two volumes of *To Know Ourselves: The Report of the Commission on Canadian Studies*. By T.H.B. Symons. Ottawa: AUCC, 1976.)

Wallin, J.H.A., ed.
The Politics of Canadian Education. Canadian Society for the Study of Education. Yearbook, vol. 4. Edmonton: Canadian Society for the Study of Education, 1977.

Wilson, J. Donald, ed.
Canadian Education in the 1980s. Calgary: Detselig Enterprises, 1981.

Zureik, Elia, and Pike, Robert M., eds.
Socialization and Values in Canadian Society. Vol. 1. The Carleton Library, no. 84. Toronto: McClelland and Stewart, 1975.

B. MINORITIES AND THE WORKING CLASS IN CANADIAN SCHOOLS

Anisef, Paul; Paasche, J. Gottfried; and Turritin, Anton H.
Is the Die Cast?: Educational Achievements and Work Destinations of Ontario Youth: A Six-Year Follow-Up of the Critical Juncture High Schools Students. Toronto: Ontario Ministry of Colleges and Universities, 1980.

Ashworth, Mary
The Forces Which Shaped Them: A History of the Education of Minority Group Children in British Columbia. Vancouver: New Star Books, 1979.

Immigrant Children and Canadian Schools. Toronto: McClelland and Stewart, 1975.

Davis, Bob
"Sifted, Sorted, Slotted and Streamed: How the Schools Manage to Divide Students into the Same Socio-Economic Groups They're in outside School Walls." *Mudpie* 4 (February 1983): 7-9, 12, 17.

Hall, Oswald, and Carlton, Richard
Basic Skills at School and Work: The Study of Albertown, an Ontario Community. Occasional Paper no. 1. Toronto: Ontario Economic Council, 1977.

Hull, Jeremy
Natives in a Class Society. 2nd ed. Saskatoon: One Sky, 1983.

Jiles, Paulette
"Reverend Wilson and the Ojibway Grammar." *This Magazine* 10 (February-March 1976): 15-17.

King, Alan J.C., et al.
Occupational/Vocational Education in Ontario Schools. Toronto: Provincial Research Committee, Ontario Secondary School Teachers' Federation, 1981.

MacFarquhar, Meredith
"A Highschool Teacher Looks at the Problem of Student 'Troublemakers'." *Mudpie* 4 (January 1984): 3-5, 16.

Martell, George
"Class Biased Streaming in Toronto Schools: A Note on Self-Contained and Part-Time Special Education." *Mudpie* 3 (October 1982): 9-11.

"Working Class Literacy: The Key Issue for N.D.P. Education Organizing: A Speech." *Mudpie* 3 (January 1982):.13-15, 18.

McDiarmid, Garnet, and Pratt, David
Teaching Prejudice: A Content Analysis of Social Studies Textbooks Authorized for Use in Ontario. A Report to the Human Rights Commission. Toronto: Ontario Institute for Studies in Education, 1971.

Osborne, Kenneth W.
"Hard-Working Temperate and Peaceable" — *The Portrayal of Workers in Canadian History Textbooks.* Edited by Alexander Gregor and Keith Wilson. Winnipeg: University of Manitoba, 1980.

Park School Community Council Brief
"Class Bias in Toronto Schools." *This Magazine Is About Schools* 5 (Fall/Winter 1971): 6-35.

Pelletier, Wilfrid
"Childhood in an Indian Village." *This Magazine Is About Schools* 3 (Spring 1969): 6-23.

Samuda, Ronald J.; Berry, John W.; and Laferrière, Michel, eds.
Multiculturalism in Canada: Social and Educational Perspectives. Toronto: Allyn & Bacon, 1983.

Simon, Roger I.
"But Who Will Let You Do It? Counter-Hegemonic Possibilities for Work Education." *Journal of Education* (Boston), no. 165 (Summer 1983), pp. 235-56.

Thomas, Barbara
"Lost in the Jungles of Multiculturalism: Immigrant Children and Canadian Schools: A Review." *This Magazine* 10 (February/March 1976): 8-9.

Wilson, J. Donald
"'No Blanket to be Worn in School': The Education of Indians in Early Nineteenth-Century Ontario." *Histoire sociale/Social History* 7 (November 1974): 293-305.

C. WOMEN AND EDUCATION

Collectif Clio
L'Histoire des femmes au Québec depuis quatre siècles. Par Micheline Dumont et al. Montréal: Les Quinze, 1982.

Dumont-Johnson, Micheline
"Des gardéries au XIXe siècle: les salles d'asile des Soeurs Grises à Montréal." *Revue d'histoire de l'Amérique française* 34 (juin 1980): 27-55.

Fahmy-Eid, Nadia, et Dumont, Micheline, éds.
Maîtresses de maison, maîtresses d'école: femmes, familles et education dans l'histoire du Québec. Montréal: Boréal Express, 1983.

Gaskell, Jane
"Gender and Course Choice: The Orientation of Male and Female Students." *Journal of Education* (Boston), no. 166 (Winter 1984), pp. 89-102.

"Education and Women's Work: Some New Research Directions." *Alberta Journal of Educational Research* 29 (September 1983): 224-41.

"The Social Construction of Skill Through Schooling: Implications for Women." *Atlantis* 8 (Spring 1983): 11-26.

Kojder, Apolonja Maria
"The Saskatoon Women Teachers' Association: A Demand for Recognition." *Shaping the Schools of the Canadian West*, pp. 177-91. Edited by David C. Jones, Nancy M. Sheehan, and Robert M. Stamp. Calgary: Detselig Enterprises, 1979.

Leduc, Constance
"Les Orientations des femmes à l'Université de Montréal en 1949-50 et en 1974-75." *Canadian and International Education* 7 (June 1978): 51-58.

Lewis, Norah L.
"Creating the Little Machine: Child Rearing in British Columbia, 1919-1939." *BC Studies*, no. 56 (Winter 1982-1983), pp. 44-60.

Prentice, Alison

"Towards a Feminist History of Women and Education." *Approaches to Educational History*, pp. 39-64. Edited by David C. Jones et al. Winnipeg: University of Manitoba, 1981.

"The Feminization of Teaching in British North America and Canada, 1845-1875." *Histoire sociale/Social History* 8 (May 1975): 5-20.

Shack, Sybil

The Two-Thirds Minority: Women in Canadian Education. Toronto: Guidance Centre, Faculty of Education, University of Toronto, 1973.

Sheehan, Nancy M.

"Temperance, Education and the WCTU in Alberta, 1905-1930." *Journal of Educational Thought* 14 (August 1980): 108-24.

Smith, Dorothy E.

"An Analysis of Ideological Structures and How Women Are Excluded: Considerations for Academic Women." *Canadian Review of Sociology and Anthropology* 12 (November 1975): 353-69.

D. CANADIAN TEACHERS

Bernier, Lucie, et al.

La Lutte syndicale chez les enseignants. Montréal: Parti Pris, 1973.

Centrale de l'enseignement du Québec

Ecole et luttes de classes au Québec. 2e éd. Ste-Foy: la Centrale, 1974. (Translation and adaptation of chapter three by Marg Bacon can be found in *This Magazine* 9 [July-August 1975]: 11-13 under the title, "Capitalist Ideology in the Schools: A CEQ Document.")

Charbonneau, Yvon

"Teachers, Workers and the Fiscal Squeeze: A View From Quebec." *Mudpie* 5 (March 1984): 4.

"Reflections and a Retrospective; An Interview with Pauline Vaillancourt and George Martell." *This Magazine* 13 (July/August 1979): 12-16.

Quotidiennement...chaque jour. [Rapport moral du président.] Québec: Corporation des enseignants du Québec, 1972.

Danylewycz, Marta, and Prentice, Alison

"Lessons From the Past: TheExperience of Women Teachers in Quebec and Ontario." *Women and Education: World Yearbook of Education.* Edited by Sandra Acker (guest editor) and Jacquetta Megarry (series editor). London: Kogan Page, 1984.

French, Doris Cavelle Martin

High Button Bootstraps: Federation of Women Teachers' Associations of Ontario, 1918-1968. Toronto: Ryerson, 1968.

Gaulin, Robert

"An Interview with Robert Gaulin: The President of the CEQ Talks with Pauline Vaillancourt and George Martell." *This Magazine* 13 (May/June 1979): 15-21.

Hennessy, Peter H.

Schools in Jeopardy: Collective Bargaining in Education. Toronto: McClelland and Stewart, 1979.

Kuehn, Larry
"From Ontario, the B.C. School Scene Looks Bad. From Here It Looks Worse." *Mudpie* 5 (March 1984): 5.

Manzer, Ronald
"Selective Inducements and the Development of Pressure Groups: The Case of Canadian Teachers' Associations." *Canadian Journal of Political Science* 2 (March 1969): 103-17.

Myers, Doug
"Teachers and Politics." *This Magazine* 11 (October 1977): 12-15.

"The Teaching 'Profession'? A Demystification." *This Magazine* 11 (May/June 1977): 14-16.

Radecki, Henry, and Evans, Susan
The Teachers' Strike Study: Sudbury, Ontario, 1980. Toronto: Ontario Ministry of Education, 1982.

Repo, Satu
"B.C. Teachers Turn Political." *This Magazine Is About Schools* 6 (Fall 1972): 8-12, 14-30.

Robinson, Stephen G.B.
Do Not Erase: The Story of O.S.S.T.F. Toronto: Ontario Secondary School Teachers' Federation, 1971.

Wilson, J. Donald
"The Teacher in Early Ontario." *Aspects of Nineteenth-Century Ontario*, pp. 218-36. Edited by F.H. Armstrong, H.A. Stevenson, and J.D. Wilson. Essays Presented to James J. Talman. Toronto: University of Toronto Press, 1974.

21

Political Parties

REG WHITAKER

The renewed interest in Marxist political economy has not extended itself to the consideration of the role of political parties within the structures of capitalist democracy. There is no shortage of pluralist literature on parties, but when one turns to political economy, two limitations immediately present themselves. First, much time has been spent on questions of the revolutionary party and on critiques of social democratic parties, but little time has been given to analyzing the much more successful bourgeois parties. Second, the renewed attention to the capitalist state has inspired very little work on the role of parties in the functioning of the state. There has been a lamentable tendency for Marxist political economy to lapse into moralistic denunciations of parties for "failing" to do this or that task assigned them by the theorist, or for mystifying the "true" consciousness of the proletariat. Such moralism is of little help in analysis. Consequently, many of the entries in this section are not by political economists at all, but by pluralists. Anyone wishing to master the issues here will have to read more pluralist writing than political economy.

One political economy approach that has had some currency is that of the "public choice" school. Inspired by Schumpeter's *Capitalism, Socialism and Democracy* over forty years ago, its classic formulation is found in Anthony Downs's *An Economic Theory of Democracy* (1957). Modelled on microeconomic theory, this school suggests that the behaviour of political parties can be predicted on the assumption that they are economically rational actors. Albert Breton's *The Economic Theory of Representative Government* (1974) is the leading Canadian statement on this theory. Public choice theory is not without its insights, but its conservative political colouration, its ahistorical bias and its unrealistic assumptions of perfect political competition have not commended it to Marxist political economists.

In fact, it is the historical dimension of the evolution of the party system that inspired the important exploratory work of Brodie and Jenson, *Crisis, Challenge and Change*. They explain the evolution of the party system, and, in particular, the failure of the CCF-NDP to achieve major party status, by a historical analysis of class forces; they emphasize the autonomous role of parties in shaping the way class issues are played out in the political system. More detailed historical work on the Liberals (Whitaker, *The Government Party* and Smith, *The Regional Decline of a National Party*) and the Conservatives (English, *The Decline of Politics*) gives some scholarly base from which larger generalizations remain to be drawn. Indeed, while there is much important literature on third parties (Macpherson's *Democracy in Alberta* and Lipset's *Agrarian Socialism* are classics), there seems compelling reason for Canadian political economy to concentrate more energy on the Liberal and Conservative parties — in the sense that it is *here* that the important clues to the activities of the federal and provincial states are to be found.

Another distinctively Canadian focus to the study of parties is the effect of federalism. Some areas have been explored (Whitaker and Smith on the Liberals; Smiley, *Canada in Question*, and Stevenson, *Unfulfilled Union*, in general) but much remains to be done. Party ideology is another area that should be rescued from the hands of idealist writers.

Perhaps the most underdeveloped area of all is that of interest groups and their intersection with political parties. This area needs much hard empirical research in order to elucidate the exact mechanisms of influence between private wealth and public power.

Empirical work, of course, requires theory to guide it. There is no doubt that theory of political parties remains badly underdeveloped in Canadian political economy (and in other countries as well). As political economy shifts from economic analysis to a new interest in cultural, ideological and political questions, it is to be hoped that this change of emphasis will result in a certain concentration on the role of political parties.

Abella, Irving
  Nationalism, Communism and Canadian Labour: The CIO, the Communist Party, and the Canadian Congress of Labour, 1935-1956. Toronto: University of Toronto Press, 1973.

Allen, Richard
  The Social Passion: Religion and Social Reform in Canada, 1914-1928. Toronto: University of Toronto Press, 1971.

Avakumovic, Ivan
  The Communist Party in Canada: A History. Toronto: McClelland and Stewart, 1975.

Beck, J.M.
  Pendulum of Power: Canada's Federal Elections. Scarborough, Ont.: Prentice-Hall, 1968.

Bourque, Gilles
  "Class, Nation and the Parti Québécois." *Studies in Political Economy*, no. 2 (Autumn 1979), pp. 129-58.

Breton, Albert
  The Economic Theory of Representative Government. London: Macmillan, 1974.

Brodie, M. Janine, and Jenson, Jane
  Crisis, Challenge and Change: Party and Class in Canada. Toronto: Methuen, 1980.

Buck, Tim
  Yours in the Struggle: Reminiscences of Tim Buck. Edited by William Beeching and Phyllis Clarke. Toronto: NC Press, 1977.

  Thirty Years, 1922-1952: The Story of the Communist Movement. Toronto: Progress Books, 1952.

Bullen, John
"The Ontario Waffle and the Struggle for an Independent Socialist Canada: Conflict Within the NDP." *Canadian Historical Review* 64 (June 1983): 188-215.

Canadian Dimension
"The NDP and the Waffle." (Special Supplement) 7 (April 1971).

Caplan, Gerald L.
The Dilemma of Canadian Socialism: The CCF in Ontario. Toronto: McClelland and Stewart, 1973.

Chi, N.H.
"Class Voting in Canadian Politics." *The Canadian Political Process: A Reader.* Rev. ed., pp. 226-47. Edited by O.S. Kruhlack et al. Toronto: Holt, Rinehart and Winston, 1973.

Clarke, Harold D., et al.
Political Choice in Canada. Toronto: McGraw-Hill Ryerson, 1979.

Conway, John
"Populism in the United States, Russia, and Canada: Explaining the Roots of Canada's Third Parties." *Canadian Journal of Political Science* 9 (March 1978): 99-124.

Creighton, D.
John A. Macdonald. 2 vols. Toronto: Macmillan, 1955.

Cross, Michael
The Decline and Fall of a Good Idea: CCF-NDP Manifestoes, 1932-1969. Toronto: New Hogtown Press, 1974.

Elkins, David J., and Simeon, Richard
Small Worlds: Parties and Provinces in Canadian Political Life. Toronto: Methuen, 1980.

Engelman, Frederick C., and Schwartz, Mildred A.
Canadian Political Parties: Origin, Character, Impact. Scarborough, Ont.: Prentice-Hall, 1975.

English, John
The Decline of Politics: The Conservatives and the Party System 1901-20. Toronto: University of Toronto Press, 1977.

Ferns, Henry, and Ostry, Bernard
The Age of Mackenzie King. Toronto: James Lorimer, 1976. (First published 1955.)

Finkel, Alvin
"Populism and the Proletariat: Social Credit and the Alberta Working Class." *Studies in Political Economy*, no. 13 (Spring 1984), pp. 109-35.

Gonick, Cy
"Schreyer's New Democrats." *Canadian Dimension* 9:6 (July 1973): 5-7.

"Socialism and the Economics of Growthmanship." *Essays on the Left: Essays in Honour of T.C. Douglas*, pp. 135-59. Edited by L. Lapierre et al. Toronto: McClelland and Stewart, 1971.

Gordon, Walter Lockhart
A Political Memoir. Toronto: McClelland and Stewart, 1977.

Graham, R.
Arthur Meighen. Toronto: Clarke, Irwin, 1960.

Granatstein, J.L.
Canada's War: The Politics of the Mackenzie King Government, 1939-45. Toronto: Oxford University Press, 1975.

The Politics of Survival: The Conservative Party of Canada, 1939-1945. Toronto: University of Toronto Press, 1967.

Horowitz, Gad
Canadian Labour in Politics. Toronto: University of Toronto Press, 1968.

"Tories, Socialists and the Demise of Canada." *Canadian Dimension* 2 (May 1965): 12-15.

Howell, Colin
"The Maritimes and Canadian Political Culture." *Acadiensis* 8 (Autumn 1979): 107-14.

Irvine, William
The Farmers in Politics. The Carleton Library, no. 114. Toronto: McClelland and Stewart, 1976. (First published 1920.)

Irving, John
The Social Credit Movement in Alberta. Toronto: University of Toronto Press, 1959.

Kilbourn, William
Pipeline: TransCanada and the Great Debate: A History of Business and Politics. Toronto: Clarke, Irwin, 1970.

Laxer, James, and Laxer, Robert
The Liberal Idea of Canada: Pierre Trudeau and the Question of Canada's Survival. Toronto: James Lorimer, 1977.

Lewis, David
Louder Voices: The Corporate Welfare Bums. Toronto: James Lorimer, 1972.

Lipset, Seymour Martin
Agrarian Socialism: The Cooperative Commonwealth Federation in Saskatchewan: A Study in Political Sociology. Rev. ed. Berkeley: University of California Press, 1971. (First published 1950.)

Macpherson, C.B.
The Life and Times of Liberal Democracy. Oxford: Oxford University Press, 1977.

Democratic Theory: Essays in Retrieval. Oxford: Clarendon Press, 1973.

Democracy in Alberta: Social Credit and the Party System. 2nd ed. Toronto: University of Toronto Press, 1968. (First edition 1955.)

The Real World of Democracy. The Massey Lectures, 4th series. Toronto: C.B.C. Publications, 1965.

Mallory, J.R.
Social Credit and the Federal Power in Canada. Toronto: University of Toronto Press, 1977. (First published 1954.)

Marchak, M. Patricia
Ideological Perspectives on Canada. 2nd ed. Toronto: McGraw-Hill Ryerson, 1981.

Martin, Patrick; Gregg, Allan; and Perlin, George
  Contenders: The Tory Quest for Power. Scarborough, Ont.: Prentice-Hall, 1983.

McCall-Newman, Christina
  Grits: An Intimate Portrait of the Liberal Party. Toronto: Macmillan, 1982.

McKenty, Neil
  Mitch Hepburn. Toronto: McClelland and Stewart, 1967.

McNaught, Kenneth
  A Prophet in Politics: A Biography of J.S. Woodsworth. Toronto: University of Toronto Press, 1959.

Meisel, John
  Cleavages, Parties and Values in Canada. London: Sage Publications, 1974.

  Working Papers on Canadian Politics. Enl. ed. Montreal: McGill-Queen's University Press, 1973.

  Papers on the 1962 Election. Toronto: University of Toronto Press, 1964.

Menzies, J.
  "Votes for Saskatchewan Women." *Politics in Saskatchewan*, pp. 78-92. Edited by Norman Ward and Duff Spafford. Toronto: Longmans, 1969.

Morton, Desmond Paul
  NDP: Social Democracy in Canada. New and rev. 2nd ed. Toronto: Hakkert, 1977. (First published 1974 under title: *NDP: The Dream of Power*.)

Morton, W.L.
  The Progessive Party in Canada. Toronto: University of Toronto Press, 1950.

Naylor, R.T.
  "The Ideological Foundations of Social Democracy and Social Credit." *Capitalism and the National Question in Canada*, pp. 251-6. Edited by G. Teeple. Toronto: University of Toronto Press, 1972.

Newman, Peter
  Renegade in Power: The Diefenbaker Years. The Carleton Library, no. 70. Toronto: McClelland and Stewart, 1973.

  Distemper of Our Times: Canadian Politics in Transition: 1963-1968. Toronto: McClelland and Stewart, 1968.

Ostry, Bernard
  "Conservatives, Liberals and Labour in the 1870's." *Canadian Historical Review* 41 (June 1960): 93-127.

Paltiel, K.Z.
  Political Party Financing in Canada. Toronto: McGraw-Hill, 1970.

Penner, Norman
  The Canadian Left: A Critical Analysis. Scarborough, Ont.: Prentice-Hall, 1977.

Penniman, Howard R., ed.
  Canada at the Polls, 1979 and 1980: A Study of the General Elections. A.E.I. Studies, no. 345. Washington, D.C.: American Enterprise Institute for Public Policy Research, 1981.

  Canada at the Polls: The General Election of 1974. Foreign Affairs Study, no. 24. Washington, D.C.: American Enterprise Institute for Public Policy Research, 1975.

Perlin, George C.
The Tory Syndrome: Leadership Politics in the Progressive Conservative Party.
Montreal: McGill-Queen's University Press, 1980.

Pinard, Maurice
The Rise of a Third Party: A Study in Crisis Politics. Scarborough, Ont.:
Prentice-Hall, 1971.

Pratt, Larry, and Stevenson, Garth, eds.
Western Separatism: The Myths, Realities & Dangers. Edmonton: Hurtig,
1981.

Pross, A. Paul, ed.
Pressure Group Behaviour in Canadian Politics. Scarborough, Ont.: McGraw-
Hill Ryerson, 1975.

Quinn, Herbert
The Union Nationale: A Study in Quebec Nationalism. Toronto: University
of Toronto Press, 1963.

Richards, John
"Populism: A Qualified Defence." *Studies in Political Economy*, no. 5 (Spring
1981), pp. 5-27.

Robin, Martin
Radical Politics and Canadian Labour, 1880-1930. Kingston, Ont.: Industrial
Relations Centre, Queen's University, 1968.

Robin, Martin, ed.
Canadian Provincial Politics: The Party Systems of the Ten Provinces. 2nd
ed. Scarborough, Ont.: Prentice-Hall, 1978.

Saywell, John
The Rise of the Parti Québécois, 1967-1976. Toronto: University of Toronto
Press, 1977.

Sharp, Paul F.
*The Agrarian Revolt in Western Canada: A Survey Showing American Paral-
lels.* Minneapolis: University of Minnesota Press, 1948.

Smart, John
"Populist and Socialist Movements in Canadian History." *Canada, Ltd.: The
Political Economy of Dependency*, pp. 197-212. Edited by Robert Laxer.
Toronto: McClelland and Stewart, 1973.

Smith, David E.
The Regional Decline of a National Party: Liberals on the Prairies. Toronto:
University of Toronto Press, 1981.

Prairie Liberalism: The Liberal Party in Saskatchewan 1905-71. Toronto:
University of Toronto Press, 1975.

Smith, Denis
Gentle Patriot: A Political Biography of Walter Gordon. Edmonton: Hurtig,
1973.

Stein, Michael B.
*The Dynamics of Right-Wing Protest: A Political Analysis of Social Credit in
Quebec.* Toronto: University of Toronto Press, 1973.

Stewart, Ian
"Of Customs and Coalitions: The Formation of Canadian Federal Parlia-

Stewart, Ian (con'd)
mentary Alliances.'' *Canadian Journal of Political Science* 13 (September 1980): 451-79.

Thorburn, Hugh
"Pressure Groups in Canadian Politics." *Canadian Journal of Political Science* 30 (May 1964): 157-74.

Thorburn, Hugh, ed.
Party Politics in Canada. 4th ed. Scarborough, Ont.: Prentice-Hall, 1979.

Underhill, Frank
In Search of Canadian Liberalism. Toronto: Macmillan, 1960.

Wearing, Joseph
The L-Shaped Party: The Liberal Party of Canada 1958-1980. Toronto: McGraw-Hill Ryerson, 1981.

Whitaker, Reginald
"The Liberal Party and the Canadian State." *Acadiensis* 12 (Autumn 1982): 145-63.

"Reason, Passion and Interest: Pierre Trudeau's Eternal Liberal Triangle." *Canadian Journal of Political and Social Theory* 4 (Winter 1980): 5-31.

"Political Thought and Political Action in Mackenzie King." *Journal of Canadian Studies* 13 (Winter 1978-79): 40-60.

The Government Party: Organizing and Financing the Liberal Party of Canada 1930-58. Toronto: University of Toronto Press, 1977.

Wise, S.F.
"Conservatism and Political Development: The Canadian Case." *South Atlantic Quarterly* 69 (Spring 1970): 226-43.

Wiseman, Nelson
Social Democracy in Manitoba: A History of the CCF-NDP. Winnipeg: University of Manitoba Press, 1983.

Wood, Louis Aubrey
A History of Farmers' Movements in Canada. Toronto: University of Toronto Press, 1975. (First published 1924.)

Young, Walter D.
The Anatomy of a Party: The National C.C.F., 1932-61. Toronto: University of Toronto Press, 1969.

Zakuta, Leo
A Protest Movement Becalmed: A Study of Change in the CCF. Canadian Studies in Sociology. Toronto: University of Toronto Press, 1964.

22

Federalism

GARTH STEVENSON

Federalism, both as a structural and a social phenomenon, has preoccupied Canadian social scientists, lawyers and historians since 1867. The preoccupation has been greatest at times when conflict between federal and provincial governments has risen to abnormally high levels, symptomatic of underlying stresses and strains, or of the difficulty in adapting old state structures to new circumstances. In their writings, Innis and Mackintosh, the leading representatives of the "old" political economy tradition, both referred to the difficulty of adapting Canadian federalism to the economic changes that occurred during the period between the two world wars. J.R. Mallory's brilliant study, *Social Credit and the Federal Power in Canada* a book Donald V. Smiley has aptly termed the best ever written on the subject of Canadian federalism, offers a retrospective look at the same subject and acknowledges its author's debt to Innis.

More recently, Canadian federalism has been affected by Quebec's Quiet Revolution, the rise of the Parti Québécois, the conflict between petroleum-producing and petroleum-importing regions of Canada from 1972 onwards, the overhaul of the formal Constitution, culminating in the "patriation" of 1982, and the so-called "western alienation" represented by the Progressive Conservative government of Alberta. These developments coincided with the revival of political economy and its increasing association with Marxism, and attracted the attention of the new generation of political economists. In recent years, most left-wing political economists have been rather uncritically sympathetic towards Quebec nationalism, and hostile towards the central government's efforts to contain it within a federal framework. Some have even sympathized with the "regionalism" promoted by anglophone provincial governments, led by ultra-conservative Alberta. The field of political economy has thus become somewhat polarized between "centralists" and "provincialists."

The major themes that run through the political economy literature on Canadian federalism are listed below, accompanied by the names of a few representative authors.

- The nature of Confederation as a historical event, particularly the class forces involved (Creighton, Naylor, Ryerson, Scott, White).
- The impact of various staple commodities, particularly natural resources falling under provincial ownership and control, on federal-provincial relations (Armstrong, Faucher, Innis, Lithwick, Mackintosh).
- External influences, particularly that of the United States, on the Canadian federal system (Innis, Mackintosh, Mallory, Naylor, Stevenson).

- Uneven development and regional underdevelopment (Bercuson, Boismenu, Faucher, Henry, Pratt and Stevenson).
- The class forces that contribute to both centrifugal and centripetal tendencies in Canadian federalism (Armstrong, Boismenu, Morrison, Stevenson, Trudeau).
- The consequences of having federal, as opposed to unitary, state structures (Corry, Mallory, Simeon, Smiley, Stevenson).

The bibliography that follows includes some works on federalism that are possibly beyond the boundaries of "political economy," whether defined as a school of thought or as a field of study. Because federalism is associated with so many aspects of Canadian life, readers should also refer to other sections of this guide, notably "Resources and Staples," "Imperialism and Dependency," "British Columbia," "The Prairies," "Atlantic Canada" and "Quebec."

Armstrong, Christopher
The Politics of Federalism: Ontario's Relations with the Federal Government, 1867-1942. Toronto: University of Toronto Press, 1981.

Arnopoulos, Sheila McLeod, and Clift, Dominique
The English Fact in Canada. 2nd ed. Kingston, Ont.: McGill-Queen's University Press, 1984.

Banting, Keith G.
The Welfare State and Canadian Federalism. Kingston, Ont.: McGill-Queen's University Press, 1982.

Banting, Keith G., and Simeon, Richard, eds.
And No One Cheered: Federalism, Democracy and the Constitutional Act. Toronto: Methuen, 1983.

Bercuson, David J., ed.
Canada and the Burden of Unity. Toronto: Macmillan, 1977.

Black, Edwin, R.
Divided Loyalties: Canadian Concepts of Federalism. Montreal: McGill-Queen's University Press, 1975.

Boismenu, Gérard
Le Duplessisme: politique économique et rapports de force, 1944-1960. Presses de l'Université de Montréal, 1981.

Boismenu, Gérard, et al.
Espace régional et nation: pour un nouveau débat sur le Québec. Montréal: Boréal Express, 1983.

Burns, Ronald M.
The Acceptable Mean: The Tax Rental Agreements, 1941-1962. Financing Canadian Federation, no. 3. Toronto: Canadian Tax Foundation, 1980.

Byers, R.B., and Reford, Robert W, eds.
Canada Challenged: The Viability of Confederation. Toronto: Canadian Institute of International Affairs, 1979.

Cairns, Alan C.
"The Governments and Societies of Canadian Federalism." *Canadian Jour-*

nal of Political Science 10 (December 1977): 695-725.

"The Judicial Committee and its Critics." *Canadian Journal of Political Science* 4 (September 1971): 301-45.

Canada. Parliament. House of Commons. Special Committee on the Federal-Provincial Fiscal Arrangements.
Fiscal Federalism in Canada: Report. Ottawa: The Task Force, 1981.

Canada. Parliament. Senate
Report Pursuant to Resolution of the Senate to the Honourable Speaker by the Parliamentary Counsel, Relating to the Enactment of the British North America Act, 1867, Any Lack of Consonance between Its Terms and Judicial Construction of Them and Cognate Matters. Ottawa: King's Printer, 1939.

Canada. Royal Commission on Dominion-Provincial Relations
The Rowell-Sirois Report: An Abridgement of Book 1 of the Commission Report. Edited and introduced by Donald V. Smiley. Toronto: McClelland and Stewart, 1963. (Report first published 1940.)

Canada. Task Force on Canadian Unity
A Future Together: Observations and Recommendations. (Co-chairmen: Jean-Luc Pepin, and John P. Robarts.) Hull, Que.: Supply and Services Canada, 1979.

Charbonneau, Jean-Pierre, et Paquette, Gilbert
L'Option. Montréal: Editions de l'homme, 1978.

Chretien, Jean
Securing the Canadian Economic Union in the Constitution. Discussion Paper published by the Government of Canada. Ottawa: Supply and Services, 1980.

Corry, J.A.
Difficulties of Divided Jurisdiction. Royal Commission on Dominion-Provincial Relations Report. Appendix 7. Ottawa: King's Printer, 1939.

Courchene, Thomas J.
"Canada's New Equalization Program: Description and Evaluation." *Canadian Public Policy* 9 (December 1983): 458-75.

Creighton, Donald
"The Decline and Fall of the Empire of the St. Lawrence." *Towards the Discovery of Canada: Selected Essays*, pp. 157-73. By Donald Creighton. Toronto: Macmillan, 1972.

Canada's First Century, 1867-1967. Toronto: Macmillan, 1970.

The Road to Confederation: The Emergence of Canada 1863-1867. Toronto: Macmillan, 1964.

British North America at Confederation. Royal Commission on Dominion-Provincial Relations Report. Appendix 2. Ottawa: King's Printer, 1939.

Dubuc, Alfred
"The Decline of Confederation and the New Nationalism." *Nationalism in Canada*, pp. 112-32. Edited by Peter Russell. Toronto: McGraw-Hill, 1966.

Dupré, J. Stefan, et al.
Federalism and Policy Development: The Case of Adult Occupational Training in Ontario. Toronto: University of Toronto Press, 1973.

Faucher, Albert
Histoire économique et unité canadienne. Montréal: Fides, 1970.

Fullerton, Douglas H.
The Dangerous Delusion: Quebec's Independence Obsession: As Seen by Former Advisor to René Levesque and Jean Lesage. Toronto: McClelland and Stewart, 1978.

Haack, Richard; Hughes, David Robert; Shapiro, R.G.
The Splintered Market: Barriers to Interprovincial Trade in Canadian Agriculture. Toronto: James Lorimer in association with the Canadian Institute for Economic Policy, 1981.

Hayes, John A.
Economic Mobility in Canada: A Comparative Study. Ottawa: Government of Canada, 1982.

Henry, Jacques
"La Dépendence structurelle du Québec dans un Canada dominé par les Etats-unis." *Choix* 7 (2e trimestre 1975): 203-23.

Hodgetts, J.E.
The Canadian Public Service: A Physiology of Government, 1867-1970. Toronto: University of Toronto Press, 1973.

Pioneer Public Service: An Administrative History of the United Canadas, 1841-1867. Toronto: University of Toronto Press, 1955.

Innis, Harold A.
A History of the Canadian Pacific Railway. Toronto: University of Toronto Press, 1971. (First published 1923.)

"Decentralization and Democracy." *Essays in Canadian Economic History*, pp. 358-71. Edited by Mary Q. Innis. Toronto: University of Toronto Press, 1956.

"Great Britain, the United States and Canada." *Essays in Canadian Economic History*, pp. 394-412. Edited by Mary Q. Innis. Toronto: University of Toronto Press, 1956.

"The Wheat Economy." *Essays in Canadian Economic History*, pp. 273-9. Edited by Mary Q. Innis. Toronto: University of Toronto Press, 1956.

Jenkin, Michael
The Challenge of Diversity: Industrial Policy in the Canadian Federation. Background study no. 50. Ottawa: Science Council of Canada, 1983.

Lamontagne, Maurice
Le Fédéralisme canadien: évolution et problèmes. Québec: Presses de l'université Laval, 1954.

Laskin, Bora
"'Peace, Order and Good Government' Re-examined." *Canadian Bar Review* 25 (1947): 1054-87.

Legaré, Anne
"Towards a Marxian Theory of Canadian Federalism." *Studies in Political Economy*, no. 8 (Summer 1982), pp. 37-58.

Lithwick, N.H.
"Is Federalism Good for Regionalism?" *Journal of Canadian Studies* 15 (Summer 1980): 62-73.

Mackintosh, W.A.
The Economic Background of Dominion-Provincial Relations. Royal

Commission Report on Dominion-Provincial Relations, Appendix III. Ottawa: King's Printer, 1938. (Reprinted by McClelland and Stewart: The Carleton Library, no. 13. Edited by J.H. Dales. Toronto: 1964.)

Mahon, Rianne
"Canadian Public Policy: The Unequal Structure of Representation." *The Canadian State: Political Economy and Political Power*, pp. 165-98. Edited by Leo Panitch. Toronto: University of Toronto Press, 1977.

Mallory, James Russell
Social Credit and the Federal Power in Canada. Toronto: University of Toronto Press, 1977. (First published 1954.)

Martin, Chester
"Dominion Lands" Policy. The Carleton Library, no. 69. Toronto: McClelland and Stewart, 1973.

"British Policy in Canadian Confederation." *Canadian Historical Review* 13 (March 1932): 3-19.

Maxwell, J.A.
"Better Terms." *Queen's Quarterly* 40 (February 1933): 125-39.

Maxwell, Judith, and Pestieau, Caroline
Economic Realities of Contemporary Confederation. Montreal: C.D. Howe Research Institute, 1980.

McWhinney, Edward
Canada and the Constitution, 1979-1982: Patriation and the Charter of Rights. Toronto: University of Toronto Press, 1982.

Quebec and the Constitution, 1960-1978. Toronto: University of Toronto Press, 1979.

Meekison, J. Peter, ed.
Canadian Federalism: Myth or Reality. 3rd ed. Toronto: Methuen, 1977.

Mintz, Jack, and Simeon, Richard
Conflict of Taste and Conflict of Claim in the Federal System. Kingston, Ont.: Institute of Intergovernmental Relations, Queen's University, forthcoming.

Morin, Claude
Quebec Versus Ottawa: The Struggle for Self-Government 1960-72. Toronto: University of Toronto Press, 1976. (First published in two parts in French 1972 and 1973.)

Morrison, K.L.
"The Businessman Voter in Thunder Bay: The Catalyst to the Federal-Provincial Voting Split?" *Canadian Journal of Political Science* 6 (June 1973): 219-29.

Morton, Desmond
"Aid to the Civil Power: The Canadian Militia in Support of Social Order, 1867-1914." *Studies in Canadian Social History*, pp. 417-34. Edited by Michiel Horn and Ronald Sabourin. Toronto: McClelland and Stewart, 1974. (Reprinted from *Canadian Historical Review* 51 [December 1970]: 407-25.)

Naylor, R.T.
"The Rise and Fall of the Third Commercial Empire of the St. Lawrence." *Capitalism and the National Question in Canada*, pp. 1-41. Edited by G. Teeple. Toronto: University of Toronto Press, 1972.

Oliver, M., ed.
Social Purpose for Canada. Toronto: University of Toronto Press, 1961.

Pratt, Larry, and Stevenson, Garth, eds.
Western Separatism: The Myths, Realities & Dangers. Edmonton: Hurtig, 1981.

Rémillard, Gil
Le Fédéralisme canadien: éléments constitutionnels de formation et d'évolution. Montréal: Québec-Amérique, 1980.

Russell, Peter H., ed.
Leading Constitutional Decisions: Cases on the British North America Act. The Carleton Library, no. 23. Ottawa: Carleton University Press, 1982.

Ryerson, Stanley
Unequal Union: Confederation and the Roots of Conflict in the Canadas, 1815-1873. Toronto: Progess Books, 1968.

Safarian, A.E.
Canadian Federalism and Economic Integration. Ottawa: Privy Council Office, Government of Canada, 1974.

Schultz, Richard
Federalism, Bureaucracy and Public Policy: The Politics of Highway Transport Regulation. Toronto: Institute of Public Administration of Canada, 1980.

Federalism and the Regulatory Process. Montreal: Institute for Research on Public Policy, 1979.

Scott, Frank R.
Essays on the Constitution: Aspects of Canadian Law and Politics. Toronto: University of Toronto Press, 1977.

Scott, Frank, et al.
Social Planning for Canada. Toronto: University of Toronto Press, 1975. (First published 1935.)

Silver, Arthur Isaac
The French-Canadian Idea of Confederation, 1864-1900. Toronto: University of Toronto Press, 1982.

Simeon, Richard
Federal-Provincial Diplomacy: The Making of Recent Policy in Canada. Toronto: University of Toronto Press, 1972.

Smiley, Donald V.
Canada in Question: Federalism in the Eighties. 3rd ed. Toronto: McGraw-Hill Ryerson, 1980.

Stevenson, Garth
Unfulfilled Union: Canadian Federalism and National Unity. Rev. ed. Toronto: Gage, 1982.

"The Political Economy Tradition and Canadian Federalism." *Studies in Political Economy*, no. 6 (Autumn 1981), pp. 113-33.

"Canadian Regionalism in Continental Perspective." *Journal of Canadian Studies* 15 (Summer 1980): 16-28.

"Federalism and the Political Economy of the Canadian State." *The Canadian State: Political Economy and Political Power*, pp. 71-100. Edited by Leo Panitch. Toronto: University of Toronto Press, 1977.

Trudeau, Pierre Elliott
Federalism and the French Canadians. Toronto: Macmillan, 1968.

Tupper, Allan
Public Money in the Private Sector: Industrial Assistance Policy and Canadian Federalism. Kingston, Ont.: Institute of Intergovernmental Relations, Queen's University, 1982.

Walker, Michael, ed.
Canadian Confederation at the Crossroads: The Search for a Federal-Provincial Balance. Vancouver: Fraser Institute, 1978.

Whitaker, Reginald
Federalism and Democratic Theory. Discussion Paper no. 17. Kingston, Ont.: Institute of Intergovernmental Relations, Queen's University, 1983.

White, W.L., et al.
Canadian Confederation: A Decision-Making Analysis. The Carleton Library, no. 117. Toronto: Macmillan, 1979.

Workshop on the Political Economy of Confederation, Queen's University, Kingston, Ont., 1978.
Proceedings. Kingston, Ont.: Institute of Intergovernmental Relations; Ottawa: Economic Council of Canada, 1979.

23

State Policy and Politics

DAVID WOLFE

One of the most significant features of all advanced capitalist societies is the expanded role of the state. Since the end of the Second World War, the state has played a major role in stabilizing fluctuations in levels of growth, employment and income. Responsibility for protecting individuals against the hazards of old age, ill health and unemployment has also been assumed by the state. Relations between capital and labour involving the certification of labour unions and the process of collective bargaining have become the focus of direct regulation by the state. As a consequence, state policies in the fields of economic stabilization, social welfare and industrial relations have taken on major proportions in contemporary capitalism.

While the role of state policies has expanded dramatically in the postwar Canadian economy, the phenomenon itself is not new. As several of the readings listed below make clear, the state has traditionally played a significant role in the development of the Canadian economy. Historically, however, the bias of state policies leaned strongly in favour of support for the profitable accumulation of capital, particularly in the resource sectors of the economy based on the staples trades. This bias has been altered in the period since the Second World War, as state policies have provided greater security for the standards of living and the conditions of work of the majority of Canadians. One of the major debates documented in the readings below concerns the question of whether these state policies have actually altered the existing structure of class relations (and to what extent) or merely served to better legitimate that structure.

As state intervention has assumed greater importance in the postwar economy, additional social and economic problems have become the focus of state policies. The following list of books and articles makes no attempt to provide a comprehensive survey of such activities. It focuses instead on policies that have been introduced to deal with the persistent problems of regional disparities, one of the fundamental characteristics of the Canadian political economy, and on policies to promote and regulate the development of energy resources. Both of these areas have become increasingly controversial, and the literature cited below documents some of these controversies.

Throughout much of the postwar period, the question of state intervention in the economy was devoid of great ideological debate, largely as a result of the consensus around the policy ideas of John Maynard Keynes. As the period of sustained economic growth came to an end in the mid-1970s, this consensus was shattered by a growing degree of strife over the continued nature of that intervention. In the past decade, many of the policies introduced in the earlier period have been subject to criticism. Canada has not experienced the full-blown effects of the neo-conservative attack on the welfare state, but the level and quality of this country's services have been steadily eroded. The current crisis concerning the role of the state raises the question of whether the historical possibilities of the postwar welfare state have been exhausted.

Armitage, Andrew
  Social Welfare in Canada: Ideals and Realities. Toronto: McClelland and Stewart, 1975.

Armstrong, Hugh
  "The Labour Force and State Workers in Canada." *The Canadian State: Political Economy and Political Power*, pp. 289-310. Edited by Leo Panitch. Toronto: University of Toronto Press, 1977.

Axelrod, Paul Douglas
  "Higher Education, Utilitarianism, and the Acquisitive Society: Canada, 1930-1980." *Readings in Canadian Social History*, vol. 5: *Modern Canada, 1930-1980s*, pp. 179-205. Edited by Michael S. Cross and Gregory S. Kealey. Toronto: McClelland and Stewart, 1984.

  Scholars and Dollars: Politics, Economics and the Universities of Ontario, 1945-1980. University of Toronto Press, 1982.

Badgley, Robin F., and Wolfe, Samuel
  Doctors' Strike: Medical Care and Conflict in Saskatchewan. Toronto: Macmillan, 1967.

Bates, Stewart
  Financial History of Canadian Governments. Study Prepared for the Royal Commission on Dominion-Provincial Relations. Ottawa: n.p., 1939.

Bird, Richard M.
  The Growth of Public Employment in Canada. Public Sector Employment in Canada, vol. 3. Toronto: Institute for Research on Public Policy, 1979.

Brady, Alexander
  "The State and Economic Life." *Canada*, pp. 353-71. Edited by George W. Brown. The United Nations Series. Berkeley: University of California Press, 1950.

Bregha, François
  Bob Blair's Pipeline: The Business and Politics of Northern Energy Development Projects. Toronto: James Lorimer, 1979.

Brewis, T.N., et al.
  Canadian Economic Policy. Rev. ed. Toronto: Macmillan, 1965.

Bryce, R.B.
  "Government Policy and Recent Inflation in Canada." *Inflation and the Canadian Experience: Proceedings of a Conference, Queen's University, Kingston, Ont., 1970*, pp. 226-43. Edited by N. Swan and D. Wilton. Kingston: Queen's University, 1971.

Bryden, Kenneth
  Old Age Pensions and Policy-Making in Canada. Montreal: McGill-Queen's University Press, 1974.

Buchbinder, Howard
"Inequality and the Social Services." *Inequality: Essays on the Political Economy of Social Welfare*, pp. 348-69. Edited by Allan Moscovitch and Glenn Drover. Toronto: University of Toronto Press, 1981.

Careless, Anthony G.S.
Initiative and Response: The Adaptation of Federalism to Regional Economic Development. Montreal: McGill-Queen's University Press, 1977.

Chandler, Marsha A.
"State Enterprise and Partisanship in Provincial Politics." *Canadian Journal of Political Science* 15 (December 1982): 711-40.

Christensen, Sandra S.
Unions and the Public Interest: Collective Bargaining in the Government Sector. Vancouver: Fraser Institute, 1980.

Corry, James Alexander
The Growth of Government Activities Since Confederation. A Study Prepared for the Royal Commission on Dominion-Provincial Relations. Ottawa: n.p., 1939.

"The Fusion of Government and Business." *Canadian Journal of Economics and Political Science* 2 (August 1936): 301-16.

Crane, David
Controlling Interest: The Canadian Gas and Oil Stakes. Toronto: McClelland and Stewart, 1982.

Craven, Paul
"An Impartial Umpire": Industrial Relations and the Canadian State, 1900-1911. Toronto: University of Toronto Press, 1950.

Crispo, John H.G., ed.
Wages, Prices, Profits and Economic Policy. Proceedings of a Conference Held by the Centre for Industrial Relations, University of Toronto, 1967. Toronto: University of Toronto Press, 1968.

Cuneo, Carl
"State Mediation of Class Contradictions in Canadian Unemployment Insurance, 1930-1935." *Studies in Political Economy*, no. 3 (Spring 1980), pp. 37-65.

"State, Class and Reserve Labour: The Case of the 1941 Canadian Unemployment Insurance Act." *Canadian Review of Sociology and Anthropology* 16:2 (1979): 147-70.

Deaton, Rick
"The Fiscal Crisis of the State and the Revolt of the Public Employee." *Our Generation* 8 (October 1972): 11-51.

Doern, G. Bruce
"The Mega-Project Episode and the Formulation of Canadian Economic Development Policy." *Canadian Public Administration* 26 (Summer 1983): 219-38.

Doern, G. Bruce, and Toner, Glen
The NEP and the Politics of Energy. Toronto: Methuen, 1984.

Donner, Arthur W., and Peters, Douglas D.
The Monetarist Counter-Revolution: A Critique of Canadian Monetary Policy,

1975-1979. Toronto: James Lorimer in association with the Canadian Institute for Economic Policy, 1979.

Dosman, Edgar J.
The National Interest: The Politics of Northern Development, 1968-75. Toronto: McClelland and Stewart, 1975.

Drover, Glenn
"Income Redistribution." *Inequality: Essays on the Political Economy of Social Welfare*, pp. 199-226. Edited by Allan Moscovitch and Glenn Drover. Toronto: University of Toronto Press, 1981.

Finkel, Alvin
Business and Social Reform in the Thirties. Toronto: James Lorimer, 1979.

"Origins of the Welfare State in Canada." *The Canadian State: Political Economy and Political Power*, pp. 344-70. Edited by Leo Panitch. Toronto: University of Toronto Press, 1977.

Foot, David K., ed.
Public Employment and Compensation in Canada: Myths and Realities. Toronto: Butterworth for the Institute for Research on Public Policy, 1978.

GATT-Fly Project
Power to Choose: Canada's Energy Options. Toronto: Between the Lines, 1981.

Giles, Anthony
"The Canadian Labour Congress and Tripartism." *Relations Industrielles/ Industrial Relations* 37:1 (1982): 93-125.

Gillespie, W. Irwin
The Redistribution of Income in Canada. The Carleton Library, no. 124. Ottawa: Institute of Canadian Studies, Carleton University, 1980.

"Postwar Canadian Fiscal Policy Revisited, 1945-1975." *Canadian Tax Journal* 27 (May-June 1979): 265-76.

In Search of Robin Hood: The Effect of Federal Budgetary Policies During the 1970s on the Distribution of Income in Canada. Montreal: C.D. Howe Research Institute, 1978.

Goffman, Irving J.
"Canadian Social Welfare Policy." *Contemporary Canada*, pp. 191-224. Edited by Richard H. Leach. Toronto: University of Toronto Press, 1968.

"The Political History of National Hospital Insurance in Canada." *Journal of Commonwealth Political Studies* 3 (1965): 136-47.

Gonick, Cy
Out of Work: Why There's So Much Unemployment, and Why It's Getting Worse. Toronto: James Lorimer, 1978.

Inflation or Depression: The Continuing Crisis of the Canadian Economy. Toronto: James Lorimer, 1975.

Gordon, Howard Scott
"A Twenty Year Perspective: Some Reflections on the Keynesian Revolution in Canada." *Canadian Economic Policy Since the War: A Series of Six Public Lectures in Commemoration of the Twentieth Anniversary of the White Paper on Employment and Income of 1945*. Sponsored by the Canadian Trade

Gordon, Howard Scott (con'd)
Committee, Private Planning Association of Canada. [Montreal: n.p., 1966.]
The Economists Versus the Bank of Canada. Toronto: Ryerson, 1961.

Gordon, Marsha
Government in Business. Montreal: C.D. Howe Institute, 1981.

Grauer, Albert Edward
Public Assistance and Social Insurance: A Study Prepared for the Royal Commission on Dominion-Provincial Relations. Ottawa: n.p., 1939.

Greenaway, William K., and Brickey, Stephen L., eds.
Law and Social Control in Canada. Scarborough, Ont.: Prentice-Hall, 1978.

Guest, Dennis
The Emergence of Social Security in Canada. Vancouver: University of British Columbia Press, 1979.

Hasson, Reuben
"The Cruel War: Social Security Abuse in Canada." *Canadian Taxation* 3 (Fall 1981): 114-47.

"Tax Evasion and Social Security Abuse — Some Tentative Observations." *Canadian Taxation* 2 (Summer 1980): 98-108.

Haythorne, George V.
"Prices and Incomes Policy: The Canadian Experience, 1969-1972." *International Labour Review*, no. 108 (December 1973), pp. 485-503.

Hutcheson, John
"The Capitalist State in Canada." *Canada Ltd.: The Political Economy of Dependency*, pp. 153-77. Edited by Robert Laxer. Toronto: McClelland and Stewart, 1973.

Huxley, Christopher
"The State, Collective Bargaining and the Shape of Strikes in Canada." *Canadian Journal of Sociology* 4 (Summer 1979): 223-39.

Jamieson, Stuart Marshall
Industrial Relations in Canada. 2nd ed. Toronto: Macmillan, 1973.

Johnson, A.W.
"Canada's Social Security Review, 1973-75: The Central Issues." *Canadian Public Policy* 1 (Autumn 1975): 456-72.

Johnson, Andrew F.
"A Minister as an Agent of Policy Change: The Case of Unemployment Insurance in the Seventies." *Canadian Public Administration* 24 (Winter 1981): 612-33.

Kent, Thomas Worrall
Social Policy for Canada: Towards a Philosophy of Social Security. Ottawa: Policy Press, 1962.

Kilbourn, William
Pipeline: Transcanada and the Great Debate: A History of Business and Politics. Toronto: Clarke, Irwin, 1970.

Kuusisto, Nils, and Williams, Rick
"Social Expenses and Regional Underdevelopment." *Inequality: Essays on the Political Economy of Social Welfare*, pp. 249-74. Edited by Allan Moscovitch and Glenn Drover. Toronto: University of Toronto Press, 1981.

Laxer, James
Oil and Gas: Ottawa, the Provinces and the Petroleum Industry. Toronto: James Lorimer, 1983.

Canada's Energy Crisis. (New updated ed.) Toronto: James Lorimer, 1975.

Lithwick, N.H.
Regional Economic Policy: The Canadian Experience. Toronto: McGraw-Hill Ryerson, 1978.

MacDowell, Laurel Sefton
"The Formation of the Canadian Industrial Relations System During World War Two." *Labour/Le Travailleur*, no. 3 (1978), pp. 175-96.

Mackintosh, W.A.
"The White Paper on Employment and Income in its 1945 Setting." *Canadian Economic Policy Since the War.* Edited by S.F. Kaliski. Montreal: Private Planning Association of Canada, 1966.

"Canadian Economic Policy From 1945 to 1957 — Origins and Influences." *The American Economic Impact on Canada*, pp. 51-68. By Hugh G.J. Aitken et al. Durham, N.C.: Duke University Press for the Duke University Commonwealth-Studies Centre, 1959.

Mahon, Rianne
"Regulatory Agencies: Captive Agents or Hegemonic Apparatuses." *Studies in Political Economy*, no. 1 (Spring 1979), pp. 163-200.

"Canadian Public Policy: The Unequal Structure of Representation." *The Canadian State: Political Economy and Political Power*, pp. 165-98. Edited by Leo Panitch. Toronto: University of Toronto Press, 1977.

Mandel, Michael
"Democracy, Class and Canadian Sentencing Law." *Crime and Social Justice* 21-22 (1984): 163-82.

Mandel, Michael, and Glasbeek, Harry J.
"The Legalization of Politics in Advanced Capitalism: The Canadian Charter of Rights and Freedoms." *Critical Perspectives on the Constitution.* Edited by Robert Martin. Winnipeg: Socialist Studies, 1985.

Mandel, Michael; Ericson, Richard; and Savan, Beth
"Law and Social Order." Ideas series, C.B.C. Radio transcripts, Toronto, 1983. (On the R.C.M.P. scandal, policing in general, and environmental regulation.)

Marsh, Leonard
Report on Social Security for Canada. Toronto: University of Toronto Press, 1975. (First published 1943.)

Martell, George
"The Schools, the State and the Corporations." *The Politics of the Canadian Public School*, pp. 1-36. Edited by George Martell. Toronto: James Lorimer, 1974.

Maslove, Allan M., and Swimmer, Gene
Wage Controls in Canada, 1975-78: A Study of Public Decision Making. Montreal: Institute for Research on Public Policy, 1980.

McDougall, John N.
Fuels and the National Policy. Toronto: Butterworth, 1982.

Molot, Maureen Appel and Laux, Jeanne Kirk
"The Politics of Nationalization." *Canadian Journal of Political Science* 12 (June 1979): 227-58.

Moscovitch, Allan
"Housing: Who Pays? Who Profits?" *Inequality: Essays on the Political Economy of Social Welfare*, pp. 314-47. Edited by Allan Moscovitch and Glenn Drover. Toronto: University of Toronto Press, 1981.

Moscovitch, Allan and Drover, Glenn, eds.
Inequality: Essays on the Political Economy of Social Welfare. Toronto: University of Toronto Press, 1981.

Nelles, H.V.
"Canadian Energy Policy, 1945-1980: A Federalist Perspective." *Entering the Eighties: Canada in Crisis*, pp. 91-117. Edited by R. Kenneth Carty and W. Peter Ward. Toronto: Oxford University Press, 1980.

Panitch, Leo
"Corporatism in Canada." *Studies in Political Economy*, no. 1 (Spring 1979), pp. 43-92.

"The Development of Corporatism in Liberal Democracies." *Comparative Political Studies* 10 (April 1977): 61-90.

"The Role and Nature of the Canadian State." *The Canadian State: Political Economy and Political Power*, pp. 3-27. Edited by Leo Panitch. Toronto: University of Toronto Press, 1977.

Panitch, Leo, and Swartz, Donald
"Towards Permanent Exceptionalism: Coercion and Consent in Canadian Industrial Relations." *Labour/Le Travail*, no. 13 (Spring 1984), pp. 133-57.

Phidd, Richard W.,and Doern, Bruce G.
The Politics and Management of Canadian Economic Policy. Toronto: Macmillan, 1978.

Plumptre, Arthur FitzWalter Wynne
Three Decades of Decision: Canada and the World Monetary System, 1944-75. Toronto: McClelland and Stewart, 1977.

Pratt, Larry
"Energy: The Roots of National Policy." *Studies in Political Economy*, no. 7 (Winter 1982), pp. 27-59.

"Petro-Canada." *Public Corporations and Public Policy in Canada*, pp. 95-148. Edited by Allan Tupper and G.Bruce Doern. Montreal: Institute for Research on Public Policy, 1981.

Rice, James J.
"Social Policy, Economic Management and Redistribution." *Public Policy in Canada: Organization, Process, and Management*, pp. 106-31. Edited by G. Bruce Doern and Peter Aucoin. Toronto: Macmillan, 1979.

Ross, David P.
The Working Poor: Wage Earners and the Failure of Income Security Policies. Toronto: James Lorimer in association with the Canadian Institute for Economic Policy, 1981.

Schecter, Stephen
"Education and Inequality: Some Strategic Considerations." *Inequality: Essays*

on the Political Economy of Social Welfare, pp. 275-92. Edited by Allan Moscovitch and Glenn Drover. Toronto: University of Toronto Press, 1981.

Shaffer, Edward H.
Canada's Oil and the American Empire. Edited by José Druker. Edmonton: Hurtig, 1983.

Strong-Boag, Veronica
"'Wages for Housework': Mother's Allowances and the Beginnings of Social Security in Canada." *Journal of Canadian Studies* 14 (Spring 1979): 24-34.

Struthers, James
No Fault of Their Own: Unemployment and the Canadian Welfare State, 1914-1941. Toronto: University of Toronto Press, 1983.

"Two Depressions: Bennett, Trudeau and the Unemployed." *Journal of Canadian Studies* 14 (Spring 1979): 70-80.

"Prelude to Depression: The Federal Government and Unemployment, 1918-29." *Canadian Historical Review* 58 (September 1977): 277-93.

Swartz, Donald
"The Politics of Reform: Conflict and Accommodation in Canadian Health Policy." *The Canadian State: Political Economy and Political Power*, pp. 311-43. Edited by Leo Panitch. Toronto: University of Toronto Press, 1977.

Taylor, Ian
Crime, Capitalism and Community: Three Essays in Socialist Criminology. Toronto: Butterworth, 1983.

Taylor, Malcolm Gordon
Health Insurance and Canadian Public Policy: The Seven Decisions that Created the Canadian Health Insurance System. Montreal: McGill-Queen's University Press, 1978.

Toner, Glen, and Bregha, François
"The Political Economy of Energy." *Canadian Politics in the 1980s*, pp. 1-26. Edited by Michael S. Whittington and Glen Williams. Toronto: Methuen, 1981.

Traves, Tom
The State and Enterprise: Canadian Manufacturers and the Federal Government, 1917-1931. Toronto: University of Toronto Press, 1979.

Tupper, Allan
"The State in Business." *Canadian Public Administration* 22 (Spring 1979): 124-50.

"Public Enterprise as Social Welfare: The Case of the Cape Breton Development Corporation." *Canadian Public Policy* 4 (Autumn 1978): 530-46.

Tupper, Allan, and Doern, Bruce G.
Public Corporations and Public Policy in Canada. Montreal: Institute for Research on Public Policy, 1981.

Van Loon, Rick
"Reforming Welfare in Canada." *Public Policy* 27 (Fall 1979): 469-504.

Wallace, M. Elizabeth
"The Origin of the Social Welfare State in Canada, 1867-1900." *Canadian Journal of Economics and Political Science* 16 (August 1950): 383-93.

Willard, Joseph W.
''Some Aspects of Family Allowances and Income Redistribution in Canada.'' *Yearbook of the Graduate School of Public Administration, Harvard University*, vol. 5: *Public Policy*, pp. 190-232. Cambridge, Mass.: Graduate School of Public Administration, Harvard University, 1954.

Wolfe, David A.
''The Rise and Demise of the Keynesian Era in Canada: Economic Policy, 1930-1982.'' *Readings in Canadian Social History*, vol. 5: *Modern Canada, 1930-1980s*, pp. 46-80. Edited by Michael S. Cross and Gregory S. Kealey. Toronto: McClelland and Stewart, 1984.

''Economic Growth and Foreign Investment: A Perspective on Canadian Economic Policy.'' *Journal of Canadian Studies* 13 (Spring 1978): 3-20.

''The State and Economic Policy in Canada, 1968-75.'' *The Canadian State: Political Economy and Political Power*, pp. 251-88. Edited by Leo Panitch. Toronto: University of Toronto Press, 1977.

24

Industrial and Commercial Policy

RIANNE MAHON

The search for the roots of Canada's "underdeveloped" industrial structure constitutes a central theme in the debates on industrial and commercial policy. The revival of Canadian political economy, in fact, can be linked to the left nationalist Waffle's challenge to the orthodox explanation, which blamed Canada's first industrial policy — the National Policy tariff — for protecting uncompetitive industries. For left nationalists such as Tom Naylor, the problem is not that the policy was "protectionist", but that it encouraged the development of branch-plant industries. It did so, moreover, because of the dominance of merchant-financiers over indigenous industrial capital.

Naylor's seminal work has been criticized primarily for ignoring the role played by other classes in Canadian development. Less has been said about his interpretation of the National Policy. Craven and Traves, however, have produced a more nuanced analysis of the political reasons for the National Policy's success: the National Policy managed to divide, and thus to conquer, the opponents of the dominant class. More recently, Glen Williams's *Not for Export* rejects the thesis that the Policy reflected the defeat of indigenous capital and instead argues that the tariff served the latter's interest: industrialization by import substitution. Williams also raises the important question of "state failures," documenting the persistent, yet unsuccessful efforts by Trade and Commerce to promote an export orientation among domestic manufacturers. Gord Laxer's comparative analysis of Canada and other countries late to industrialize, brings out another, more state-specific, consequence of Canada's imperial ties. He suggests that Canada's relative failure to fully industrialize is, in part, due to the lack of stimulation an independent military policy might have provided.

The impact of war on Canadian commercial and industrial policy structures has been explored in two recent doctoral dissertations. In the latter chapters of his thesis, David Wolfe examines the process through which W.A. Mackintosh's synthesis of Keynesian and staples theory became the basis of postwar reconstruction planning. Wolfe also traces the impact of joint Canada-U.S. wartime production planning on postwar policy. Hugh James has analyzed the development of the state's capacity to coordinate growth in the capital and consumer goods sectors. Although James argues that such changes in the role and structure of the state are characteristic of "monopoly capitalism," he is careful to note that in Canada's case this meant state involvement in a continental industrial structure.

Continental integration has clearly remained on the state's agenda. The government's publication of *Canadian Trade Policy for the 1980s* indicates that a revamped Department of External Affairs is likely to pursue this option. Yet the state has also attempted more nationalistic policies such as the "megaprojects" strategy, which promised to capture the industrial spinoffs from major resource projects for domestic manufacturers. The forces behind such contradictory responses to the crisis require analysis.

One of the pressures for new policy initiatives stems from the "new international division of labour" emerging as a result of the opening of new, low-wage industrial sites in Asia and Latin America. Canada's traditional industrial policy — the tariff — is largely ineffective against such import competition; yet the latter poses a potentially greater threat of deindustrialization than did the Nixon administration's attempt to bring the branch plants home in the early Seventies. The publication of *Canada and the New International Division of Labour* should stimulate debate among political economists on this question.

The changing role of the Canadian state needs also to be examined in relation to the crisis of the "Keynesian" or "Fordist" mode of state intervention. Both Chernomas (1983) and Houle (1983) seem to suggest that the state's "nationalist" initiatives are a response to this crisis that involves an attempt to shift to a "post-Keynesian" mode of intervention. Recent publications of the Canadian Institute for Economic Policy and the Science Council (French, 1980; Clarkson, 1982; Jenkin, 1983; Thorburn, 1983), however, throw into question the Canadian state's capacity to implement such policies. Yet, these studies fail to consider the relationship between state structure and class power that Mahon's analysis of the state's involvement in the restructuring of the textile industry — *The Politics of Industrial Restructuring* — highlights.

Finally, Canadian political economists have not yet begun to debate seriously the question of a socialist alternative to the current industrial policy options. It is, in fact, ironic that while the Waffle was among the first to raise the spectre of deindustrialization, Canadian political economists have not kept pace with their British and American counterparts, who are involved in a lively debate on this question. Of course, we do have the publications of the Canadian Institute for Economic Policy as well as the Laxer report, *Rethinking the Canadian Economy*. Yet although these publications have maintained the nationalism of the Waffle, the socialist element has been dropped in favour of an anti-labour variant of post-Keynesianism.

Acheson, T.W.
"The National Policy and the Industrialization of the Maritimes, 1880-1910." *Acadiensis* 1 (Spring 1972). (Reprinted in D.J. Bercuson. *Canada and the Burden of Unity*. Toronto: Macmillan, 1977.)

Bacon, Robert William, and Eltis, Walter
Britain's Economic Problem: Too Few Producers. London: Macmillan, 1976.

Barber, C.L.
"Canadian Tariff Policy." *Canadian Journal of Economics and Political Science* 21 (November 1955): 513-30.

Beigie, Carl E., and Stewart, James K.
"New Pressures, Old Constraints: Canada-United States Relations in the 1980s." *Behind the Headlines* 40:6 (1983): 1-28.

Biggs, Margaret A.
The Challenge: Adjust or Protect? Canada and Third World Trade, no. 1. Ottawa: North-South Institute, 1980.

Binhammer, H.H.; McDonough, L.C.; and Lepore, G.
Government Grants to Private Sector Firms. Discussion Paper 0225-8013, no. 227. Ottawa: Economic Council of Canada, 1983.

Blackaby, Frank, ed.
De-industrialisation. London: Heinemann, 1979.

Blais, André, and Faucher, Philippe
"La Politique industrielle dans les économies capitalistes avancées." *Canadian Journal of Political Science* 14 (March 1981): 3-35.

Bliss, Michael
The Evolution of Industrial Policies in Canada: An Historical Survey. Discussion Paper no. 218. Ottawa: Economic Council of Canada, 1982.

"Canadianizing American Business: The Roots of the Branch Plant." *Close the 49th Parallel, Etc.: The Americanization of Canada*, pp. 27-42. Edited by Ian Lumsden. Toronto: University of Toronto Press, 1970.

Bluestone, Barry, and Harrison, Bennett
The Deindustrialization of America: Plant Closings, Community Abandonment, and the Dismantling of Basic Industry. New York: Basic Books, 1982.

Bourgault, Pierre
Innovation and the Structure of Canadian Industry. Science Council of Canada. Special Study no. 23. Ottawa: Information Canada, 1972.

Bowles, Samuel; Gordon, David M.; and Weisskopf, Thomas E.
Beyond the Waste Land: A Democratic Alternative to Economic Decline. Garden City, N.Y.: Anchor Books, 1984.

Brecher, Irving
"Burying Industrial Strategy." *Policy Options* 4 (September-October 1983): 19-21.

Britton, John N.H., and Gilmour, James M.
The Weakest Link: A Technological Perspective on Canadian Industrial Underdevelopment. Background Study no. 43. Ottawa: Science Council of Canada, 1978.

Brown, Douglas, and Eastman, Julia
The Limits of Consultation: A Debate Among Ottawa, the Provinces and the Private Sector on Industrial Strategy. A Discussion Paper prepared by the Institute of Intergovernmental Relations, Queen's University. Ottawa: Supply and Services, 1981.

Buckley, Kenneth
Capital Formation in Canada, 1896-1930. The Carleton Library, no. 77. Toronto: McClelland and Stewart, 1970. (First published 1955.)

Cameron, Duncan, and Houle, François
Canada and the New International Division of Labour. Ottawa: University of Ottawa Press, 1985.

Campbell, Robert Malcolm
"Post-Keynesian Politics and the Post-Schumpeterian World." *Canadian Journal of Political and Social Theory* 8 (Winter 1984): 72-91.

Canada. [Commission of] Inquiry into the Automotive Industry
The Canadian Automotive Industry: Performance and Proposals for Progress. (Simon Reisman, Commissioner.) Ottawa: Industry, Trade and Commerce, 1978.

Canada. Economic Council of Canada
The Bottom Line — Technology, Trade and Income Growth. Ottawa: Economic Council of Canada, 1983.

Looking Outward: A New Trade Strategy for Canada. Ottawa: Economic Council of Canada, 1975.

Canada. External Affairs
Canadian Trade Policy for the 1980s: A Discussion Paper. Ottawa: Supply and Services Canada, 1983.

A Review of Canadian Trade Policy: A Background Document to Canadian Trade Policy for the 1980s. Ottawa: Supply and Services Canada, 1983.

Canada. Science Council of Canada
Hard Times, Hard Choices: Technology and the Balance of Payments. A Statement by the Science Council Industrial Policies Committee. Ottawa: Science Council of Canada, 1981.

Chernomas, Bob
"Keynesian, Monetarist and Post-Keynesian Policy: A Marxist Analysis." *Studies in Political Economy*, no. 10 (Winter 1983), pp. 123-42.

Clarkson, Stephen
Canada and the Reagan Challenge: Crisis in the Canadian-American Relationship. Toronto: James Lorimer in association with the Canadian Institute for Economic Policy, 1982.

Conference of Socialist Economists. London Working Group
The Alternative Economic Strategy: A Response by the Labour Movement to the Economic Crisis. London: CSE Books, 1980.

Cordell, Arthur J.
The Multinational Firm, Foreign Direct Investment and Canadian Science Policy. Science Council of Canada. Special Study no. 22. Ottawa: Information Canada, 1971.

Craven, Paul, and Traves, Tom
"The Class Politics of the National Policy: 1872-1933." *Journal of Canadian Studies* 14 (Fall 1979): 14-38.

Creighton, D.G.
"Economic Nationalism and Confederation." *Towards the Discovery of Canada*, pp. 122-36. Toronto: Macmillan, 1972.

Dales, John H.
"'National Policy' Myths, Past and Present." *Journal of Canadian Studies* 14 (Fall 1979): 92-94.

The Protective Tariff in Canada's Development: Eight Essays on Trade and Tariffs When Factors Move, with Special Reference to Canadian Protection-

ism 1870-1955. Toronto: University of Toronto Press, 1966.

De Vos,Dirk
Governments and Microelectronics: The European Experience. Background Study no. 49. Ottawa: Science Council of Canada, 1983.

Doern, G. Bruce, ed.
How Ottawa Spends Your Tax Dollars: National Policy and Economic Development, 1982. Toronto: James Lorimer, 1982.

How Ottawa Spends Your Tax Dollars: Federal Priorities 1981. Toronto: James Lorimer, 1981.

Drache, Daniel, and Kroker, Arthur
"The Labyrinth of Dependency." *Canadian Journal of Political and Social Theory* 7 (Fall 1983): 5-24.

Faucher, Philippe; Blais, André; and Young, Robert
"L'Aide directe au secteur manufacturier au Québec et en Ontario, 1960-1980." *Journal of Canadian Studies* 18 (Spring 1983): 54-78.

Forster, Ben
"The Coming of the National Policy: Business, Government and the Tariff, 1876-1879." *Journal of Canadian Studies* 14 (Fall 1979): 39-49.

Fowke, V.C.
The National Policy and the Wheat Economy. Toronto: University of Toronto Press, 1957.

"National Policy and Western Development in North America." *Journal of Economic History* 16 (December 1956): 461-79.

"The National Policy — Old and New." *Canadian Journal of Economics and Political Science* 18 (August 1952): 271-86. (Reprinted in *Approaches to Canadian Economic History: A Selection of Essays*. Edited by W. T. Easterbrook and Mel Watkins. Toronto: McClelland and Stewart, 1967.)

Freeman, Christopher; Clark, John; and Soete, Luc
Unemployment and Technical Innovation: A Study of Long Waves and Economic Development. Westport, Conn.: Greenwood Press, 1982.

French, Richard D., and Van Loon, Richard
How Ottawa Decides. Rev. ed. Toronto: James Lorimer in association with the Canadian Institute for Economic Policy, 1984.

Goldspink, Frank, et al., eds.
"The Labour Movement, Corporatism and the Economic Crisis." *Canadian Dimension* 15 (December 1980): 37-44. (One of two articles in the section "Towards a Corporatist Canada".)

"Slipping in the Back Door: Tripartism Today — Corporatism Tomorrow?" *Canadian Dimension* 15 (December 1980): 30-36. (One of two articles in the section "Towards a Corporatist Canada".)

Gonick, Cy
"Boom and Bust: State Policy and the Economics of Restructuring." *Studies in Political Economy*, no. 11 (Summer 1983), pp. 27-47.

Hill, O. Mary
Canada's Salesman to the World: The Department of Trade and Commerce, 1892-1939. Montreal: McGill-Queen's University Press, 1977.

Houle, François
"Economic Strategy and the Restructuring of the Fordist Wage-Labour Relationship in Canada." *Studies in Political Economy*, no. 11 (Summer 1983), pp. 127-47.

Hunter, W.T.
"Toward Free Trade? The Dilemma of Canadian Trade Policy." *Journal of Canadian Studies* 13 (Spring 1978): 49-62.

James, Hugh Mackenzie
"Monopoly Relations in the Canadian State, 1939-1957 (How the Coordinative and Recuperative Functions Peculiar to the Monopoly State Became Established in the Canadian Civil Service)." 2 vols. Ph.D. dissertation, University of British Columbia, 1983.

Jenkin, Michael
The Challenge of Diversity: Industrial Policy in the Canadian Federation. Background Study no. 50. Ottawa: Science Council of Canada, 1983.

"Prospects for a New National Policy." *Journal of Canadian Studies* 14 (Fall 1979): 126-41.

Jenkins, Glenn P.
Costs and Consequences of the New Protectionism: The Case of Canada's Clothing Sector. Ottawa: North-South Institute, 1980.

Laxer, Gordon
"The Social Origins of Canada's Branch Plant Economy, 1837-1914." Ph.D. dissertation, University of Toronto, 1981.

Laxer, James
Rethinking the Economy. Toronto: NC Press, 1984.

"The Aftermath of the Autopact." *Canadian Forum* 60 (June-July 1980): 6.

Laxer, Robert, ed.
(Canada) Ltd.: The Political Economy of Dependency. Toronto: McClelland and Stewart, 1973.

Lazar, Fred
The New Protectionism: Non-Tariff Barriers and Their Effects on Canada. Toronto: James Lorimer in association with the Canadian Institute for Economic Policy, 1981.

Lyon, Peyton V.
Canada-United States Free Trade and Canadian Independence. Ottawa: Economic Council of Canada, 1975.

Mahon, Rianne
The Politics of Industrial Restructuring: Canadian Textiles. Toronto: University of Toronto Press, 1984.

Mahon, Rianne, and Mytelka, Lynn Kriegen
"Industry, the State, and the New Protectionism: Textiles in Canada and France." *International Organization* 37 (Autumn 1983): 551-81.

Massey, Doreen B., and Meegan, Richard
The Anatomy of Job Loss: The How, Why, and Where of Employment Decline. London: Methuen, 1982.

Masters, D.C.
The Reciprocity Treaty of 1854. The Carleton Library, no. 9. Toronto:

McClelland and Stewart, 1963.

Reciprocity, 1846-1911. Historical Booklet no. 12. Ottawa: Canadian Historical Association, 1961.

McDiarmid, Orville John
Commercial Policy in the Canadian Economy. Cambridge, Mass.: Harvard University Press, 1946.

Naylor, R.T.
The History of Canadian Business, 1867-1914. 2 vols. Toronto: James Lorimer, 1975.

"Rise and Fall of the Third Commercial Empire of the St. Lawrence." *Capitalism and the National Question in Canada*, pp. 1-41. Edited by G. Teeple. Toronto: University of Toronto Press, 1972.

Parker, Ian
"The National Policy, Neoclassical Economics, and the Political Economy of Tariffs." *Journal of Canadian Studies* 14 (Fall 1979): 95-110.

Perry, Ross
The Future of Canada's Auto Industry: The Big Three and the Japanese Challenge. Toronto: James Lorimer in association with the Canadian Institute for Economic Policy, 1982.

Phillips, Paul
"The National Policy Revisited." *Journal of Canadian Studies* 14 (Fall 1979): 3-13.

Porter, B., and Cuff, R., eds.
Enterprise and National Development: Essays in Canadian Business and Economic History. Toronto: Hakkert, 1973.

Ritchie, Gordon
"Government Aid to Industry: A Public Sector Perspective." *Canadian Public Administration* 26 (Spring 1983): 36-46.

Scheinberg, Stephen
"Invitation to Empire: Tariffs and American Economic Expansion in Canada." *Business History Review* 47 (Summer 1973): 218-38.

Shepherd, John J.
The Transition to Reality: Directions for Canadian Industrial Strategy. Ottawa: Canadian Institute for Economic Policy, 1980.

Steed, Guy P.F.
Threshold Firms: Backing Canada's Winners. Background Study no. 48. Ottawa: Science Council of Canada, 1982.

Stegemann, Klaus
Canadian Non-Tariff Barriers to Trade. Montreal: Canadian Economic Policy Committee, Private Planning Association of Canada, 1973.

Swimmer, Eugene
"Six and Five." *How Ottawa Spends: The New Agenda, 1984.* Edited by Allan Maslove. Toronto: Methuen, 1984.

Thorburn, Hugh G.
Planning and the Economy. Toronto: James Lorimer in association with the Canadian Institute for Economic Policy, 1984.

Traves, Tom
The State and Enterprise: Canadian Manufacturers and the Federal Government, 1917-1931. Toronto: University of Toronto Press, 1979.

Tucker, Gilbert N.
The Canadian Commercial Revolution, 1845-1851. The Carleton Library, no. 19. Toronto: McClelland and Stewart, 1964.

Tupper, Allan
Public Money in the Private Sector: Industrial Assistance Policy and Canadian Federalism. Kingston, Ont.: Institute of Intergovernmental Relations, Queen's University, 1982.

Warnock, Jack
"Free Trade Fantasies: The Case of the Farm Implements Industry." This Magazine 9 (November-December 1975): 36-40.

Wilde, Jim de
"Modern Capitalist Planning and Canadian Federalism: The Case of High-Technology Industries." Ph.D. dissertation, McGill University, 1979.

Williams, Glen
Not For Export: Toward a Political Economy of Canada's Arrested Industrialization. Toronto: McClelland and Stewart, 1983.

"The National Policy Tariffs: Industrial Underdevelopment Through Import Substitution." Canadian Journal of Political Science 12 (June 1979): 333-68.

Willson, Bruce F.
The Energy Squeeze: Canadian Policies for Survival. Toronto: James Lorimer in association with the Canadian Institute for Economic Policy, 1980.

Wolfe, David
"The Delicate Balance: The Changing Economic Role of the State in Canada." Ph.D. dissertation, University of Toronto, 1980.

Wonnacott, Ronald J.
"Controlling Trade and Foreign Investment in the Canadian Economy: Some Proposals." Canadian Journal of Economics 15 (November 1982): 567-85.

Young, J.
Canadian Commercial Policy. Royal Commission on Canada's Economic Prospects. Ottawa: Queen's Printer, 1957.

Zohar, Uri
Canadian Manufacturing: A Study in Productivity and Technological Change. 2 vols. Toronto: James Lorimer in association with the Institute for Economic Policy, 1982.

25

Urban Politics

CAROLINE ANDREW

The earliest writings on urban politics in Canada, dating from the urban reform era of the late nineteenth century, are primarily concerned with analyzing relationships between the economic situation, living conditions and politics, and are marked by a strong concern for social justice. Following this initial period, writings on urban politics tended to give greater emphasis to descriptions of the formal political institutions, devoting less attention to situating these institutions within a socio-economic context.

The return to the political economy tradition in urban politics has been greatly influenced by developments in social history. Studies on city building, municipal economic development strategies, boosterism, working-class politics, etc., have provided insights into the links between class and urban politics and reawakened interest in studying the impact of political decisions and political forces on economic development in Canadian cities.

Recent writing on urban politics has been influenced by two theoretical perspectives: a radical interpretation centred on analysis of the property industry and neo-Marxist interpretations concerned with urban social movements and state intervention. The first, associated with James Lorimer both as author and publisher, has described local politics as the servicing of the property industry and has provided abundant material on links between developers, municipal politicians, municipal bureaucrats and local media and, as well, on the impact that these links have on urban policies and on the physical shape of cities.

Neo-Marxist interpretations of urban politics, heavily inspired by the writings of French Marxists and particularly by Manuel Castells, were predominant in Quebec writing on urban politics from the early 1960s and emerged somewhat later in English-language studies in Canada. These studies led to research on the class nature of state intervention, on the relationships between different levels of the state, on the impact of leadership within social movements and on the political significance of a variety of urban social movements.

Recent studies in urban politics have developed a number of research areas. Although they remain dominated by studies that examine individual cities or individual municipalities in isolation, a growing number deal with individual cities as actors or units within the larger economy or overall political system. Urban policy studies are also increasingly numerous, with housing and transportation being the most studied areas. Class and gender bias are examined, and here again, intergovernmental relations often form one of the centres of research interest. Finally, while the majority of studies focus on the impact of politics on the urban form, a certain number examine the influence of the built form on the individual, the society and the policy.

Ames, H.B.
The City Below the Hill: A Sociological Study of a Portion of the City of Montreal, Canada. Toronto: University of Toronto Press, 1972. (First published 1897.)

Andrew, Caroline
"Les Femmes et la consommation collective: les enjeux de l'engagement politique." *Politique* 5 (hiver 1984): 107-22.

Andrew, Caroline; Bordeleau, Serge; et Guimont, Alain
L'Urbanisation: une affaire: l'appropriation du sol et l'Etat local dans l'Out-aouais québécois. Ottawa: Editions de l'Université d'Ottawa, 1981.

Armstrong, Christopher, and Nelles, H.V.
The Revenge of the Methodist Bicycle Company: Sunday Streetcars and Municipal Reform in Toronto, 1888-1897. Toronto: Peter Martin Associates, 1977.

Artibise, Alan F.J.
Winnipeg: A Social History of Urban Growth, 1874-1914. Montreal: McGill-Queen's University Press, 1975.

Artibise, Alan F.J., ed.
Town and City: Aspects of Western Canadian Urban Development. Regina: Canadian Plains Research Centre, University of Regina, 1981.

Artibise, Alan F.J., and Stelter, Gilbert A., eds.
The Usable Urban Past: Planning and Politics in the Modern Canadian City. The Carleton Library, no. 119. Toronto: Macmillan, 1979.

Aubin, Henry
City For Sale. Montréal: Editions l'Etincelle in association with James Lorimer, Toronto, 1977.

Axworthy, L., and Gillies, J.M., eds.
The City: Canada's Prospects, Canada's Problems. Toronto: Butterworth, 1973.

Barker, G.; Penny, J.; and Seccombe, W.
Highrise and Superprofits. Kitchener, Ont.: Dumont Press Graphix, 1973.

Bird, Richard M., and Slack, N. Enid
Urban Public Finance in Canada. Toronto: Butterworth, 1983.

Blumenfeld, H.
The Modern Metropolis. Montreal: Harvest House, 1971.

Brownstone, Meyer, and Plunkett, T.J.
Metropolitan Winnipeg: Politics and Reform of Local Government. Berkeley: University of California Press for the Institute of Governmental Studies and the Institute of International Studies, University of California, Berkeley, 1983.

Bryant, R.W.G.
Land: Private Property, Public Control. Montreal: Harvest House, 1972.

Budden, S., and Ernst, J.
The Movable Airport: The Politics of Government Planning. Toronto: Hakkert, 1973.

Cameron, Kenneth D.
"Tenth National Seminar [Municipal Government in the Intergovernmental

Maze, 1979]: Summary of Discussions.'' *Canadian Public Administration* 23 (Summer 1980): 195-221.

Carver, H.
Compassionate Landscape: Places and People in a Man's Life. Toronto: University of Toronto Press, 1975.
Cities in the Suburbs. Toronto: University of Toronto Press, 1962.

Caulfield, Jon
The Tiny Perfect Mayor. Toronto: James Lorimer, 1974.

Chorney, Harold
''Amnesia, Integration and Repression: The Roots of Canadian Urban Political Culture.'' *Urbanization and Urban Planning in Capitalist Society*, pp. 535-64. Edited by Michael Dear and Allen J. Scott. London: Methuen, 1981.

Clairmont, Donald H., and Magill, Dennis W.
Africville: The Life and Death of a Canadian Black Community. Toronto: McClelland and Stewart, 1974.

Clark, Samuel D.
The New Urban Poor. Toronto: McGraw-Hill Ryerson, 1978.

Colton, Timothy J.
Big Daddy: Frederick G. Gardiner and the Building of Metropolitan Toronto. Toronto: University of Toronto Press, 1980.

Copp, Terry
The Anatomy of Poverty: The Condition of the Working Class in Montreal, 1897-1929. Toronto: McClelland and Stewart, 1974.

Deachman, Helen, and Woolfrey, Joy
''Les Terrasses de la Chaudière: How the Liberal Federal Government Did Business for Us with Campeau Corporation.'' *Our Generation* 14 (Winter 1981):7-34. (Reprinted as ''Highrises and Super Profits — The Marriage of State and Capital.'' in *The City and Radical Social Change*, pp. 301-44. Edited by Dimitrios Roussopoulos. Montreal: Black Rose Books, 1982.)

Dear, Michael, and Scott, Allen J., eds.
Urbanization and Urban Planning in Capitalist Society. London: Methuen, 1981.

Dennis, M., and Fish, S.
Programs in Search of a Policy: Low Income Housing in Canada. Toronto: Hakkert, 1972.

Divay, Gérard, et Richard, Louise
Les Institutions financières et les types de logements dans les années 1970 au Québec. Etudes et documents, no. 31. Montréal: Institut national de la recherche scientifique, I.N.R.S.-Urbanisation, 1982.

L'Aide gouvernementale au logement et sa distribution sociale: bilan sommaire pour les années soixante-dix au Québec. Institut national de la recherche scientifique. Etudes et documents, no. 26. Montréal: I.N.R.S.-Urbanisation, 1981.

Dupré, J. Stefan
''Intergovernmental Relations and the Metropolitan Area.'' *Politics and Government of Urban Canada*, pp. 151-61. Edited by Lionel D. Feldman. Toronto: Methuen, 1981.

EZOP-Québec
Une Ville à vendre. Laval, Qué.: Editions coopératives Albert Saint-Martin, 1981.

Faculty of Environmental Studies, York University
Women and Environments, vol. 4, no. 1 and 2- (June 1980). (Continues *Women and Environments International Newsletter*.)

Feldman, Lionel D., and Graham, Katherine A.
Bargaining For Cities: Municipalities and Intergovernmental Relations: An Assessment. Montreal: Institute for Research on Public Policy; Toronto: distributed by Butterworth, 1979.

Feldman, Lionel D., ed.
Politics and Government of Urban Canada: Selected Readings. 4th ed. Toronto: Methuen, 1981.

Fraser, Graham
Fighting Back: Urban Renewal in Trefann Court. Toronto: Hakkert, 1972.

Freeman, Bill, and Hewitt, Marsha, eds.
Their Town: The Mafia, the Media and the Party Machine. Toronto: James Lorimer, 1979.

Garner, Hugh
Cabbagetown. Toronto: Ryerson, 1968. (First published 1950.)

Godbout, Jacques
La Participation contre la démocratie. Montréal: Editions coopératives Albert Saint-Martin, 1983.

Gold, Gerald L.
Saint-Pascal: Changing Leadership and Social Organization in a Quebec Town. Toronto: Holt, Rinehart & Winston, 1975.

Gutstein, Donald
Vancouver Ltd. Toronto: James Lorimer, 1975.

Hamel, Pierre; Léonard, Jean-François; et Mayer, Robert, éds.
Les Mobilisations populaires urbaines. Montréal: Nouvelle optique, 1982.

Harris, Richard
Class and Housing Tenure in Modern Canada. Research Paper no. 153. Toronto: Centre for Urban and Community Studies, University of Toronto, 1984.

Higgins, Donald J.H.
Urban Canada: Its Government and Politics. Toronto: Macmillan, 1977.

Hodge, Gerald, and Qadeer, Mohammad A.
Towns and Villages in Canada: The Importance of Being Unimportant. Toronto: Butterworth, 1983.

Jacobs, Jane
Canadian Cities and Sovereignty Association. Toronto: Canadian Broadcasting Corporation, 1980.

Johnson, Leo A.
History of Guelph, 1827-1927. Guelph, Ont.: Guelph Historical Society, 1977.

Katz, Michael B.
The People of Hamilton, Canada West: Family and Class in a Mid-Nineteenth

Century City. Cambridge, Mass.: Harvard University Press, 1975.

Kealey, Gregory S.
Toronto Workers Respond to Industrial Capitalism 1867-1892. Toronto: University of Toronto Press, 1980.

Kealey, Linda, ed.
A Not Unreasonable Claim: Women and Reform in Canada, 1880s-1920s. Toronto: Women's Press, 1979.

Keating, D.R.
The Power to Make It Happen: Mass-Based Community Organizing: What It Is and How It Works. Toronto: Green Tree, 1975.

Leo, Christopher
The Politics of Urban Development: Canadian Urban Expressway Disputes. Toronto: Institute of Public Administration of Canada, 1977.

Léveillée, Jacques, et Trépanier, Marie-Odile
"Evolution de la législation relative à l'espace urbain au Québec." *Revue juridique Thémis* 16:1/2 (1981-82): 19-121.

Léveillée, Jacques, éd.
L'Aménagement du territoire au Québec: du rêve au compromis. Montréal: Nouvelle optique, 1982.

Linteau, Paul-André
The Promoters' City: Building the Industrial Town of Maisonneuve, 1883-1918. Toronto: James Lorimer, 1985.

Lithwick, N.H.
Urban Canada: Problems and Prospects: A Report. Ottawa: C.M.H.C., 1970.

Lorimer, James
The Developers. Toronto: James Lorimer, 1978.

Citizen's Guide to City Politics. Toronto: James Lorimer, 1972.

The Real World of City Politics. Toronto: James Lorimer, 1970.

Lorimer, James, and MacGregor, Carolyn, eds.
After the Developers. Toronto: James Lorimer, 1981.

Lorimer, James, and Phillips, Myfanwy
Working People: Life in a Downtown City Neighbourhood. Toronto: James Lorimer, 1971.

Lorimer, James, and Ross, Evelyn, eds.
The Second City Book: The Planning and Politics of Canada's Cities. Toronto: James Lorimer, 1977.

Magnusson, Warren
"Urban Politics and the Local State." *Studies in Political Economy*, no. 16 (Spring 1985), pp. 111-142.

"Community Organization and Local Self-Government." *Politics and Government of Urban Canada*, pp. 61-86. Edited by Lionel D. Feldman. Toronto: Methuen, 1981.

Masson, Jack K., and Anderson, James D.
Emerging Party Politics in Urban Canada. Toronto: McClelland and Stewart, 1972.

McClain, Janet
Women and Housing: Changing Needs and the Failure of Policy. Ottawa: Canadian Council on Social Development in association with James Lorimer, 1984.

McGraw, Donald
Le Développement des groupes populaires à Montréal 1963-1973. Montréal: Editions coopératives Albert Saint-Martin, 1978.

Moscovitch, Allan
"Housing: Who Pays? Who Profits?" *Inequality: Essays on the Political Economy of Social Welfare*, pp. 314-47. Edited by Allan Moscovitch and Glenn Drover. Toronto: University of Toronto Press, 1981.

O'Connell, Dorothy
Chiclet Gomez. Ottawa: Deneau & Greenberg, 1977.

Palmer, Bryan D.
A Culture in Conflict: Skilled Workers and Industrial Capitalism in Hamilton, Ontario, 1860-1914. Montreal: McGill-Queen's University Press, 1979.

Pasternak, J.
The Kitchener Market Fight. Toronto: Hakkert, 1975.

Piva, Michael J.
The Condition of the Working Class in Toronto, 1900-1921. Ottawa: University of Ottawa Press, 1979.

Powell, A., ed.
The City: Attacking Modern Myths. Toronto: McClelland and Stewart, 1972.

Quesnel-Ouellet, Louise
"Structural Changes at the Municipal Level in Quebec: Analysis of a Policy-Making Process." Banff Conference on Alternate Forms of Urban Government, 1974. *Problems of Change in Urban Government*, pp. 125-46. Edited by M.O. Dickerson, S. Drabek and John T. Woods. Waterloo, Ont.: Wilfrid Laurier University Press, 1980.

"Régionalisation et conscience politique régionale: la communauté urbaine de Québec." *Canadian Journal of Political Science* 4 (June 1971): 191-205.

Richardson, N.H.
"Insubstantial Pageant: The Rise and Fall of Provincial Planning in Ontario." *Canadian Public Administration* 24 (Winter 1981): 563-86.

Rose, Damaris
"Accumulation Versus Reproduction in the Inner City: The Recurrent Crisis of London Revisited." *Urbanization and Urban Planning in Capitalist Society*, pp. 339-82. Edited by Michael Dear and Allen J. Scott. London: Methuen, 1981.

Roussopoulos, Dimitrios, ed.
The City and Radical Social Change. Montreal: Black Rose Books, 1982.

Roweis, Shoukry T.
"Urban Planning in Early and Late Capitalist Societies: Outline of a Theoretical Perspective." *Urbanization and Urban Planning in Capitalist Society*, pp. 159-78. Edited by Michael Dear and Allen J. Scott. London: Methuen, 1981.

Roweis, Shoukry T., and Scott, Allen J.
"The Urban Question." *Urbanization and Conflict in Market Societies*, pp. 38-75. Edited by Kevin R. Cox. Chicago: Maaroufa Press, 1978.

Roy, Gabrielle
Bonheur d'occasion. Montréal: Editions internationales A. Stanké, 1978. (First published 1945. English translation: *The Tin Flute*. Toronto: McClelland and Stewart. 1980.)

Rudin, Ronald
"Boosting the French Canadian Town: Municipal Government and Urban Growth in Quebec, 1850-1900." *Urban History Review* 11 (June 1982): 1-10.

Rutherford, P.
Saving the Canadian City, the First Phase 1880-1920: An Anthology of Articles on Urban Reform. Toronto: University of Toronto Press, 1974.

Schecter, Stephen
The Politics of Urban Liberation. Montreal: Black Rose Books, 1978.

Sewell, John
"The Suburbs." *City Magazine* 2 (January 1977): 19-55.

Up Against City Hall. Toronto: James Lorimer, 1972.

Spelt, Jacob
Urban Development in South-Central Ontario. The Carleton Library, no. 57. Toronto: McClelland and Stewart, 1972. (First published 1955.)

Spurr, Peter
Land and Urban Development: A Preliminary Study. Toronto: James Lorimer, 1976.

Stelter, Gilbert A., and Artibise, Alan F.J., eds.
Shaping the Urban Landscape: Aspects of the Canadian City-Building Process. The Carleton Library, no. 125. Ottawa: Carleton University Press, 1982.

The Canadian City: Essays in Urban History. The Carleton Library, no. 109. Toronto: McClelland and Stewart, 1977.

Taylor, John
"'Relief From Relief': The Cities' Answer to Depression Dependency." *Journal of Canadian Studies* 14 (Spring 1979): 16-23.

Tennant, Paul
"Vancouver Civic Politics, 1929-1980." *BC Studies*, no. 46 (Summer 1980), pp. 3-27.

Tennant, Paul, and Zirnhelt, David
"The Emergence of Metropolitan Government in Greater Vancouver." *BC Studies*, no. 15 (Autumn 1972), pp. 3-28.

Tindal, C.R., and Tindal, S. Nobes
Local Government in Canada: An Introduction. Toronto: McGraw-Hill Ryerson, 1984.

Walker, David C.
The Great Winnipeg Dream: The Re-Development of Portage and Main. Oakville, Ont.: Mosaic Press, 1979.

Weaver, John C.
Shaping the Canadian City: Essays on Urban Politics and Policy, 1890-1920.
Toronto: Institute of Public Administration of Canada, 1977.

Wekerle, Gerda R.; Peterson, Rebecca; and Morley, David, eds.
New Space for Women. Boulder, Colo: Westview Press, 1980.

Wharf, Brian, ed.
Community Work in Canada. Toronto: McClelland and Stewart, 1979.

Wismer, Susan, and Pell, David
Community Profit: Community-Based Economic Development in Canada.
Edited by Maureen Hollingworth. Toronto: Is Five Press, 1981.

Yeates, Maurice
Main Street: Windsor to Quebec City. Toronto: Macmillan, 1975.

26
The Staples: Basic Readings in Canadian Political Economy

Armstrong, Pat, and Armstrong, Hugh
The Double Ghetto: Canadian Women and Their Segregated Work. Rev. ed. Toronto: McClelland and Stewart, 1984.

Baum, Gregory, and Cameron, Duncan
Ethics and Economics: Canada's Catholic Bishops on the Economic Crisis. Toronto: James Lorimer, 1984.

Berger, Thomas
Northern Frontier, Northern Homeland: The Report of the Mackenzie Valley Pipeline Inquiry. Ottawa: Supply and Services Canada, 1977.

Britton, John N.H., and Gilmour, James M.
The Weakest Link: A Technological Perspective on Canadian Industrial Underdevelopment. Background Study no. 43. Ottawa: Science Council of Canada, 1978.

Brym, Robert J., and Sacouman, R. James, eds.
Underdevelopment and Social Movements in Atlantic Canada. Toronto: New Hogtown Press, 1979.

Clarkson, Stephen
Canada and the Reagan Challenge: Crisis and Adjustment, 1981-85. 2nd ed. Toronto: James Lorimer, 1985.

Clement, Wallace
Continental Corporate Power: Economic Elite Linkages Between Canada and the United States. Toronto: McClelland and Stewart, 1977.

Craven, Paul
An Impartial Umpire: Industrial Relations and the Canadian State, 1900-1911. Toronto: University of Toronto Press, 1980.

Creighton, D.G.
Empire of the St. Lawrence. Toronto: Macmillan, 1956. (First published 1937.)

Easterbrooke, W.T., and Watkins, Mel, eds.
Approaches to Canadian Economic History: A Selection of Essays. Toronto: McClelland and Stewart, 1967.

Grant, George
Lament for a Nation: The Defeat of Canadian Nationalism. Toronto: McClelland and Stewart, 1965.

Innis, Harold A.
Essays in Canadian Economic History. Edited by Mary Q. Innis. Toronto: University of Toronto Press, 1956.

The Fur Trade in Canada: An Introduction to Canadian Economic History. Rev. ed. Toronto: University of Toronto Press, 1956. (First published 1930.)

Kealey, Gregory S.
Toronto Workers Respond to Industrial Capitalism, 1867-1892. Toronto: University of Toronto Press, 1980.

Kroker, Arthur
Technology and the Canadian Mind: Innis/McLuhan/Grant. Montreal: New World Perspectives, 1984.

Levitt, Kari
Silent Surender: The Multinational Corporation in Canada. Toronto: Macmillan, 1970.

Lumsden, Ian, ed.
Close the 49th Parallel Etc.: The Americanization of Canada. Toronto: University of Toronto Press, 1970.

Marshall, Herbert; Southard, Frank; and Taylor, Kenneth W.
Canadian-American Industry: A Study in International Investment. The Carleton Library, no. 93. Toronto: McClelland and Stewart, 1976. (First published 1936.)

McCallum, John
Unequal Beginnings: Agriculture and Economic Development in Quebec and Ontario Until 1870. Toronto: University of Toronto Press, 1980.

McRoberts, Kenneth, and Posgate, Dale
Quebec: Social Change and Political Crisis. Rev. ed. Toronto: McClelland and Stewart, 1980.

Naylor, R.T.
The History of Canadian Business, 1867-1914. 2 vols. Toronto: James Lorimer, 1975.

Niosi, Jorge
Canadian Capitalism: A Study of Power in the Canadian Business Establishment. Toronto: James Lorimer, 1981.

Palmer, Bryan
A Culture in Conflict: Skilled Workers and Industrial Capitalism in Hamilton, Ontario, 1860-1914. Montreal: McGill-Queen's University Press, 1979.

Panitch, Leo, ed.
The Canadian State: Political Economy and Political Power. Toronto: University of Toronto Press, 1977.

Pentland, H. Clare
Labour and Capital in Canada 1650-1860. Edited by Paul Phillips. Toronto: James Lorimer, 1981.

Phillips, Paul, and Phillips, Erin
Women and Work: Inequality in the Labour Market. Toronto: James Lorimer, 1983.

Richards, John, and Pratt, Larry
Prairie Capitalism: Power and Influence in the New West. Toronto: McClelland and Stewart, 1979.

Rotstein, Abraham
Rebuilding From Within: Remedies for Canada's Ailing Economy. Toronto: James Lorimer in association with the Canadian Institute for Economic Policy, 1984.

Ryerson, Stanley
Unequal Union: The Roots of Crisis in the Canadas, 1815-1873. 2nd ed. Toronto: Progress Books, 1973.

Stevenson, Garth
Unfulfilled Union: Canadian Federalism and National Unity. Rev. ed. Canadian Controversies Series. Toronto: Gage, 1982.

Teeple, Gary, ed.
Capitalism and the National Question in Canada. Toronto: University of Toronto Press, 1972.

Traves, Tom
The State and Enterprise: Canadian Manufacturers and the Federal Government 1917-1931. Toronto: University of Toronto Press, 1979.

White, Julie
Women and Part-Time Work. Ottawa: Canadian Advisory Council on the Status of Women, 1980.

Williams, Glen
Not For Export: Toward a Political Economy of Canada's Arrested Industrialization. Toronto: McClelland and Stewart, 1983.

Index by Author

Underhill, Frank 135, 175, 194
United States. President's Materials Policy Commission 8
Université du Québec à Montréal. Laboratoire sur la réparation de la sécurité du revenue, pour le Conseil du statut de la femme 43
Upton, L.F.S. 161
Usher, Peter J. 146, 151, 161
Usiskin, Roz 73

Vaillancourt, Jean-Guy 35, 172, 176
Vaisey, Douglas 51
Vallières, Pierre 33, 35
Van Kirk, Sylvia 9
Vance, Catherine 59, 70
Vandycke, Robert 176
Van Kirk, Sylvia 59
Van Loon, Richard 97, 209, 215
Vano, Gerard S. 169
Vaughn, W. 110
Veeman, Michele, 9, 126
Veeman, Terry 9, 126
Veltmeyer, Henry 92
Vernon, Raymond 88
Vézina, J.-P. 29
Vigod, B.L. 169
Vincenthier, Georges 35
Vinet, Alain 43

Waddell, Eric 27
Wade, Mason 35
Wade, Susan 59
Wadel, Cato 144
Wales, Terence J. 118
Walker, David C. 225
Walker, David F. 135
Walker, Michael A. 82, 84, 201
Wallace, M. Elizabeth 209
Wallerstein, M. 78
Wallin, J.H.A. 183
Walters, Vivienne 75
Wanstall, Adrienne 117
Warburton, Rennie 118
Ward, Norman 126
Ward, W. Peter 118, 119
Warkentin, Germaine 135
Warkentin, John 135

Warme, Barbara 56
Warnock, Jack 9, 101, 126, 218
Warren, Bill 92
Warrian, Peter 20, 52
Warriner, G. Keith 9, 119
Warskett, George 56
Watkins, Mel x, 1, 9, 84, 151, 161, 169, 227
Watson, Louise 59
Watt, F.W. 21, 61, 73
Wearing, Joseph 194
Weaver, John C. 226
Weaver, Sally M. 161
Weiler, Paul 75
Weinrich, Peter 51, 73
Weinstein, Michael 171, 179
Weisskopf, Thomas E. 79, 80, 213
Wekerle, Gerda R. 226
Weldon, J.C. 110
Wells, D. 44, 167
Western Canada Studies Conference 126-27
Wetzel, Judy 151
Wharf, Brian 226
Whitaker, Reginald xi, 73, 175, 188, 189, 194, 201
White, Julie 43, 229
White, Pam 151
White, W.L. 195, 201
Wilber, Charles K. 90
Wilde, Jim de 218
Wilkins, Mira 89, 101, 110
Will, R.M. 114
Willard, Joseph W. 210
Willes, John A. 75
Williams, G. 19, 99, 110, 211, 218, 229
Williams, Rick 9, 206
Willoughby, William 110
Willson, Bruce F. 9, 218
Wilson, Alan 49
Wilson, Barry F. 9, 127
Wilson, C.R. 158
Wilson, Charles F. 127
Wilson, J. Donald 183, 185, 187
Wilson, James Wood 119
Wilson, Susannah Jane Foster 43
Wise, S.F. 49, 135, 194
Wiseman, Nelson 127, 194
Wismer, Catherine 15
Wismer, Susan 226

Wolfe, David x, xiv, 84, 210, 211, 218
Wolfe, Eric Robert 92
Wolfe, Margie 39, 177
Wolfe, Samuel 203
Wolforth, John 161
Wood, Louis Aubrey 9, 22, 127, 194
Woodcock, George 161, 170
Woodward, Frances M. 119
Woolfrey, Joy 221
Wonnacott, Ronald J. 218
World Council of Indigenous People 151
Worlsey, Peter 92
Wortman, Peter 161
Wright, J.B. 151
Wright, Erik Olin 80
Wright, Judy 169
Wylie, William N.T. 61
Wynn, Graeme 110, 144

Yandle, Sharon 84
Yantz, Lynda 38
Yanz, Lynda 80
Yeates, Maurice 226
Young, Bert 49
Young, Brian J. 110
Young, J. 218
Young, John H. 118
Young, Robert 215
Young, Walter D. 127, 194
Younge, Eva R. 122
Yves, Roby 106

Zaidi, Mahmood A. 53
Zakuta, Leo 194
Zaslow, Morris 135
Zerker, Sally F. 69
Zinhlet, David 225
Zohar, Uri xv, 218
Zureik, Elia 183
Zwelling, Marc 70